Bagman to Swagman

To Romilly, My Wife

Bagman to Swagman

Tales of Broome, the North-West and
other Australian Adventures

Alistair McAlpine

ALLEN & UNWIN

First published in 1999 by
Allen & Unwin
9 Atchison Street
St Leonards NSW 2065
Australia
Phone: (61 2) 8425 0100
Fax: (61 2) 9906 2218
E-mail: frontdesk@allen-unwin.com.au
Web: http://www.allen-unwin.com.au

National Library of Australia
Cataloguing-in-Publication entry:

McAlpine, Alistair, Lord, 1942– .
    Bagman to Swagman: tales of Broome, the North-West and
    other Australian adventures.

Includes index.
ISBN 1 86508 389 5 (pbk.).

1. McAlpine, Alistair, Lord, 1942–. 2. Collectors and
collecting—Australia. 3. Australia, Northwestern—
Description and travel. 4. Australia—Politics and
government. 5. Australia—Social life and customs. I. Title.

919.41

Set in 10.5 on 13 Sabon by Midland Typesetters, Maryborough
Printed and bound by McPherson's Printing Group, Maryborough, Vic

10 9 8 7 6 5 4 3 2

Contents

Preface

For forty years I have travelled to and from Australia, sometimes staying only a week or so, sometimes as long as a few
months. One year in particular I visited Australia eight times,
but since 1964 I have been in the habit of visiting during each
quarter of the year.

These are the memories of those visits—events in my
social, business and artistic life, recalled as accurately as I am
able, given the vagaries of memory and the embellishments of
imagination created by the passing of time.

These memoirs are more than a travelogue, or a catalogue
of the people, places and objects I have come across during
my travels around this fascinating and beautiful country—
this is the story of my love affair with Australia.

I

Early Days in Perth

If it is wildflowers that you dream of, go to Perth in Western Australia in September. There, in Kings Park, in over eight hundred hectares of natural bush in the middle of the city, are eight thousand species of wildflower. On those cool September mornings, their combined scent has a beauty I have never experienced elsewhere. Kangaroo paw, native iris, the banksia shrub—plants so exotic they have been collected for years and were growing in conservatories in Europe long before the State was settled.

In this peaceful and strange park there are also avenues of ghost gums, each with a plaque to commemorate a Western Australian soldier killed in the First World War. It is a moving experience just to read them: Hall, George F., 10th Australian Light Horse, killed in action, Palestine 19.4.17; Fred Thomas, killed, Pozières, France, 1916. No war memorial can be more poignant than these great white gums, bearing the names of men killed at Gallipoli, the Somme, North Africa, and at Beersheba. These men died on a faraway continent more than thirty years before the centenary of their State.

Under the gums, the wildflowers grow in plumes not unlike the emu feathers that decorated the slouch hats these dead men wore. The flowers are like a great posy at their memorial. The white-tailed black cockatoos circle and shriek in the wind. The blackfellas in the north say that the different varieties of cockatoo call their own names; for me, they are the unquiet spirits of men buried far from the home they loved. Around the trees, children play. On Sunday afternoons, their parents, whose grandparents had never heard of Western Australia, walk in the park. Never is the idea of war more beautiful, never is the futility of war more certain, than when you stand here in one of the most remote cities in the world.

It was to Perth in Western Australia, a State the size of Western Europe—with nothing much but desert lying between it and most of Australia's population in the east—that I came in 1958. The SS *Oriana* was on her maiden voyage, the first of a new generation of ocean liners built to carry both freight and passengers to Australia. This voyage, that I was on with my parents, stopped at many ports before arriving in Australia. The *Oriana* was a fine ship with luxurious first-class accommodation. My parents' cabin had both a balcony and a sitting room attached to it. My accommodation was a comfortable cabin on a lower deck with a porthole bolted closed against the sea. In the event, the sea treated us well as we sailed through still waters in the Mediterranean and the Red Sea and out into the Indian Ocean. At night, the moon reflected on their calm surfaces and the algae disturbed by the liner's wake glowed, a silver slipstream marking our passage. It was a romantic trip, with stops at Port Said, Suez, Aden and Colombo. As each day passed, I became more and more excited. The ship was full: the first-class passengers, mostly elderly, had boarded at Southampton; the steerage passengers, at Nice and Naples. There were few teenagers on the outward voyage. Aged sixteen, I made no shipboard friendships—the balmy nights and romantic silvered seas were wasted as far as I was concerned. However, my excitement on this great journey was such that I did not need the company of contemporaries, seeking instead the companionship of old men and the tales of their youth.

Brigadier Shearer, perhaps the most polite man I have ever met, travelled with his wife, Mary, and my parents. Shearer was a Highland Scot, with all the romance of his people in his soul. As a young man, he had joined the Indian Army. Often engaged in intelligence work, he saw the last acts of what Kipling called 'The Great Game', the battle of wits to keep the Russians from outflanking British India. During the First World War, he was a cavalryman, and fought with Allenby's cavalry in the desert. On the *Oriana*, he was full of stories of the places that we passed. During the Second World War, he had been head of British Military Intelligence for the Middle East based in Cairo. It had been his duty to tell King Farouk of Egypt that the British no longer required his services. At the time, the British were engaged in the desert war with Germany, and their General Rommel was sweeping across the desert with his forces—Egypt, and particularly Cairo, were threatened. Farouk was a dissolute man whose hobby was collecting pornography. He was also a weak king who could not be relied upon, so the British determined to remove him from the throne and govern the country. Each day, it was John Shearer's habit to breakfast with Farouk's uncle at a café overlooking the palace. At one of these breakfast meetings, Farouk's uncle, not much taken with the idea that his nephew be dethroned, said so. Shearer, now aware that the dethroning was not going to be done quietly, took a white handkerchief from his sleeve—it was the habit of British officers of the regular army to carry a handkerchief concealed in the sleeve of their uniforms—and waved it in the morning air. A nearby British tank fired one shot, demolishing the palace gates. So went the last king of Egypt.

Back in London for a while, Shearer was spotted at a railway station by General Montgomery who realised that Shearer was reporting directly to Churchill. Before long, Shearer had been relieved of his command and left Cairo. He then became the managing director of the French couturier Molyneux. An unlikely post for an ex-general, Molyneux, however, was the cover for British intelligence working in Occupied France. I spent much time with John Shearer, his stories and his adventures inspiring in me a restlessness that has been with me all my life.

Another passenger, Lord Morley, was a singular old man. His family had once owned Dorchester House in London, the mansion that once stood where the Dorchester Hotel now stands. In 1928 my family acquired Lord Morley's London home, pulled it down and built a hotel in its place. The gateway to the old Dorchester House was bought by Rosa Lewis, better known as the Duchess of Jermyn Street, who specialised in finding nice clean girls for gentlemen. She also sold them, when they were in their cups, large pieces of masonry too large to be taken away. One of these pieces of stone was the arch that once had formed the gateway to Dorchester House. In the 1960s, my family rebuilt her hotel in Jermyn Street. The Dorchester arch now stands in the garden of my brother William's house, and very well it looks.

Lord Morley was old and doddery, but he had been a fine young fellow in his time. A Guards Officer at the time of the Boer War, he recalled his departure from Southampton. His regiment was paraded on the dock, as Queen Victoria was to inspect them before they left. Up and down the ranks the Queen progressed, stiff as a ramrod until she came opposite the young Lord Morley. Turning to an aide, she rested her hand on his shoulder and dabbed tears from her eyes. 'My fine young men all going to war', the Queen murmured, 'so few of them will ever come back'. Lord Morley told me that he did not find the Queen's words reassuring as he boarded the liner that was to take him and his regiment to South Africa.

Happily, while the Queen was right as a generality and

many of her fine young men did not return, she was wrong in the specific, for Lord Morley survived well into his nineties. Old and doddery he may well have been on that trip out to Australia, but when we reached that great continent and a number of extremely elegant young ladies boarded the *Oriana* for its return voyage to England, he perked up no end.

⊷

As we crossed great oceans, shipboard life fell into a routine until the night came when it was announced that the next morning we would see Australia. My first sight of this most ancient continent in the world was the long, flat coastline of Western Australia. As the *Oriana* closed with that coastline, the Island of Rottnest, which guards the entrance of the Swan River, and the port of Fremantle came into view. When we arrived in Fremantle, the great liner's decks were crowded with migrants—migrants who had left so little and arrived expecting so much, their white skins burned red by the Indian Ocean's sun. The migrants, dragging their children by the arm, walked towards the immigration officers who were seated behind desks; children who looked around, and carried their world in a basket. A lone piper stood and played as the passengers came ashore. This was Australia, the lucky country, the 'Golden West': that is what these people had been told by those paid to persuade them to travel there for ten pounds a head. The Cinderella State: that is what those who lived and worked there called Western Australia. But Cinderella did go to the ball, and what a ball those forty years have been. I had no idea then that I would fall in love with this great continent, let alone with Western Australia, its landscape, its people, and join in its hectic dance.

A ship's officer came towards my father and with him a young man in military uniform, wearing a kilt. We were to take morning tea with the Governor of Western Australia.

The young man took us quickly to his waiting car. The government driver saluted; customs officials stood aside. We set out from Fremantle and in a moment were out of the town among the bush that then tracked the Swan River. In those days, the Swan River ran at the edge of the escarpment on which stands Kings Park.

At that time, Perth was barely a city, more a big farming town where you expected to see cattle and drovers in the main street. An elegant street, nonetheless, with buildings of the 1930s seldom more than three or four storeys high, built in soft, yellow Donnybrook stone. Offices were fitted out with dark-brown panelling of jarrah, a tree that grows in Western Australia and can reach several hundred feet in height.

The Governor, Sir Charles Gairdner, was an old friend of my family's travelling companion, John Shearer. We took tea with him and talked about nothing in particular, for Perth was a town where nothing in particular ever happened. There was no talk of an exciting future; indeed, there was no talk about any future. We drove back up St George's Terrace, Perth's comfortable main street. At one end, there was a red brick fortress known as the Barracks, built in the early years of the colony, which blocked the view of Parliament House. The Barracks looked for all the world like a child's toy castle. Back along the road under the escarpment, to our left, a squadron of small yachts sailed on the Swan River.

We did not linger in Perth—just morning tea and then we were away. That night, we rounded the bottom of Western Australia and with the old whaling port of Albany on our port side, we set out across the Great Australian Bight. It was by now the end of January, and the weather in Perth had been hot, extremely hot. You can imagine my surprise when, just twenty-four hours out of Fremantle, I came on deck and found it covered in snow. Wind blew and it was bitterly cold; the sun was nowhere to be seen. The next day we arrived at

Melbourne. In my view, it was not as pretty as Perth, but a place of substance; where there had been farming in Perth, there was business in Melbourne. This was no lazy country town, rather a city with a cultural hinterland and prospects. The tide of development was stirring in Melbourne and you could feel it as you walked the streets. The museums, the theatres, the Parliament buildings, even the hotels, had about them a permanence. This was a place where history had been made and, as you listened to the people talk, a place where history would be made again.

Twenty-four hours in Melbourne, lunch at the Windsor Hotel, a drive round the city, each important feature pointed out to us, and then a dinner party at the house of a grand family that had been forewarned of our coming. A fine house, built in the style of a late nineteenth-century manor, set in large gardens where exotic plants grew in profusion. A generous dinner, with Australian wines and excellent food, a dinner conducted with a formality that my mother claimed reminded her of pre-war Britain.

Back on our ship, where all had remained the same, day in, day out, there was a change. The Campbell family had joined the passengers: Mrs Campbell, a pretty woman with blonde hair, and her husband, a good-looking man, tall and strong, but now walking with sticks. It was, however, the Campbell daughters who made the difference: Virginia, a blonde, not tall, pretty with shortish curling hair, very like her mother, and her sister, Susan, a tall, fine-looking girl with long blonde hair. At first, I regarded these girls from afar; in time, we became friends.

A day or so sailing from Melbourne, we arrived at Sydney. Sydney was in 1958 a city caught between the formality of its past—long white gloves and picture hats to be worn on all occasions—and the hurly-burly of its future. Already the foundations of its Opera House were in place, a building which, at that time, was probably the most remarkable under-taking in the world. My father and I were shown over the building site of what was to become the world's most spec-tacular opera house. The contractor, whose manager was our guide, intended to embark on casting some immensely com-plicated post-stressed concrete beams. 'Have you ever worked with post-stressed concrete?' my father asked. Post-stressing concrete involves placing wet concrete around piano wires, which are stressed or tightened as the concrete surrounding them sets. Timing in this is everything, and great skill is needed to conduct such an operation successfully. 'No,' replied the site manager, 'there shouldn't be any real problem.' My father, who had seen a great deal of post-stressed concrete used in the nuclear power stations that we were building, was of a different view, but refrained from comment until we were alone.

⚜

After Utzon, its Danish architect, had been dismissed, those charged with the construction of the Opera House had to discover how on earth they were to build the cluster of giant shells that are both roof and building. How could Utzon's vision, that had been sketched in the sand of a beach on the other side of the world, become a reality? The reality of human life, however, is cruel, just as is the reality of nature. In the end, Ove Arup and Partners, a fine partnership of engi-neers, adapted Utzon's designs to ease the task of construc-tion. Sadly, the architect's light touch was lost; the natural caution of the engineers made the building heavier than was originally intended. What had started with Utzon drawing nautilus shells in the sand became a solid edifice on the edge of Sydney's harbour. Utzon's Opera House would have seemed likely to fly away with the wind. Still a remarkable building, the Opera House is, and always will be, a thing of beauty, but how much more beautiful it could have been if the politics of ambition and greed had not played their dubious role.

For there can be no doubt that, had Utzon's Opera House been built, the building would have been the masterpiece of this millennium and, indeed, most other millennia as well. For years now, the world at large has been content to praise Sydney's great Opera House. It is only the advent of the museum in Bilbao, built for the Guggenheim Foundation, that makes one wonder whether Utzon and the people of Australia weren't cheated out of the chance to truly make architectural history.

༻ৠ༺

Later that first day in Sydney, my father and I visited the local chairman of the Caltex Oil Company in his office beside Sydney Harbour Bridge. John Shearer, recently retired as chairman of Caltex in Europe, took us to see this man who was a friend of his. We were shown what seemed to us stunning views of Sydney and its harbour from the windows of this multistorey building. Today, the old Caltex building is but a pygmy among the serried ranks of skyscrapers that make up Sydney's central business district.

The next day, the *Oriana* sailed from the wharf at Woolloomooloo where we were berthed. We sailed, however, not without a slight delay. The ship's doctor had been called from his bed to attend on various members of the crew arrested by the local police force and charged with drunken behaviour. 'Are these seamen drunk?' asked the police sergeant in charge of the station where they were being held. 'Certainly not,' replied the ship's doctor. 'In which case, if you take that view, you must be drunk,' responded the sergeant and, without much ado, locked up the ship's doctor with the crew.

While the *Oriana* might well have sailed without members of her crew, there was no possibility of sailing without the doctor. So we all waited for the matter to be resolved. Fines paid, restitution made for damage done and apologies given all round, the *Oriana* set off from Sydney for New Zealand. As the liner swung away from the wharfs of Woolloomooloo, we passed Mrs Macquarie's Chair, a headland jutting into Sydney's beautiful harbour. Along the side of this headland ran a group of school children accompanied by nuns, their black robes flying in the wind. They waved at the ship, we waved back and the ship's band played 'Anchors Away'. During the voyage across the Pacific, I became friends with Susan and Virginia Campbell, a friendship that lasted while they lived in London. A pair of good-looking girls, they were popular among both the passengers and the officers. Their father had his work cut out keeping an eye on them. As for myself, I was too young to enter into a romantic situation with these beautiful women; I was also short, fat and far from articulate.

New Zealand was, in the words of Marlene Dietrich, 'always closed'. When we reached its shores it seemed as if she was right! Ms Dietrich may never have known how accurate she was when she made that damning observation. In Auckland, we could get neither dinner nor a drink after six o'clock in the evening. Fiji was exotic and wonderful; Hawaii, the most fantastic place that I had ever visited. It was crossing the Pacific that Susan Campbell one day turned up on the upper deck bar wearing the briefest of bikinis. These were, of course, the days before the Swinging Sixties, days when girls dressed with caution and young men behaved with the best of manners. Even the barman, a cockney of considerable experience, was slightly shocked. 'Miss Campbell, how wonderful it is that we are seeing more and more of you in this bar.'

In time, we reached Vancouver. My mother was brought up in Vancouver, so our stay there was an emotional one. She had told us about the town, only to find that the place was not as she remembered it at all. We visited the places of her youth, now changed beyond recognition. My parents and I left the ship at Vancouver to take the train through the Rockies. Fond goodbyes were said all round, addresses exchanged and promises made to meet again, sincere promises as shipboard promises always are. In the event, I did see much of Virginia and Susan in London in the following years, and then our paths drifted apart as the paths of travellers do. My mother had made the trip through the Rockies many times and was much reassured that nothing had changed in this remote but beautiful place. Then across the plains of Canada to Toronto, where we were met by the Canadian manager of my family's business. We were soon looking at building sites, all thoughts of Australia forgotten.

There was, however, one fellow traveller on the *Oriana* who might have changed my life: a woman from Texas who was in the business of building roads across that State. 'Send your son to spend a couple of years with me, it will be great experience for him.' My father agreed but, in the event, I went to work in my family's business and Texas was forgotten as well. This, as I look back, is not surprising, for my family were contractors and they lived for their work. As a child, I had ridden on the foreman's shoulders, seen concrete mixers as big as four-storey buildings and cranes that towered hundreds of feet into the air, and been terrified of the rattle of the giant air compressors. As a young man, I was caught in the excitement of our trade.

My family lived construction and talked construction, and, as a youth, I dreamt construction. Power stations and docks, skyscrapers and hotels were to be built. The construction boom of the late 1950s and early 1960s was well under way. I had neither the time nor the inclination to go to Texas to build roads and neither had my father the inclination to send me, for this woman and her construction business were never mentioned again.

2

It might have been that I would never have returned to Australia and, in particular, to Perth, for on that first visit I came across nothing that would draw me back, met no-one with whom I fell in love, saw nothing so remarkable that I felt compelled to return. My interest in Australia and my association with that continent could have been all over, but for one man and the fact that, by chance one day in the mid-1960s, my father was on holiday when he telephoned. He was Sir Halford Reddish, then the chairman of Rugby Portland Cement. A customer of my family's, Sir Halford Reddish and his reasons for me to undertake the journey to Australia are well-described in my memoir *Once a Jolly Bagman*. Suffice to say here that I knew that if Sir Halford Reddish asked you to go somewhere, you went—and went as quickly as possible.

So it was that I found myself on a long and incredibly tedious journey. The flights took ages and the breaks at various cities along the way were curtailed by the fact that I had miscalculated the time changes, with the result that no sooner had I arrived, for instance, in San Francisco or Sydney, than I had to leave again. Tired beyond belief, I found myself ensconced in Perth's Adelphi Hotel. Built in the 1930s, the Adelphi Hotel was a solid building of local stone, four floors in height. Its doorway was recessed from the street, with a short flight of stone steps leading up to it. These steps were guarded by a pair of knights in armour, knights taken from the romantic fantasies of the Pre-Raphaelites. Each of the knights carried an electric light disguised as a flaming torch. The hallway was brown and dark, and led onto a dining room that owed more to a penal establishment than a first-class hotel, let alone a luxury one. The rooms were small, the service and the bathroom, I felt at the time, defied description.

The highlight of the Adelphi Hotel was a Steak and Oyster Restaurant located in the basement; you could eat a plate of oysters and a steak for less than three dollars. Cheesecake was an optional extra, but as it was served by a voluptuous young Western Australian woman, my friends and I usually ate cheesecake. Swan lager was readily available, also wine, I believe, but I never drank any there. Wine did not then enjoy the popularity it has since achieved. In the bar that adjoined the restaurant was a remarkable cartoon by Rigby. It caricatured many of Perth's notable figures—sportsmen, politicians, lawyers and judges. Later, the cartoon was moved to one of the bars in the new Parmelia Hotel. It is interesting today to look at it and reflect on how the people of Perth have changed in the last 40 years.

☙

Sir Halford Reddish had promised Charles Court, then the Minister for Industrial Development in Western Australia, that he would build a first-class hotel in Perth. To achieve this, he and my family acquired the Adelphi and the Riviera, a block of flats behind the Adelphi. The Riviera was to be demolished first and the Parmelia Hotel built on the site. After the Parmelia had opened for business, the plan was to demolish the Adelphi and build a multistorey office building, Hamersley House. The whole of this development was carried out in partnership with Sir Halford Reddish's company, Rugby Portland Cement. The architect for the Parmelia Hotel and Hamersley House was Peter Arney, a partner of Oldham

15

Boas Ednie-Brown, a firm working in association with the British firm of architects, T.P. Bennett & Partner. Michael Metcalf and Philip Bennett, the son of Sir Thomas Bennett, the firm's founder, looked after these projects.

One afternoon, Peter Arney took me to meet his retired partner, Harold Boas. We took tea, in the proper sense of the word, at this gentleman's house. Harold Boas poured the tea and Peter Arney offered the sandwiches—delicate things were these sandwiches. The house stood on the edge of the escarpment that edged Kings Park, one of four or so that stood there with a breathtaking view out over the City of Perth and the Swan River. Most of these houses have now been pulled down and replaced with apartments. Harold Boas explained to me that it was only 30 years since he had designed the Adelphi Hotel and now I was going to pull it down. He believed that to pull down this fine old hotel was a shame and, as I reflect on the matter, I am inclined to agree with him in his judgement with, however, one caveat. I believe that to have pulled down that wonderful hotel was, in fact, a crime—among the first of a succession of crimes that systematically destroyed St George's Terrace.

෴

Perth in the early 1960s was a large, sprawling country town with a main street of commercial buildings where the lawyers and other professionals worked. St George's Terrace was at that time a noble street. Slowly over the last 40 years, its grand buildings have been knocked down and replaced by pale images of skyscrapers taken from the pages of glossy magazines devoted to the world's architecture. These buildings have neither elegance nor originality. Parliament House, that stands on the hill at the end of St George's Terrace, is a building of solidity, as Parliament buildings should be. It looks out over a motorway beyond which now stands only the brick gateway to the long-demolished toy castle, the

Barracks. That gateway stands lonely, lost, irrelevant, a rebuke to the Western Australian parliamentarians who were responsible for an architectural tragedy. I do not refer to the loss of the fine buildings in St George's Terrace—that loss was due only to the natural course of commerce, ignorance and the short-sighted pursuit of greed—but rather to the pulling down of the Barracks, an impediment to the view from Parliament House.

In the days when I first came to Perth, the Barracks housed the civil servants. It was no architectural masterpiece; in fact, it was a nineteenth-century utilitarian building, not unlike the brick armouries that you still find scattered among the buildings of New York. It is true that in this building the civil servants had accommodation of rather a poor quality: they had no views or at least none to compare with those they now have from their office in the block on the hill. Of course, the Barracks had to go and the new motorway that surrounds Perth provided the perfect excuse. With the Barracks gone and its view secured by sinking the vast motorway into a trench, Parliament intended to sit with the bureaucracy in new office towers at its back. Happily, only one of five hard-faced, multistoreyed office blocks to house civil servants was ever built. On seeing the first of these monoliths, some intelligent politician must have realised that civil servants, a prolific but generally unpopular species in Australia, would not enhance the popularity of politicians with so dominant a presence.

They, the ubiquitous they, caused the peaceful bays of the Swan River to be filled with earth so they could build this motorway. The foreshore of the river's north bank became a spaghetti junction. To ease the pain of the motorway, they planted gardens between its coils, with little bridges and little ponds—small trite gardens that nestle among roads that curl like a tortured snake. Then a grateful Government gave the planner who did all this the Order of Australia. With time, a car park and a bus station have been added, and the trees around the motorway have grown. Even with the motorway, the Barracks could have been saved, though it blocked the views of politicians down the once-grand St George's Terrace. It could have been saved, but it was pulled down. The plan was carried out with precision; the cries of residents in the area went unheard. Only one mistake was made—that fortress's gateway was left standing, a permanent memorial to the folly of planners and their masters in the Parliament behind it.

Now the great motorway, an act of conceit by a Government that saw the future of the State as grand, but not as grand as it became, runs through the city rather than around it, and the politicians' great vision, their desire to be modern, has become, 40 years later, a folly. The true beauty of the city, its peace, is shattered by traffic that another generation will try to eliminate by spending more taxpayers' money. As for the city's foreshore, that is long gone. Try as they may and, indeed, they seem to be trying, there is little option but to start again.

Perth is a great city, its people different from those of other great cities—Perth should have been proud of that difference. Sadly, for some years, it lost its way, seduced by the idea of being modern but ending up being much the same as everywhere else. Where once the architects of Western Australia benefited from their isolation and built small new buildings in scale with their town, in the 1980s they started to read glossy architectural magazines and build glossy buildings. In the depths of the recession of the 1990s, the emptiness of these buildings stared through shiny glass that once reflected the greed of the men who owned them. Their concrete piazzas, emptied of people, had concrete pots and windswept trees— the main street, the once-beautiful St George's Terrace, became a wind-filled canyon. The State Government should take the opportunity that came out of the recession to turn empty city sites into gardens before their value increases with the demand for space. A new road system must be planned and the concrete of the old motorway demolished, its tarmac torn up. Kings Park must be allowed to escape from its escarpment and filter down through the city. The hard core of Perth must be softened before it is too late. As for the gateway to the old Barracks, rebuild the walls that flanked it and use it as an auditorium. In retrospect, one can see that a new centre for the city's business district should have been created away from St George's Terrace. No part of the city centre of Perth is more than 20 minutes' walk from another. It is ridiculous, when you think about it, to pull down buildings just because they are too small. Often I call to mind the image of Harold Boas watching, with a grandstand view, the building that he designed being pulled apart. Now that a building is given a lifespan of thirty years, I wonder when I will see the first of the buildings that were the children of my imagination suffer the blows of the demolition contractor's ball.

❧

The Riviera flats, despite their grand name, were quite another kettle of fish. If anything deserved to be pulled down, it was that godforsaken block of jerry-built flats standing in a jungle of bamboo decorated with the waste of successive tenants. The Riviera flats belonged to Alan Bond; they were his first and only property holding within the City of Perth at that time. Bond was known to my lawyer, John Adams, and others, as being a pretty sharp customer. Before he vacated the Riviera, he stripped it of light switches and fittings, water heaters—anything that could be detached. After completion of the contract of sale on the Riviera, Bond offered himself as a partner to Sir Halford Reddish and myself, an offer that Sir Halford turned down quite simply with the words, 'No, thank you, Mr Bond,' and then, before Alan Bond could protest, 'Goodbye, Mr Bond.'

It was many years before I met Alan Bond again, and by this time he was well on his way towards the top of the dung heap created by a small group of corrupt businessmen in Western Australia. Crowing like crazy, flapping his arms, barely a day passed that this consummate publicist did not make out that he was the best thing to happen to Western Australia in years. What is more, many highly intelligent people believed Bond's line. Bankers were falling over themselves to lend him money, the State Government, both Liberal and Labor administrations, treated the man as if he were a king and, in a way, Bond was a king. Tycoons went in fear of him, his holdings in the media were powerful, his holdings in industry and property impressive, his efforts to win the America's Cup admired. His success in winning the America's Cup was applauded by all and sundry, and even sceptics began to soften in their criticism of him. Bob Hawke, the then prime minister, announced that anyone who did not give their work force the day off when 'Bondy' won the Cup was 'a bum'.

For many years, the Swan Brewery had been the greatest industrial force in Western Australia, and the chairman of this institution wore the crown in Perth. Alan Bond needed to own the Swan Brewery, he needed to wear that crown. The Perth business establishment desperately needed to stop him from owning the Swan Brewery and all the prestige that went with it, not to mention the brewery's abundant flow of cash. The Swan Brewery had at this time just completed a brand-new brewing plant some miles outside Perth. This left it with two redundant breweries in the city itself. Both breweries sat on prime sites, and on the site occupied by the Emu Brewery, I had my eye—fourteen acres of land tucked under the escarpment of Kings Park, just across the road from the Bishop's See development, the jewel in my family company's crown. The Bishop's

See development was on about four acres of near-derelict land on which sat several old buildings. I had these buildings, which included the particularly fine Bishop's House, restored, and a large area of land became an important West Australian garden. A multistorey office building occupied the balance of the site.

Alan Blanckensee was then the chairman of the Swan Brewery. He was also a partner of John Adams, my chairman, and a good friend of both John and myself. In time, we did a deal: my family company formed a joint company with the Swan Brewery to develop the Emu Brewery site. Plans were under way for a hotel, and Inter-Continental Hotels were keen to be our partners. Enter Alan Bond—suddenly he had a stake of some size in the Swan Brewery, then he had a seat on its board and, before many months passed, he appeared on the board of our joint company. Until this time, the company had been run with a considerable amount of informality, decisions were taken after only a telephone call. John Adams and I ran the company, consulting frequently with our partners. With the presence of Bond on the board, however, formality became the order of the day, as careful note needed to be taken of every word that was spoken and every decision that was made. A board meeting was called and, for convenience, it was arranged to hold that meeting in Europe. For most of my life I have admired the City of Venice, so that was where the meeting was to be held, in the Gritti Palace Hotel. Rooms were booked, all was arranged. I flew into Venice and waited on the arrival of Mr Alan Bond. The weather was perfect, a warm spring, the sun bright, the sky a clear blue, the waters of the lagoon cool.

We met at ten o'clock that morning. The meeting, which should have finished by twelve-thirty in time for lunch with our wives, lasted until two o'clock as Bond argued over every detail. Alan Blanckensee, always an elegant dresser, wore a beige linen suit. We sat down for lunch, a tense affair. Bond was boastful and often rude but, no matter, the strategy was to humour the beast. My wife Romilly asked after his art collection. He told her of it in some detail, rather more detail than her polite enquiry had required. 'But where do you keep all these paintings?' she asked. 'I don't tell people where I keep my pictures, they might steal them,' was the reply. At last, lunch was coming to an end. 'Could you please pass the coffee?' Alan Blanckensee asked Bond. Bond passed the coffee, spilling it all over his chairman's elegant suit. The end was obviously near for Alan, and within weeks, Bond gained control of the Swan Brewery and became its chairman in his place. As for our joint company, John Adams and I withdrew from the board and appointed Alan Blanckensee and another lawyer as our nominees. Their instructions were to make life as difficult as possible for Bond and they set about this task with relish. In about a year, Bond bought out our interest for a remarkably satisfactory price. After this experience, I began to take a close interest in the affairs of Alan Bond, as indeed did most of Western Australia's population. Bond had become something of a local hero, the local boy who made good; he had become the ambassador of Western Australia's success to the rest of the world. We heard of his triumphs in America and in China; in Britain, his native land, he bought a village and set out to become its squire.

My next encounter with Alan Bond was during the America's Cup in Perth in 1987, a time when he was at the height of his fame and, as it turned out, at his most vulnerable financially. For the Cup, my family's company took over the dock previously used by the Italian team, Italia, which had been knocked out at an early stage. John Adams arranged to have a tent set up the length of the dock. Large television sets were strategically placed so that my guests could eat their lunch and watch the racing at the same time. That dock was a wonderful spot to be in during the week of the Cup; we were at the heart of the action and in great comfort, as well. Unfortunately, the Americans won so convincingly that the racing took a day less than had been expected. Suddenly it was all over and Australia had lost. Frantic negotiations took place to keep the Cup in Australia by offering such advantageous terms to the victors that they would choose Fremantle as the venue for the next challenge. The Government of Western Australia and its supporters from business nearly pulled it off. The reality of life, however, was that had the victorious Americans gone home to Newport and announced that the America's Cup would once again be competed for at Fremantle, instead of a victory parade, there would have been a lynching. Since the tycoons of Perth were at a loose end that day, I invited them all to lunch. It was extraordinary to see the likes of Laurie Connell, Alan Bond and other members of what was to be called 'Western Australia Inc.' sitting all together at the same table. To cheer them up, I told the story of Alan Bond and how he had taken the hot water heaters from the Riviera flats after he had sold the property to me. He really seemed quite proud of what he had done. The others thought it was a great joke, particularly Laurie Connell. For some years after that lunch, I did not meet Alan Bond again; indeed, there was no reason for our paths to cross.

In a few years, however, his name came up at a board meeting of Imre Properties, a public company whose chairman was the charismatic and brilliant financier, David Davis. It was suggested that Alan Bond would buy 50 per cent of the property development that we were undertaking on the site of the old St George's Hospital at London's Hyde Park Corner. Never in my whole business career had I been so definite about anything at a board meeting. Alan Bond was a man with whom I did not wish to be in partnership under any circumstances. There was not a price that Bond could offer that would make me change my mind. On this I was quite clear—Bond should buy the whole scheme or nothing. A few days later, he came back with a highly acceptable offer for the whole development.

While Bond in those days was a man of mercurial moods, one aspect of his character was always constant: he could not resist a gamble, especially in a field that he knew nothing about. At the outset of what turned out to be by any standards a remarkable career, Alan Bond succeeded in cheating me out of the hot water heaters in the Riviera flats. I suppose he felt that he could go on behaving in the same way towards everyone else with whom he did business. Events, however, moved against him—his gambles had been a little too wild and his business practice a little too sharp. His decline was short, his struggle to avoid the consequences of his actions protracted but its result inevitable. While Western Australia was the richer for having Bond as a citizen, it's just a shame that he directed himself towards business rather than politics.

3

My hosts were kind in my first days in Perth. Each evening I was entertained by different people. While the people who entertained me were different, the restaurant that they took me to was always the same one. It was Luis, the city's best restaurant. In those days, it was decorated with printed colour reproductions of the great paintings of Degas, Monet and Renoir—'I am told that these pictures are extremely valuable,' said one of my hosts. The food was awful and the pictures imitation; the proprietor of Luis knew little about French art or cooking. The citizens in those days all seemed to be big men, well over six feet tall, with heads like shopping baskets and faces burned brown by the sun and the wind. They wore grey suits and brown fedora hats, looking at you from under wide brims that made no attempt to hide their eyes.

By chance, I met in Perth in the mid-1960s a man who was to become one of a small group of four or five people whom I consider to be my closest friends. I do not make real friends easily, although I have many acquaintances that others might call friends. I had in London been introduced to the Agent-General for Western Australia, a former Government minister of that State, Gerry Wild. He gave me an introduction to a lawyer friend of his in Perth, called Adams. One morning I went to the office of Mr Adams and asked to see him. Perth was like that then: you just turned up at somebody's office and they would see you; appointments seemed unnecessary. It was the same even with senior politicians. The whole place was extremely casual; there was no noticeable security nor, for that matter, any need for security. The office of premier of Western Australia was about the equivalent of that of mayor of a small European city; the premier's budget for a state the size of Western Europe would at that time have been smaller than that of most large towns in Britain.

Seeing before her a young man, the receptionist assumed that I wanted the young Mr Adams, rather than the older and rather grander Mr Adams to whom I had an introduction. Young Mr Adams, John, appeared and even he did not mention his father. I explained what I wanted done and John explained that he could save my family a lot of tax if we made our land purchases in a particular way. I did not really understand tax then—and I still do not understand it now—so I thought it better if John came to England to talk to experts. 'I am pretty busy,' he told me but, once in the street, as he told me years later, he ran all the way to the travel agent to get a ticket for the next day's flight. When we arrived in England, I took John to my home at Fawley Green, arriving there at about midday on a Sunday. I showed John his room, left him to have a bath and change, and returned with a dry martini. My family prided itself on its dry martinis and I had been taught the art in a hard school: pour a few drops of vermouth into a shaker full of ice, shake it about and throw the liquid away, then add a large quantity of gin, shake it up, pour the liquid into an ice-cold glass, rub a slice of lemon peel around the edge of the glass and serve. John drank the cocktail and said that he would be down for lunch in a few minutes. Time passed and still there was no sign of John. Lunch was delayed and delayed again. After the second delay, I went upstairs to find out what had happened to him. John was fast asleep; he woke only in time for breakfast on Monday morning.

A month after this first visit to London, John Adams joined the board of my family's Australian company and stayed there until 1990, when he left to become a Master of the Supreme Court of Western Australia. In late March 1996, John died of cancer. His death took much of the joy out of my visits to Australia; we had, for thirty years, been extremely close friends. My memories of him are legion but, like so many memories of friendship, they are full of the jokes of fleeting moments, the joinings of two people's sense of humour that, when written down, lose their energy. In print, the events that made us laugh become too laboured to seem humorous at all. Numerous were the travels we made together in those early days, carrying a giant model of the new Parmelia Hotel and the adjacent office block, visiting government office after government office, endlessly answering the question, 'Why would you want to build this hotel in Perth?' The answer was that I had faith in Western Australia—I saw something in the economic climate that attracted me to the place.

ॐ

In those days in Perth the city did not have much in the way of entertainment, and at a weekend it was a place of peace and particularly quiet. As for vice and crime, they barely existed. In those days, you never saw a policeman; crime was, as a citizen of Perth might say, 'as rare as hens' teeth'. If you saw a girl standing on a street corner late at night, and you often did, she was waiting for a bus. Walking in the streets at any time of day or night was totally without danger. John Adams and I used to set out looking for fun. I was, at the time, a mere twenty-two years old. We liked to drink and, if possible, we liked to drink where women were to be found. Drink was not easy to come by then and the women of Perth were respectable. The morals of the promiscuous society had not reached Perth from London's Kings Road. There was a motel in south Perth, I forget its name, where airline crews stayed on overnight stops. They drank a lot in those days and then the fun and games began. A favourite trick was for two male members of such a crew to hold a woman upside down so she could walk up a wall and across the ceiling, leaving footprints of boot polish on the paintwork, much to the amazement of the room's next occupants. This was considered the height of entertainment.

The airport was popular because the bar was open for longer hours than were the bars in the city hotels. When I first visited the airport, it was packed with people whom I imagined were waiting for their flights but, in fact, were waiting for another drink. Pinocchios, a nightclub in Murray Street was, I believe, dry but full of young women. One night, John and I, tiring of Pinocchios, decided to move on. The car was parked some way off and rain was pelting down; water ran about a foot deep in the gutters. Believing that there was no point in us both getting soaked, John ran to fetch the car while I waited in front of the club's door. Without warning, a customer was ejected from the club. He came out horizontally, hitting me in the small of the back. I was pitchforked into the water rushing down the gutters. That was about as wild as nightlife was likely to become in the Perth of the 1960s.

As a result of the laws restricting drinking, rather than eliminating drunkenness, it became common. On my first stay in the old Adelphi, I was sitting one afternoon in the lounge when a middle-aged woman fell down the stairs from the first floor. I looked on in amazement as she scrambled to her feet, swaying like a galleon in a heavy sea, top-heavy with a large hat not unlike a cream bun, balancing herself with hands hidden in long white gloves. In a flash, the woman spotted my amazement. 'What the —— —— are you staring at?' Then, as an afterthought, 'You'd be drunk if it was your son getting married.' Too stunned to apologise, I watched in silence as she felt her way along the wall to the hotel's front door.

On a Sunday, there was no drinking except for a couple of hours in the afternoon. This was called 'the Session'. The beer was served in jugs, each member of the party taking a couple of jugs in each hand, going into the garden of the hotel and drinking long after the place closed. This restriction on a person's right to drink was clearly not designed to attract foreign tourists and it certainly would not help an international hotel earn a living. After much negotiating with the State Government, John Adams and I managed to agree a formula for a liquor licence that would be satisfactory for the new Parmelia Hotel. There was, at that time, no such thing as, for instance, a banqueting licence, and the hours in which a hotel guest was allowed a drink were restricted to the same hours as those allowed the patrons of its bars. The Government had been as helpful as one might expect, bearing in mind that a luxury international hotel in this unlikely city was the idea of Sir Charles Court, then the Minister for Industrial Development, who sold the idea to Sir Halford Reddish, who then sold it to me. I in turn had sold it to my family, none of whom realised quite how bizarre a suggestion this was for the City of Perth in 1965.

John Adams and I were confident that, with the government on-side, we would have little trouble in the matter of this special licence. In due course, John and I set off across the street from the old Adelphi to the Licensing Court. The judge was an old man, or so he seemed to be—in retrospect, he was probably in his mid-fifties. He looked at us with total contempt. 'I have read your submission to the court and I see that you intend to build a five-star hotel. We do not have five stars in this State; we do have four stars but no four-star hotels. You can build a four-star hotel if you have a mind to, although I would not advise it. As, however, we have not got five stars, you cannot build a five-star hotel.' This was an unpromising start, to say the least. He continued, 'I have studied your plans for this hotel and I cannot find any single bedrooms nor can I find a reading room on each floor'.

John explained in a deferential manner that it was the habit these days to build hotels where all the rooms were doubles and there were no reading rooms in modern hotels. 'That may very well be your habit to build hotels in that fashion but it is not my habit and this hotel will have single rooms and reading rooms if it is to have a licence.' John rose to protest. 'Sit down,' the judge snapped. John sank to his seat as if he had been shot. 'What is more, the single rooms will be so small that only one single bed fits in there. The reading rooms will be fitted out with armchairs and all the bedside lights will be screwed to the wall.' I stood up to protest and was firmly shot down. 'You, sir, are clearly unaware of how things are done in Western Australia so I will explain them to you just once. The single bedrooms will be small as I do not want you putting another bed in there after I inspect your premises. I insist on this because you might put two people in the same room who do not know each other and the bedside lights will be screwed to the wall as I don't want you taking them out once I have inspected the place.'

I protested that this was a luxury hotel and there was no possibility of two strangers being forced to share a room. 'That may sound ridiculous to you,' said the judge with some passion, 'but only last week I booked into a hotel in Port Hedland. When I went to sleep, I was alone in my room. When I awoke in the middle of the night, there were two other men sleeping there, and by morning one of them had left taking my wallet. As for the reading rooms, there are a number of people, of whom I might say I am one, who do not want to spend their time in bars. These reading rooms are for us and, what is more, the law provides that we shall have our reading rooms.'

I left the building and had, once again, to seek the help of Sir Charles Court, the dynamo behind the mega-leap to prosperity that Western Australia took during the late 1960s. Sir Charles recognised the problems that I faced with the Licensing Board: Western Australia was to have a five-star hotel and so, in time, work started on the Parmelia Hotel.

༄

Travelling around with that giant model of the Parmelia became the bane of my life. When I first brought it into Australia, the customs officers made me unpack it, which involved removing almost fifty brass screws that held the lid of its travelling box in place. Then they pronounced: 'This thing is made of wood. You can't bring it into Australia!' Happily, John had met my plane and I was able to say, 'Hold on a moment while I fetch my lawyer.' John persuaded them to allow the model into Australia provided we had it sprayed. Determined, however, to stop something coming into Australia, they picked on the fur coat of my then wife, Sarah. 'How long has that been dead?'

This box travelled with us from Canberra to Sydney, then to Melbourne and then back again to Canberra. Every time we showed the wretched thing, all its screws had to be undone. Every time we changed State, quarantine and health officials would ask, 'What's in that box?' We travelled from banks to borrow money, to the government to ask permission to borrow money, and always we were asked the same question: 'Why would you want to build that hotel in Perth?' Even when our travels around the capitals of the Australian

States were over, the problems with the Parmelia Hotel persisted. Even in Perth itself, officials did not believe that the badly needed hotel of international quality would ever be built.

There can be no doubt that the Parmelia was planned to be as no other hotel in Australia. Sir Halford Reddish wanted the best. 'A small version of London's famous Dorchester Hotel' was how he described his vision of the Parmelia. Sir Halford, apart from being a considerable industrialist, was a man who knew 'the best' when he came across it, and the Parmelia was to be his home in Australia. What is more, he had just the right manager in mind to run the place—Donald Mclean, who ran the Sheraton East in New York, the hotel where Sir Halford always stayed when in that city. The Sheraton East had about this time just been sold and was due to be demolished. Donald Mclean was ready to make a change, although I do not imagine that he ever expected that change to be from New York's Park Avenue to Mill Street in a small Australian city. When Donald Mclean arrived in Perth, he oversaw the outfitting of the building and also hired and trained staff.

A large, florid-faced man in, I suppose, his mid-thirties, he wore the formal clothes of a hotel manager. It seemed, however, that these clothes had been made for another person, as nothing that he wore really seemed to fit him. Mclean was, if nothing else, a great enthusiast. He entered into life in Perth with gusto, gave parties and went to parties. It must, of course, be remembered that by the standards of the world's great capitals, in those days the wild set of Perth was extremely tame. At Donald Mclean's parties, champagne and canapés were served; at everyone else's, beer—and you cooked your own steak or prawns.

Dancing furiously at a beach party on a hot summer's evening, Mclean began to sweat profusely, and damp patches began to appear on the front of his pink shirt. A fellow reveller, a prospector just out of the bush for a week's holiday in the metropolis, took a dislike to Mclean from the moment that he set eyes on him. Walking up to this florid and sweaty hotel manager, he brought Mclean's dancing to an abrupt halt by poking him in the chest. It seemed as if a fight was about to ensue. Mclean, who was winded from the dancing and always had a certain trouble getting the words from his brain into general circulation, stood gasping. The prospector looked him up and down and then remarked, 'It seems to me that your pink shirt and your pink face were both washed in the same bucket.' Before Mclean could reply or strike a blow, the prospector weaved his way off into the night.

Donald Mclean's efforts at setting up the Parmelia were remarkable: in a city that had never heard of interior decoration and had no tradition of service, he gave Sir Halford the hotel he sought. The Parmelia became a hotel of considerable character, furnished with decorative antiques and a fine collection of Australian paintings all displayed with great style. Most of the paintings were bought from Rose Skinner, who dominated the art market in Western Australia. Mclean's budget was modest but the results he achieved were very grand. While many in Perth bemoaned the loss of the old Adelphi Hotel, the Parmelia was the first sign of the affluence that was to grip Perth in the following decades. Perth was still a long way from everywhere but it now boasted a hotel that people wanted to stay in.

Donald Mclean pleased Sir Halford Reddish in almost every respect except one—Mclean liked a drink. Sir Halford was a teetotaller; no-one who worked around him mentioned drink, let alone took one when he was present. The staff Christmas party at Rugby Portland Cement, the company that Sir Halford chaired and ran as a virtual dictator, was a dry occasion—dry, that is, until some enterprising managing director switched the fruit punch for Pimm's and then convinced Sir Halford that Pimm's was a non-alcoholic drink. Sir Halford was not often in Perth, so the fact that Donald Mclean liked a drink or two went unnoticed for a couple of years. The end came suddenly. Mclean had been to a highly successful party and, although tired, he decided to drive himself home in the early hours of the morning. After a long day's work and a long night's drinking, he fell asleep in his car. But for where it was, I doubt if the police would have noticed him, sleeping quietly in the early hours of the morning. Perth, after all, was in those days a city where the police presence was almost invisible. Mclean was incensed at being woken from a deep sleep by two policemen. 'Drunk, how dare you say that I am drunk?' he said, or words to that effect. The policemen stared at him in total amazement and then asked how he came to be asleep in a car that was parked in the middle of a highway and, what was more, a car that was facing the wrong way? There was no answer. Mclean rang his lawyer who had him released from the police station. At first, it was judged best not to inform Sir Halford of Mclean's indiscretion. It was, after all, a personal matter and did not happen during working hours. Besides, in the nature of their job, hotel managers either drink nothing or rather a lot. However, in every organisation there is someone who delights in passing on bad news. So it was with Donald Mclean—he left his job and left Australia the richer for having known him and the poorer for his going.

❧

After Mclean's departure, my family sold its interest in the Parmelia to Sir Halford Reddish's company. The hotel was for some years never quite the same; profits were given priority over style. Perth grew and the Parmelia grew with Perth, its customers were no longer farmers uncomfortable amongst the hotel's fashionable decor. Business was booming in Perth. Business people from overseas stayed at the Parmelia, business people used its bars and its restaurants, a nightclub was opened and the place prospered.

In every hotel, stories abound, and the Parmelia was no exception in this respect. It became a step in the career of a number of stars in Perth's hotel and catering industry, among them Gavino Achenza. Gavino is a champion among enthusiasts; for him, every day starts well and can only get better. He is also the sort of man who attracts the unusual as inevitably as dead fish attract flies on a hot day. On his first day as a trainee waiter, he entered the kitchen of the hotel where he was working with his usual enthusiasm, whistling gaily. Seeing the stacked tray of dishes that were ready for serving, he picked them up and, still whistling, moved towards the service door. Almost at the door, he felt a stab of pain in his left buttock and, with his free hand, searched for the cause. Gavino was somewhat surprised when he found a serving fork sticking out of his bottom and blood running down his hand. Putting down the tray, he pulled the fork out and then looked around to find out how it got there. The cause was self-evident—the head chef was standing there with a face of thunder. 'You ignorant young fool,' he shouted at Gavino. 'Don't you know that it's the worst kind of luck to whistle in a kitchen?' Gavino did not know that it was bad luck to whistle in a kitchen but he did now know that the chef was amazingly adept at throwing a two-pronged serving fork a long distance at a small target.

Gavino later took over the management of the Garden Restaurant at the Parmelia. In a restaurant, Gavino moves about the place like a tennis champion. Trained in Britain, he is the sort of head waiter who makes you feel that he has waited all year for you to come to his restaurant, even if you last dined there only the day before. Nothing is too much trouble for him when it comes to his customers. Even if he doesn't have the dishes that they require on his menu and the ingredients are not in the kitchen, he leaves them feeling satisfied, simply by convincing them that they did not really want those dishes in the first place. While Gavino was at the Parmelia, the hotel had an important customer: an elderly gentleman, a local businessman who lunched there every day; his lunch, always just a plate of smoked salmon. He was undemanding and his habits were as regular as clockwork. He would arrive at the same time Monday to Friday, sit at the same table, look at the menu and order smoked salmon. On this particular day, Gavino had greeted the customer and, as usual, asked him how he was. 'Very well, thank you,' the customer replied. He was seated, his smoked salmon ordered and, in the twinkling of an eye, it was served. Gavino, moving around the restaurant attending other customers, noticed that the elderly gentleman only sat and looked at his smoked salmon, making no attempt to eat it. Concerned lest the customer was upset, Gavino wondered how he should approach this problem.

Pulling himself to his full height and selecting his broadest smile, Gavino swung nonchalantly across the room, looking everywhere except at the man and his untouched smoked salmon. 'Well, how is everything today?' he said, as he patted the man on his back. In place of a reply, the man fell forward, his face four-square in the plate of smoked salmon; clearly, he was dead. Gavino quickly pulled him into a seated position and then, sliding his arm around the waist of the corpse, raised it to its feet. Determined not to spoil the lunch of his other customers, Gavino walked with the corpse towards the kitchen. The head waiter and the dead customer appeared to be in animated conversation. It was then that Gavino's problems really began: the chef, Gavino knew, wouldn't have the corpse in the kitchen, and he couldn't leave it in the restaurant.

Chefs, as Gavino well knew, are highly superstitious, and if whistling causes bad luck, heaven alone knows what sort of bad luck a corpse would cause in a kitchen. Gavino was not unresourceful, so he propped the corpse up between the double swing doors of the kitchen's service entrance and went off to ring for an undertaker. Undertaking, however, is not a trade where hurry is of the essence; corpses can usually be counted upon to wait for the undertaker, unlike customers in a restaurant who expect to get fed promptly. When Gavino returned from the telephone, he discovered that the corpse had collapsed and was jammed between the two sets of swing doors. What was worse, the waiters now all knew that the customer who had been lurking in between the swing doors for the last fifteen minutes was dead and not just taking a nap. Gavino was right about the chef—he refused to have the corpse even pass through his kitchen. In addition, the waiters refused to step over the body as they went in and out of the kitchen. Gavino ended up performing a shuttle service between the waiters in the kitchen and those out in the restaurant.

In time, Gavino left the Parmelia to open his own restaurant. With a partner, he ran the Mediterranean in Perth. It soon became the epicentre of Western Australia Inc. His customers planned deals, buying and selling companies as they ate their lunch and drank what in those days appeared to be an endless supply of Dom Perignon champagne.

⌘

At the time of my sojourn in the old Adelphi Hotel, I used to be shaved every morning. The barber was an Italian migrant to Australia, Tony Sgro. In the early days, he was a travelling barber with no shop of his own. Tony shaved me every day that I was in Perth for the best part of 25 years. When the Parmelia was built, he took premises in the shopping arcade and I would remove myself each day from my hotel suite to his barber's chair. As I sat there, behind me, in the centre of the arcade, was a shallow pond that was supposed to stop people bumping their heads on the cantilevered stairway to the ground floor of Hamersley House. Tony Sgro, always helpful, explained to me that far from helping people, this pond was a hindrance—customers coming out of the hotel's bar often as not stepped into the pond which, to be fair, was hard to see. Then, concerned only with their wet feet, these irate customers banged their heads on the stairway. Much as he found this a great entertainment, he believed that we should fill in the pond. Ponds always appear on architects' drawings; in reality they seldom work, becoming either full of litter or people—I took Tony Sgro's advice.

On one visit to his barber's shop, he looked particularly carefully at my chin as the whole surface was badly lacerated. Even his natural politeness could not constrain Tony from asking me what had happened. 'Last night I was waiting in Singapore airport,' I told him. In those days, Singapore airport was a very different place to the all-singing, all-dancing airport it is today. In fact, it was just a large hangar with merchants selling mechanical toys that performed all over the floor. Bored with waiting for the flight and the toys, I noticed a barber's stall. Sitting high in his chair, the barber asked me if I would like a back massage. Foolishly, I accepted the offer. The barber then asked for a small coin, which he slipped into a slot in the side of the chair. The coin deposited, my chair began to vibrate and the barber began to shave me with a cutthroat razor. The result was the chin that Tony Sgro did his best to repair.

∽

In time, the movers and shakers took over from the tall men in grey suits and brown fedora hats who ran Western Australia. The movers and shakers were short and fat, with bald heads and, if they wore a hat, it was a yachting cap.

Their suits were blue, too bright a blue, with too much silken thread in the weave—these were shiny men. The America's Cup came and Perth became a party; the State changed the slogan on its car number plates from 'The wild-flower State' to 'The State of Excitement'. Still a small city, the whole world now knew about Perth, the place where the tycoons came from, the place where the deals were done. In time, both the champagne and the luck of Western Australia ran out. Cinderella was about to leave the ball and Western Australia was about to be beset by terrible scandals and the deepest recession that Australia has seen this century. The boom of the 1980s, when anything went, came to an end.

However, Australia is built on bankruptcy, with an endless supply of optimistic Australians waiting to take over where others have failed. Nowhere is this more apparent than in Western Australia, for the West is a hard country and her people hardened by her; as fast as a shop failed, a restaurant or café opened. By the mid-1990s, the whole population of Perth seemed to have given up shopping and taken up eating. There can be nowhere else with so few people and so many restaurants. Not the plush paint and velour of the past, these new places were decorated with whatever came to hand, and all the better for it. The city, for all its changes, again had the feel of the 1960s; the citizens still played bowls dressed in their whites, the peppermint trees still stood in the suburb of Peppermint Grove. The lucky country? The people of Western Australia have learned that the ball is over—Cinderella is back in the kitchen and luck comes only with effort. In truth, both the people and the place are the better for it.

4

The bureaucrats who did not believe the Parmelia Hotel would ever get built were wrong. Not only did it get built but it became the first of a number of buildings that John Adams and I worked on in Perth. Hamersley House, perhaps the least distinguished of them, was the next. In time, everything was in place for the building of Hamersley House; all that remained to be done was the pulling down of the old Adelphi Hotel which occupied the site. As the Adelphi closed, so would the new Parmelia open. On the last night of my visit to make the final arrangements for this demolition to commence, Donald Mclean gave a party, and what a party it was. I drank too much and ate too little. My head would, I believe, be considered hard and the quantity of alcohol that I drank that night was no greater than I had often drunk in an evening before and most certainly no more than I have often drunk in an evening since, without a great effect. Perhaps I had been poisoned by a defective bottle of champagne, or maybe in the general excitement I had eaten a bad oyster. Whatever the cause, its effect was dramatic. When I returned to my hotel room, I was desperately sick. Feeling awful, I decided for some reason to have a bath, so, putting in the bath plug and turning on the taps, I lay on my bed.

Next morning, I awoke to find the room ankle-deep in water. As I believed my room was on the first floor, and the hotel would close the next week, I did not worry too much about the damage. Dressing quickly, I set off for some fresh air. Standing in the street by the hotel entrance, my head aching as never before, I watched guests coming and going. In time, a smart, well-built man in a formal black suit of old-fashioned cut, black tie and a black Homburg hat, descended the steps from the hotel's entrance. He gave me a vicious scowl, and at that moment I remembered that my suite was not on the first floor but on the second. The gentleman scowling at me with such ferocity was the occupier of the first-floor suite, a client who had lived in the hotel for many years. He, poor fellow, must have been soaked during the night. In any event, he had booked out of the hotel that morning. Overcome with an aching head, weak legs and the general lethargy of a terrible hangover, my mind was working too slowly for me to be able to apologise for this terrible accident.

ॐ

This all happened so very long ago and it is only as I write that the events of some of those years become a reality. It was during that week, so long ago, when I was sitting in John Adams's office that John's brother came in to say goodbye as he set off to the Vietnam War. Richard Adams looked a fine figure of a man, wearing the uniform of the Australian Army and carrying a kitbag. It all seemed so natural, this parting of brothers. John did speculate, after Richard had left, whether or not he would ever see his brother again. That war changed Australia—the sense of duty to fight other people's wars, in other people's lands, was for the last time stretched to its very limit. At the same time, prosperity came with the sale of wool, whose price rose to a figure never since repeated, and the influx of American servicemen for rest and recuperation in Australian cities. Sydney changed beyond belief; nightclubs opened as never before and the city was filled with manufactured gaiety. Prostitutes lined the streets around Kings Cross, and traffic accidents were caused by cruising cars which came to a sudden halt to pick up an attractive woman, while the driver of the car behind was also watching the same woman rather than the vehicle in front. The roads in that part of Sydney were like the dodgems at a fair—one car after another bumping into the car in front. Hotels opened and restaurants flourished as, for the first time, tourists really came to Sydney.

Time flies, yet we barely notice that it is happening nor its impact on us. When I was young, I believed people my age were ancient; now, I look at people half my age and believe them older than I was at the same age. A few months ago, I lunched with a childhood friend, a woman a couple of years younger than me. When I mentioned the Vietnam War, she held her hands up in horror. 'Never mention that you remember that war, and on no account ever tell anyone where you were when President Kennedy was assassinated. Young people will think that you are geriatric if you say such things. Just drop into the conversation that you remember the Falklands War; it is socially much safer.'

༄

Hamersley House was built and I tried to decorate it with paintings and sculpture, without much enthusiasm from my colleagues. Glass and brass were the touchstones of modern taste in the Perth of 1968. They hated my modern pictures and detested my contemporary sculpture. Although the plans for Hamersley House included an arcade to join onto one that was to cross the City of Perth, it never happened. Its gardens never really worked: the wind killed the plants and filled its ponds with litter from the street. When a creeper that had been planted in the building's forecourt really took off and had reached the fifth storey—for some unknown reason it liked wind and pollution—despite direct instructions to the contrary, some child in an estate agent's office instructed that this adventurous plant be cut at the roots.

With the death of this plant, the last piece of friendliness was stripped from the barren face of the building. No-one that I employed was remotely interested in making this building look better than its neighbours; they could not see the sense in such an idea.

Across the road, a brick building was erected. I was beginning to win the battle to make my buildings people-friendly. Oliver Ford, whom I knew from London, was employed to design the foyer of this building. His job was to give it a dramatic quality—'Make it seem like an old hotel,' I told him, 'forget that it's an office building.' So he did, with a sweeping staircase in the foyer and panelling on its walls. Then we decorated the inside with antique furniture, modern Australian paintings and a variety of strange objects, from farm implements to equipment from Perth's old Mint. It was not a masterpiece but the result was far better than Hamersley House.

Two blocks down was London House, a concrete monster built by others at the time that I was planning the Parmelia. We bought it in partnership with the family store, Boans, then we pulled it down. In its place went New London House, a tall, red-brick building with a grand foyer, again designed by Oliver Ford, with high ceilings, its walls covered by Sidney Nolan's paintings and large Chinese pots placed in the corners. On a carpet in the centre, its design taken from an Aboriginal painting, sat eighteenth-century English furniture. In a smaller foyer off to the side, an entire wall was covered with Aboriginal artefacts and weapons, which made a stark contrast to the elegance of eighteenth-century England. The result was a sensation, the building let at once and in the weeks after opening, thousands of people came just to look at the foyers.

At least three of the foyers that I built in Perth were designed by Oliver Ford. Over many years, he was a great

43

help to my family's business. Not only was he in charge of redecorating the Dorchester Hotel when renovation was needed, but each week he inspected all the suites to check that the furnishings had not been muddled up by careless housekeepers. Through my association with Oliver came the idea to make the foyers of our buildings portable. Instead of designing the foyers of office buildings so that they were all marble and brass, we used paint and plaster, adding expensive paintings and furniture. Oliver was a master at getting just the right colours to make the plaster look expensive, then I would hang often very valuable paintings on his beautifully finished walls. The furniture was always antique; the carpets, often copied from Aboriginal paintings, were woven in Thailand. The total cost of these buildings per square foot was about the same as the ones with the marble and brass foyers, but the scale and the feel of our foyers was domestic. The beauty of the whole scheme was that when we sold our buildings, we could move the pictures, the furniture and the carpets on to the next building that we were developing. No-one so far has discovered a convenient way of shifting marble and brass. Oliver Ford gave me the idea, for he used to make immensely beautiful gardens by acquiring wonderful tubs and planting them with shrubs and flowers. When he moved house, his garden moved with him.

∞

John Roberts, the intuitive contractor who runs and owns the highly efficient Multiplex Construction Company, built many buildings for me in Australia. Over the years, he has become one of my closest friends. A consummate storyteller, John once told me one that involved Ray O'Connor, the man who succeeded Charles Court as premier of Western Australia. They were together in London with Alan Bond. Bond, born in London, claimed that he knew how they should behave. First, they must buy English suits, then English shoes, and then English shirts and ties. Perversely, Bond insisted that they make these purchases at the Scotch House. Equipped to appear as Englishmen, they set out from the Hilton Hotel. On their walk, they passed through Shepherd's Market in London's West End. On a corner about a hundred yards from them was a street musician with an accordion. As they approached, he broke off the tune he was playing and burst into a spirited rendering of 'Waltzing Matilda'.

John Roberts, for all his good humour and funny stories, is one of the smartest contractors that I have ever come across. A man of endless generosity, he has helped many friends when they were in need despite the fact that he is totally focused on his own occupation. Generous with both money and, more importantly, his time, he does not, however, squander either. When you come to choose a builder to work for you, a good question to ask is: 'How long have your key staff been with you?' In the case of John's company, the answer to this question is, in most cases, since he started business. However well-qualified a building business is in a technological respect, a builder is only as good as his or her staff. In the case of John Roberts, they could not be better. In the choice of a builder, another important feature is to decide how you believe that builder would behave if unexpectedly things go wrong. The construction of the buildings on which John worked for me did not always run smoothly; sometimes there were problems but never a crisis, because John always dealt fairly and in good humour with every problem before it even approached the serious stage, let alone a crisis. There is no piece of paper printed with the phrases of lawyers, and signed by all participants in a deal, that I would value above a handshake with John Roberts.

The slogan of Multiplex is 'The Well-Built Builder'. John is just that, like so much about him. His size is deceptive—what at first passes as overweight is in fact strength. I once watched him run down St George's Terrace on his tiptoes, moving with great speed and surprising agility. When I first met him, John was one of Australia's smaller builders; now he is its largest with a successful international business. It wasn't by chance, however, that I met John Roberts—he sought me out. There was no need of his services as I already had a builder, a fine firm named Edwards and Taylor. I had never met Taylor but Vic Edwards was a builder of the old school while John Roberts was a builder of the modern world. When John came to see me in London, I was impressed, for I have always believed that it is a builder's job to seek out customers before they have work to let. In the world of building, persuading a customer to give you a contract is the very essence of your work. So important is this function that I always told my friends that in order to get a contract, I would crawl on my stomach from my family's London offices in Bloomsbury to Tower Bridge in the City of London. Having neither a crawling shape nor the inclination, this would be for me a considerable feat. All my life I was a builder from a family which for generations had been builders. When John Roberts came into my office and we had spent time together, I recognised a builder who was interested in his customers. Soon after John's visit, Vic Edwards died and I had need of a new builder to construct an office block at 90 St George's Terrace so I engaged John Roberts to handle that contract. Later, when my family company was about to build the Intercontinental Hotel in Sydney, I turned again to John Roberts for his help. Even though he had no business in that city, I preferred him to the local builders and how right that decision turned out to be. It would be wrong to say that the contract was completed without a hitch—there were hitches—but, as I have written, John has the ability to resist the temptation of turning a problem into a drama. My man in Australia, at that time, was Laurie Dunn, a highly experienced manager who had completed the construction of several hotels for the American Group Loewes Hotels. Together, Laurie Dunn and John Roberts's staff worked out the problems that arose and with mutual goodwill solved them. By the end of the 1980s, John Roberts had become an extremely rich man and his business, Multiplex, was flourishing.

When the Queen came to Australia, John Roberts was her host during her visit to Western Australia. The Queen and Prince Philip stayed with John and his wife, Angela, at their stud farm in the Swan Valley. Walking with John across his fields one morning, Prince Philip strode ahead of his wife, while John lagged behind with the Queen and a member of the Western Australian police force which was looking after her security. Police were stationed all over the farm and constantly spoke to one another on their mobile radios. Soon the Queen was gaining ground on the Prince, who was striding ahead. Meanwhile, John and the policeman were left far behind. 'There's an old woman following the Prince.' John could hear the words quite clearly as they came over the air from the radio of the officer walking beside him. 'I don't know how she got past us, but she has been following him for some time.' 'Where exactly is she and what does she look like?' went the conversation. 'About a hundred yards behind him dressed in an old mackintosh and a head scarf.' 'Is she any danger?' 'Well, she's gaining on him.' It was only when the police officers began to talk of 'taking her out' that John realised that they were referring to the Queen. At this point, he drew their attention to this fact.

The Queen wasn't the only world figure John Roberts entertained in Perth. When the Pope paid a visit to Australia, John was chosen to greet him. The welcoming ceremony was at the WACA stadium in Perth, and John was selected to lead the procession to the dais in the centre of the stadium. As he walked out, there was no applause; as he came near the dais, there was no applause. Becoming concerned, John quickly looked over his shoulder to find himself alone in the middle of the stadium. For some reason, the Pope had delayed his exit from the reception rooms under the stand, and John had been sent out just before this decision had been made. He was the only member of the procession who was not told what was happening.

It is entirely typical that John Roberts is usually the butt of his own humour. He tells both these stories and many others with considerable relish. He is a man who survived the scandals and the crash in the Western Australia of the early 1990s, coming through the former as fresh and as lily-white as a recently laundered handkerchief, and the latter with both his business and his fortune intact.

The buildings that my family's company owned in Perth let quickly for good rents. My idea of changing the face of foyers in Perth from cold marble halls to human habitations seemed to have worked. By now, I had a team around me who believed, as I did, in conserving the best and rebuilding the rest. There should only be one rule in the matter of conservation—'never knock anything down no matter how badly that building is regarded, unless you can replace it with something that you are convinced is aesthetically superior'. I suppose as a rider to that rule, an open space is far better for a city than a mediocre building. My feelings about conservation and town planning are strong, as the reader of this book will by now be only too aware. Writing about those feelings, I could not help wondering where they have come from. Neither my mother nor my father held these views; possibly theirs would even have been the reverse of mine. Searching, however, through my writings of the past, I came across this piece. It exactly sums up how I feel about the conservation of buildings and the human dimension in planning towns. It goes thus:

A flight to Australia is a long and tedious affair, which I thought could be eased by three days in Singapore to break the boredom. After leaving its mega-airport—a labyrinth of moving staircases, fresh-decked with fluorescent orchids, like some Eastern shrine to the modern world—the traveller encounters, on each side of the road into town, rows of hibiscus, rows of lilies. In fact, serried ranks of tropical plants that seems at first enchanting then monotonous—vast quantities of trees and plants, but of only half-a-dozen varieties.

Singapore is a difficult city to arrive at, for there are so many trees in the city that it seems like the countryside and so many buildings in the countryside that it seems like the city. No smell of exotic perfume here, no smell of oriental spice, just petrol. Its now expensive aroma hangs in the hot and sweaty air, kept captive by banks of cloud, washed almost daily by heavy rain. It is a good rule of thumb that if a country has a large quantity of lush greenery, it always gets a large quantity of rain. There is a monotony about Singapore found, I believe, nowhere else. The shops—Chanel, Cartier, Louis Vuitton, not one, but multiple agencies of these great houses—selling their products half a season behind the rest of the world. Twelve hours by aeroplane from winter to summer, but in Singapore it is hard to tell one from the other. Seasons here become irrelevant and so the fashions in these fashionable shops trail behind, unsold goods lingering on the shelves.

Its buildings, built with all the advantages of blatant commerce, have failed—towers, scaled down from other towns, clippings from architectural magazines pasted into this city then hidden with trailing bougainvillea and filled with potted palms. The highceilinged foyers of the early Sixties with their overgrown chandeliers of cascading glass. New buildings that were once Singapore's pride now seem like a reproach. Systematically they have, for nearly twenty-five years, destroyed everything that was old. Hotels everywhere, snatched from any American city and built in Singapore, everywhere there are orchids—in every foyer, in every room, on every table, tucked in napkins on trays, delivered with the morning papers—there is nowhere to go, nothing to do, that does not involve orchids, always the same sort of orchid.

To be fair to Singapore—a city that offers no real reason to be fair to it—the mood has changed. They are now rebuilding the old buildings as quickly as they can. Chinese merchants and Malay traders are being moved back into reproductions of the shops that they occupied before they were decanted into modern blocks. Bugis Street is being rebuilt—rebuilt somewhere else, for its original site is now the headquarters of the Urban Transit Authority. The Tourist Authority feels the need to recreate some local colour and no doubt a Bugis Street Authority will be created to do just this. The days when you had to kick the pipes in Raffles Hotel to start the flow of water are long gone. The days of the old Bugis Street—a street closed to traffic, opened to food, and the world's greatest form of theatre: the accident of large numbers of people enjoying themselves. Tables all over the pavement, tables all over the street. Food that crosses the borders of the Far East. Nothing that you could not buy in that street, nothing, I suppose, that you could not sell. Packed with travellers, drinking, eating, laughing and, very much later, tears and fights. The nightly parade of transvestites, quite beautiful in their way, posing for photographs with the diners, poking fun at drunks who perhaps did not realise that the beautiful girl they hugged had more to her than met the eye. A visit to Bugis Street was an event. Nothing really to do with the buildings, it was about people—not special people but special I suppose because of their ordinariness. A drunken sailor standing on a table pouring beer over himself. How can you rebuild this? Better let it go.

To wake after a night flight to Australia and to look down on the blue fingers of Sydney Harbour, its white Opera House and grey steel bridge, a city of clean air, a dry city with roofs poking like red pimples through its greenery, a sight that caused some great figure visiting from Europe to exclaim to the press at the airport: 'My first impression of Sydney?— Impetigo.'

Life is about the humans who each play their various roles; when their actions are set in a sterile efficient surrounding, the wonder and the beauty goes from their performances. It is not a matter of surprise that the perfect city, the ambition of the renaissance world, is portrayed empty of a human population.

By the mid-1970s, I had learned that rule of conservation, knocking down bad buildings while keeping the unusual, the bizarre and the beautiful and always trying to give my new buildings a human scale. I also set about actively restoring existing heritage buildings. First in Perth, where the former Bishop's House was restored to its original glory and, at the same time, three houses in Mount Street, as well as the 'Gingerbread House' in Fremantle, so-called because of the architectural feature created by the use of patterns made with different-coloured bricks. Later, twenty or so old pearling masters' homes in Broome were restored: it was, I believe, these old buildings that started my love affair with the North-West.

༄

In truth, looking at Western Australia from a distance, it has become clear that the place is getting out of balance. Conservation has become too dominant and practised in the wrong places. While the Government hurries to transform the vast empty spaces of Australia into National Parks that people are not allowed to visit, where conservation is most needed, however, amongst Western Australia's historic buildings, it is barely practised at all. The people live in a land and the people must be served by that land, but equally the people must realise that if they abuse their land, that land can no longer serve them. We are merely life tenants of this planet and it is worth remembering that we have a full repairing lease with that tenancy agreement. The transportation system of Western Australia is still, by comparison with other places, primitive. This, however, is a considerable advantage, for now is the time to integrate the use of sea, air, road and rail. Western Australia is a State, so its transport system not only should be thought of in the context of a State. When travelling north to south, railways are not an option, travel by sea extremely limited, travel by road still primitive due to the lack of good hotels, and travel by air expensive. Travelling west to east, railways are inefficient and slow, by world standards; road travel is limited, travel by sea is also limited, and again, by air, expensive. This all must surely be wrong. Australia cannot develop until efficient railways link all the State and territorial capitals. Urban railways must be made competitive with cars and lorries, small airlines encouraged, and the excesses of large airlines curbed. Airports need to be built to allow aircraft to carry freight from north to south and, in particular, overseas. The population should be encouraged to spread rather than to mass in one spot. Isolation in a modern world should not exist. The cost of creating a proper transport system may seem prohibitive but the alternative is a brake on prosperity and a terminal act to the quality of life in Australia by confining people and the means by which they earn their living into a series of small spaces.

II

Broome

5

It was John Adams who first took me to the town of Broome in north-west Australia in 1974. John and I had decided to get out of town. I wanted to visit Kalgoorlie because I had heard there were large quantities of old farm equipment lying around the place. I had started a collection of farm machinery and was keen to discover a neglected source of rare pieces. John, however, knew that if I travelled to a new town, I would likely buy something. 'Kalgoorlie,' opined John, 'is far too hot. Let's go to Broome, it's by the sea.' I also collected seashells at that time and, being a cautious man, John preferred that the 'something' be a small shell rather than a gargantuan tractor or plough. He knew only too well that it would be his task to organise this monster's travel to my house in Hampshire.

That day we lunched in Broome, the guests of the local chemist, David Hutchinson, and his wife, Thea. I enjoyed the atmosphere of the town greatly. It was, I believe, love at first sight and I did, indeed, buy some seashells in Broome. I bought them from Barry and Kerry Sharp. Their shop was a disused part of premises that belonged to a local butcher, a man often suspected of cattle rustling. It was filled with disused fishing tackle, old anchors, giant clams and diving suits. Also displayed among all this was Kerry Sharp's collection of shells. In a flash, I was on to this collection—was it for sale? Under no circumstances would she sell her shells, despite the efforts I made over the following years to persuade her to the contrary. For the time being, however, I rummaged around among piles of coral and eventually came up with an Aboriginal carving. This carving was of a barramundi; it was about 70 centimetres long, painted with ochre, a dull red. Spots were made on this wooden fish by flaking off pieces of the timber's surface, leaving patches of unstained wood exposed. I made my purchase and then Kerry produced a small parcel of shells and offered them to me at a reasonable price. I bought these as well as the wooden fish, at which point she gave me some other decorative shells. I always enjoyed the company of Barry and Kerry Sharp: when I bought a home in Broome, we became firm friends. As for Kerry's shell collection, it was offered to me after her death and became part of my collection which I subsequently sold to Chris Mitchell, who worked for a number of years at the Broome Zoo.

In January 1981, the year after I married Romilly Hobbs, we set off for Australia. I had determined to take Romilly to Broome, so we arrived there towards the end of that month. Again, we had lunch with the Hutchinsons and their son, Tony, in the same Chinese restaurant. John and Liz Adams were with us, as were John Taylor, an architect, and his wife, Sue. Michael Szell, a well-known London fabric designer, who designed and worked on the fountain in the driveway behind 190 St George's Terrace, was also with us.

The town of Broome was empty. It was the wet season, and the temperature was several degrees below that in Perth. Despite that, the myth that the north-west of Australia is a hellhole of heat in 'the wet' still persists. The climate in Broome, though, is quite different from the rest of the North-West. Cool breezes blow across Broome's peninsula, one way in the morning and the other in the evening. Often the summer temperature in Broome is considerably less than that in Perth.

In any case, air-conditioning has changed the whole business of living in the North-West. Now, with better communications and facilities—the Internet, faxes, mobile telephones, regular air flights, sealed roads, hospitals and medical attention—what was once a remote and unbearably hot area has now become an accessible and pleasant place to live.

At the time of my visit with Romilly, the golden rain and tulip trees bloomed, the frangipanis scented the air and the flowers of the bush were bright. There were no tourists and the locals were lounging in the sun on the beach, a twenty-kilometre beach that is among the most spectacular in the world. Cable Beach, which owes its name to the fact that it is where the international telegraph cable, completed in 1889, came ashore, is six kilometres from Broome on the ocean side of the peninsula and is Broome's main tourist attraction, apart from the Japanese graveyard where generations of pearl divers are buried, most of them killed in the course of their work. Who could not love this lazy place with its ramshackle buildings and eccentric population?

The old buildings of Broome fascinated me; raised on stumps, so that cool breezes could circulate around them, with only latticework to separate them from the outside world. I loved their spacious verandas and long sloping roofs of corrugated iron. In the hot days of Broome's summer, these houses, cooled by slowly revolving fans, made pleasant habitations. Newcomers to Broome, however, preferred air-conditioning and pile carpets and, as a result, these homes had become neglected. Timber in the tropics does not last if left to its own devices; unprotected by paint, rust consumes corrugated iron.

After lunch, Romilly went to Cable Beach with the Taylors, the Adamses and David and Thea Hutchinson. I set out with Tony Hutchinson and Michael Szell. We drove around the dirt roads that were Broome's streets, looking at the old pearling masters' houses that stood among the mango trees with bare earth around them. I was very taken by these houses, built by boat builders for men who sailed boats. One we came across, on the corner of Louis and Herbert Streets, had the sign '4 sale' outside. We knocked on the door, first Michael, then myself. No answer. We called and then we shouted. Yes, the house was for sale, the owner's wife told us. Her husband was at the hotel, but he would come back in an hour. Could we return?

The house belonged to Jeanie and Peter Haynes. Jeanie was cooking lights for the cat when we arrived at her front door; Peter was spending lunchtime and much of the afternoon at the Continental Hotel, or Conti as it was called in Broome. Jeanie, a pillar of Broome society, was president of the historical society and much else as well. Peter, her husband, had been a pearling master and shire president, a man much respected in the community. He was famous for having eluded the Japanese at the fall of Singapore and then making his own way down to Australia by small boat. Peter Haynes was, as were a number of Broome's citizens, inclined to come up with schemes that were close to pure fantasy; he made a highly entertaining drinking companion. The property had been on the market for some time and my interest was unexpected but extremely welcome. The house was large and rambling, and well-kept inside, where a considerable amount of polishing had clearly gone on over the years. Outside, however, the timbers of the old building were showing their age. As for the garden—or yard, for there was not a flower or plant in sight—that was filled with the remnants of Peter's career as a pearling master. The earth of the yard was bare and bright red, but you could not see it on account of heaps of corrugated iron, old and rusting anchors, coils of cable and a whole lot of equipment the purpose of which I was completely unaware. This, however, was the scene that greeted Romilly on her return from the beach. As I told her that I had bought a house in Broome, her face fell. When she saw the Haynes's backyard and smelt the noxious odour of the boiling lights, her face became a picture of misery. The place's only redeeming features were the vast mango trees that grew out of the heap of rusting iron and rotting timber.

Despite Romilly's misgivings, I bought the house. We signed the contract, drawn up by the bank manager, in the bar of the Roebuck Hotel, so named because of its proximity to Roebuck Bay. Roebuck did not graze its shores, rather it was named after HMS *Roebuck*, the ship commanded by Sir William Dampier, a man the British might call an explorer but the rest of the world a buccaneer. In 1699, Dampier was on his second voyage to New Holland, as Indonesia was then known, when he dropped anchor off the southernmost part of the Kimberley coast of Western Australia. We were intrigued as we arrived at the Roebuck Hotel to see a line painted on the street, parallel with its veranda—'No drinking past this line' was printed in large letters on the pavement. Inside was a sign that advertised a 'Hairy Arse Competition. Judging on Sunday'. John Adams, my lawyer, checked the contract and, as a round of drinks was delivered, he asked, 'What's this about a cinema?' 'Oh, you have bought that as well,' was the bank manager's reply. The Sun Pictures, now advertised as the oldest operating cinema in the world, became mine in this way. John had been right: I do tend to buy things when I visit towns for the first time.

I did not see my new house in quite the same way that Romilly and my travelling companions saw it. To me, the house was a wreck—smelly, tired, falling apart—but it was a lovely house and, standing restored among a grove of giant mangoes, it would be wonderfully romantic. You could find that kind of house described in a dozen Somerset Maugham novels. The Haynes house became my home. I set about restoring it and, over a period of years, I added a freestanding kitchen, a drawing room and double-storey bedroom, bathroom and dressing room for Romilly and myself, as well as a Chinese tearoom and a treetop bedroom in the garden. Nowadays, my former home has been turned into a small hotel.

The Sun Pictures was really no more than a spacious timber shed, with rows of deckchairs to accommodate the customers and ceiling fans lazily moving the hot night air of Broome during films. Between the audience and the screen is a stretch of long grass. On exceptionally high tides, the sea came into the picture house and flooded this stretch of grass. The local airport is behind the cinema and the planes of early evening flights out of Broome often appear over the top of the screen, the screech of the engines blotting out the film's soundtrack, the plane's lights dazzling the audience. There can be few places in the world more exotic and extraordinary to watch a film than the Sun Pictures.

For me, it was love at first sight when I visited Broome. I loved the colours, the freshness of the air and, above all, the laziness of the place. When I lived there, I found Broome to be wonderfully romantic—the buccaneers still seemed to wander the town's streets. Pearls were sold in the town's bars: a pearler would pull a handkerchief from his pocket, not to blow his nose but to show the pearls tied in its corners. At that time, I used to buy property in the Pearlers Rest Bar of the Roebuck Hotel. The drinking there began at about ten in the morning. The days were hot and everyone rose early. Most work was done by the time that people in Perth took their morning break for coffee. The system for drinking in the Pearlers Rest was easy. The customers stood at the bar, placing their money in front of them. The barmaid decided whose round it was and took the appropriate amount of money from the pile in front of that customer. After a multitude of beers, the dealing began. A property was mentioned and then a price; an ordinance survey plan was produced and the price debated; a deal struck. John Adams, who had not drunk alcohol at that stage, drew up a contract of offer and acceptance on the back of a beer mat; both parties signed this contract and the land was mine. It is hard to prove but I am sure that I was sold property by its owners just so they would have a beer-mat contract.

Soon my family company and I owned a great many properties in the township of Broome. The architecture of the town was as architecture nowhere else. The old buildings were ungainly and all the better for that. It was not only their shape and size, however, that interested me, but also their colours, often garish in the bright sunshine of the North-West. It was how these buildings related to the people who lived in them that attracted not only me, but also many of the painters who have portrayed Broome's streetscapes. In time, I discovered that you can restore buildings easily enough if you have the will to save them, but you cannot convincingly place the patina of age on new timber.

༄

It was only a question of time before I became fascinated by Broome and my vision for that town's future. My every move, my every investment, was dominated by the desire to change a tired old town into a modern tourist resort without destroying the soul of the place. It has been my experience in Australia that old homes restored to their original condition only attract speculators who, seeing something beautiful, set about changing them into buildings that are commercially useful. This happened to the houses in Mount Street in Perth that I had saved and to many of my former properties in Broome; it is not an edifying spectacle. This, however, is not an argument for allowing buildings to rot, rather an observation on the attitude to conservation in Western Australia in the 1990s.

In time, the idea caught on that money could be made out of development in Broome. New developers came to town, supermarkets were built and shopping arcades. A town with previously one of the highest records of unemployment in Australia has become prosperous. In all such schemes, there are losers, and in Broome it is the old people who have lost. The town has changed beyond their recognition. Change, however, was inevitable—I just happened to realise what was going to happen because I had seen the same phenomenon before in other places, and it was my intention to try and make the change happen in as orderly and civilised a manner as possible.

There can be no doubt, however, that the scale of my efforts at conserving buildings in Broome has altered the general attitude to architecture in that town. While the old buildings may well have been changed in both their appearance and usage, the new buildings that have gone up in the last decade have, at least, paid lip service to the style of Broome's distinctive architecture. It must be remembered that without a contemporary use an old building is of no more use than an empty bottle, decorative perhaps, but useless. Today, however, the coastline of the Broome peninsula is not cluttered with concrete towers and the other effluent of a tourist boom. No building taller than a palm tree is the rule. It will be interesting to see if that rule stands firm when the commercial pressure is really on. If, indeed, that rule can be kept, then the town will have no choice but to spread, and then it will be the time for satellite towns to appear further up the Dampier peninsula. Each of these satellite towns should be surrounded by an expanse of bush, each of them set back from the sea's shore. Communications will then become a problem and the answer to that problem will, of course, be a railway. A railway that links towns and then links these towns with villages on the coast, villages with small populations that supply the access to the sea that tourists and residents both will demand.

∽∾

Mrs Wing's restaurant was a long, brick building that might, if it had not had tables and chairs in it, have been mistaken for a warehouse. The food, however, was wonderful, quite the best food in town. Today, Mrs Wing has moved to another brick restaurant and the good food moved with her. Even inside this brick shed, to the casual diner, the original building did not seem like a restaurant, for it was not unusual to find a dozen tables occupied and nobody eating. Service was extremely slow, largely due to the fact that Mrs Wing also ran a takeaway. Since customers are more inclined to walk away if there is a delay in food they are waiting to take home than if there is a delay in service at a table, where they are settled with a bottle, takeaway customers were given precedence. The seated customers did not seem to mind, however, for Wing's was as good a place to play cards as anywhere else. Men and women drank, children became fractious and the evening wore on. As a result, I suppose, of plenty to drink and little to eat, fights broke out. These fights would have been objectionable in a restaurant in Sydney, or in any of the other State capitals, but in Wing's in Broome they only added to the general enjoyment of those waiting to eat. It was, I suppose, a tribute to Mrs Wing's cooking that so many were prepared to wait for so long to eat her food. The menu was copious, but there was plenty of time to study it before making up your mind. The item that caught my attention, however, was 'Chicken Wings'. What exotic dish could this be that Mrs Wing had dignified with her own name? What dish of oriental fantasy had Mrs Wing invented? I asked the surly waitress, a waitress so surly that if I did not attach that adjective to her name, I would have to apologise to anyone else whom I have ever called surly. She was a young girl who was working at Wing's before setting off on the next leg of her journey around Australia. 'It's chicken,' she replied. 'I know that, but how is it cooked?' 'Fried.' 'Fried' did not seem to have a ring of the exotic Orient. Watching my bewilderment, the girl explained with a considerable touch of sarcasm, 'It's bits of chicken.' As I was about to question her further, she began to flap her arms in the manner of a chicken that was hyperventilating. At the same time, she emitted loud cries of, 'Wings! Wings! Wings!' My question died in my throat; this dish owed nothing to the culinary imagination of Mrs Wing.

My mistake, I suppose, underlines the great cultural divide between those used to eating at restaurants in great cities and life in the outback of Australia; the waitress had merely pointed out my inadequacy. Later that week, Romilly and I returned to eat at Mrs Wing's, in fact, at that time when in Broome, we nearly always ate at Wing's. The waitress took her time coming over to our table and when eventually she did arrive, she gave me a look of total contempt. Romilly had obviously decided to humour the beast. 'Hello', 'How are you?', and that kind of remark, ending, on looking around the restaurant and seeing it empty, a good-natured 'Which is the best night here?' Quick as a flash, the girl replied, 'Monday.' Romilly fell into the trap. 'Why is Monday such a good night?' 'Because no-one comes here,' snapped the waitress, and then headed for the kitchen.

After an interminable wait, during which time I felt certain she had taken time to eat her dinner, the waitress reappeared. By this time, one other table was filled by a pleasant-looking family. Father, mother, two boys who seemed to be aged around twelve and ten respectively, a small girl who looked about six years old and a babe in arms. The waitress headed for them straight as a well-aimed arrow and, as it turned out, just about as deadly. 'It's a long time since I've seen you,' she said to the man. His wife looked surprised, but said nothing. 'I've never been here before,' the man protested. 'I recognise you,' the waitress accused. 'But I've never met you before, I don't know you. I know I don't know you.' The man's wife began to bridle and then, as the waitress pressed home her attack, 'That beard's a good disguise but it's your boots that have given you away,' she rose in anger. The waitress turned and headed for the kitchen. The woman slapped her husband, gathered up her children and left. Romilly and I sat and waited for someone to take the order for our dinner.

6

Perhaps it is the weather in Broome that makes you feel so good. The inhabitants of that small north-western town rise in the morning to a clear blue sky. 'Oh, hell,' they say to each other, 'it's another perfect day.' On the other hand, perhaps it is the heat of the wet that makes the people of the North-West a trifle eccentric. Whatever, be it their eccentricity or the boredom of good weather for most of the year, Broome is a place where I always found laughter. Joy, tragedy, success, failure, they all have their funny side and in that remote place, I discovered that it was the humour that people looked for. The tale of the town's baker who, finding an Aboriginal had broken into his bakery, sought the man out and shouted at him in a thoroughly abusive fashion. As the baker caught his breath, the Aboriginal replied, 'You are only saying these things to me because I am a blackfella.' 'Hold on a moment.' The baker turned, picked up a barrel of flour and tipped it over the Aboriginal. 'Now,' said the baker, 'you are a white fella.' He then continued to curse the poor man.

Almost the first day after I had moved into my house in Broome in the winter of 1981, I set out to find Paddy Roe, an important Aboriginal elder. His address had been given to me by Mary Macha, a considerable expert in Aboriginal art and other matters. Paddy lived in the Aboriginal camp at the end of Dora Street. The camp was composed of tin houses with corrugated iron roofs and no glass in their windows. Beds were laid out between these huts, iron beds with old mattresses. In the centre of the camp stood a large shady tree, the earth all around it bare and red. An old man was sitting beneath the shade of this great tree carving a mother-of-pearl shell at which he peered intently through old, misty eyes. His hands and bare feet were gnarled and knotted, and he wore a pair of shorts and an open check shirt. An old man of considerable dignity, he took no notice as I approached.

'Can you please direct me to Paddy Roe?' said I. 'Patrice,' he replied. 'Patrice, Patrice,' he kept insisting as he climbed into my car. 'Patrice, yes,' I replied as he directed me along the wide red earthen tracks that were then Broome's streets. First left, then left again and right, straight on—his directions were mostly given with hand signals. Every time I tried to speak to him, he replied, 'Patrice, Patrice,' and urged me on with frantic movements of his hands. In time, we passed a low white building; its most impressive aspect a sign describing it as a hospital. 'Stop, stop,' the old man said and jumped out of the car, quickly disappearing into the hospital. It cannot have been more than a minute or two before he reappeared, fitting a hearing aid into his ear. 'That more better,' he announced. 'I can hear you now, my patrice were dead.'

I enquired where Paddy Roe was to be found. 'Paddy Roe,' he replied, 'no worries,' and he took me back to the encampment where I had first met him and went off among the tin houses. Soon the old man reappeared from between a pair of tin homes and with him Paddy Roe. A man of commanding presence, Paddy wore a wide-brimmed hat that shaded his eyes. Arms hanging at his side, baggy trousers held in place with a wide leather belt, his face broad, with generosity in his eyes, he had a gentleness about him as he spoke, his mind as quick as his hearing. In that first meeting with Paddy, I felt the man's great strength. Paddy often seemed a simple man. I doubt, however, that there is any aspect of his character that ranks akin to simplicity. I knew him well for seventeen years and I was endlessly fascinated by how his mind worked. In the days that we first met, he was an Aboriginal leader of consequence and his manner carried the natural authority of a true leader, an authority that comes not from money or privilege, appointment or position. Paddy Roe's authority came from within the man himself.

At the time, I did not realise that the old man I had come across in the Aboriginal camp was Joe Nangan, or 'Butcher Joe', as he was called by the locals. Joe Nangan was a considerable artist who worked in crayon on sheets of paper taken from an exercise book. He recorded the myths and legends of the Kimberley. His pictures have an immense power that comes from an age-old people and the giant landscape that surrounds them. They are not the paintings that have caught the popular imagination, the abstractions of ceremonies long performed, nor are they the work of an artist urged on by art advisers of European stock in the pay of the State. These pictures are, however, in the European tradition, and they record the traditions of the Broome Aboriginals. Small, serious works, they would be categorised as primitive art. They are not eye-catching, flamboyant paintings, useful to a Western interior decorator to hang in a socialite's drawing room, but small, well-considered works whose primary purpose is to record tradition as that tradition is seen by the artist. In this, they succeed wonderfully and, in their success, they have become important works of art.

Joe Nangan and Paddy Roe were partners: Joe would dream the dreams and Paddy would make the costumes for the small corroborees that they performed. Paddy is not of pure Aboriginal blood, and had been taken from his mother as a small child to be reared by the State. It became a driving force in his life to recover the traditions of the Aboriginal people and somehow to be a bridge between black and white Australians. Paddy patiently guided me through a quagmire of traditions and rivalries in Broome, endlessly explaining why a particular mound or group of trees was important to the Aboriginals, and telling me why, when faced with the same proposition, one person would behave in a particular way and another would behave in the diametrically opposite fashion. Paddy is a serious repository of Aboriginal history and tradition. His face would break into a wide smile and then he would quite literally slap his thighs with delight as he burst into laughter at some memory that tickled his sense of humour.

Paddy Roe carved small wooden lizards. As the new lizards were finished, he would bring them to sell in my shop at the zoo, that I had recently opened. 'These little fellows keep breeding,' he would say as he broke into laughter at his joke. 'What will you have to drink, Paddy?' 'I'll have just an orange juice.' And we would sit in the shade and gossip. Over the years, most of Paddy's relatives worked for me in one form or another; fine, strong young men, often leaders in their community. In the days when I first went to Broome, there was little crime, nobody locked their cars, homes were left open. There were only drunken fights and a bit of grievous bodily harm; theft was unknown. Sadly, as the town grew and access to the outside world became easier, the curses of that world came to Broome as well as its benefits.

I can recall leaving Mrs Wing's Chinese restaurant one night to find three men beating up a fourth on a vacant lot. They had him on the ground and were kicking him. Happily, the police arrived at the same moment as myself. As the constables sauntered towards the combatants, the fight broke up, the four men moved on and the police left. Out of sight of the law, the fight began again and soon the fourth man was back on the ground again, getting another good kicking. Dr Reid, for some time the town's doctor, once told me how he had treated Aboriginals with injuries to their heads that would have killed a white man. The women used to fight with heavy sticks, smashing them together and destroying any part of the human body that got in the way. Dr Reid used to treat hands where the knuckles had been beaten to pulp. Dr Reid was a considerable, if controversial, figure. He became Shire president, a position roughly equivalent to that of an English mayor.

Right through the 1960s and 1970s, the town of Broome hibernated—there was little happening there. It wasn't that the inhabitants were naturally lazy, just that there were very few jobs available. In the wet, the grass grew and the people of Broome moved around on bicycles: cars were a menace, I was told when I first arrived in Broome. A bicycle could be thrown down in the long grass and it disappeared, but a car was another matter—everyone knew where you were. Often, when I received telephone calls from England, the calls would be put through the local switchboard and the caller informed of my whereabouts. In Broome in those days everyone knew everyone else's business or, if they didn't, they invented it.

৵৹

In fact, so quiet was the place at that time, the only serious crime, apart from grievous bodily harm, was a bank robbery— that and a bit of cattle rustling. The bank in Broome was robbed by two men on bicycles. The teller was so shocked that the money was handed over without even a murmur. The thieves left the bank's premises and, climbing on to their bicycles, pedalled like mad up the road towards the Continental Hotel. As soon as they were out of sight of the angry bank employees, who by then were searching for a policeman, the thieves ducked into the mangroves that grew along the shoreline. Hiding their bicycles, they waded through the mud and mangroves until they were opposite the Continental Hotel. It was their plan to return to their hotel rooms, wait a few days, and then quietly leave town with the loot. All went well until they crossed what passed as the Continental Hotel's foyer. Normally, the receptionist would have paid these villains about as much attention as she paid the other customers: service in the North-West was merely a concept in those days, one so foreign to the nature of those who worked in hotels that it was barely, if ever, put into practice. Leaving dirty footprints on a recently cleaned floor, however, was another matter. 'Hey!' she called. 'What do you blokes think you're doing?' The thieves took no notice, which infuriated the receptionist, and a ferocious argument ensued. The receptionist, whose anger was, to say the least, considerable, called the police. For the sake of wiping their boots, the thieves found themselves in Fremantle jail. Strange as this tale may seem, a far stranger matter occurred the night the fire brigade were called out to a serious fire. There was not a lot they could do about it, however, for the building on fire was the fire station and the fire engine was safely locked away inside it.

⤔

While Paddy Roe put on small corroborees, Roy Wiggin, from the Bardi people of One Arm Point was, of this genre, a true Diaghilev. I had over the years become very friendly with Roy. He had a dream about an epic journey made by his father and he was determined to turn his dream into a corroboree. The Aboriginal corroboree is not a sacred or secret ceremony; in fact, its character is not too different from Italian nineteenth-century opera. These corroborees are often filled with tales of heroes, triumph and tragedy. A popular corroboree might be performed for many years; an unpopular corroboree does not make it past its first performance.

⤔

I arranged with Roy Wiggin to put on a performance of his own corroboree. However, as so often with Roy, there was a problem. He had lost his totems. These totems were held in

73

the hand and helped to differentiate between one performer and another. They took the place of costumes and moved the narrative of the drama forward. Roy Wiggin needed money to make new ones for the performance. I arranged with Roy that I would pay him a generous sum for each totem that he made. I would own the totems and look after them, and he and his performers could have the use of them whenever they were to perform. Roy saw this deal as a regular source of income; whenever he was a little short of the ready, he turned up with a bundle of totems. By the end of our association, Roy had sold me over three hundred of these wooden frames with coloured wool stretched between nails, much as a spider makes a web. The totems, like much innovative art, did not cost a lot to make—just the price of some balls of coloured wool, nails and a small quantity of timber. The totems for this corroboree were truly objects of beauty, the variety of designs endless. The time spent making these totems could not have been too great either, it was the idea that really counted. The inspiration for the designs was a dream Roy had about his long-dead father's experiences during a fishing expedition from One Arm Point. In his dream about his father's journey, Roy had seen tide races, whirlpools, dangerous rocks, islands, sharks and dugongs, birth and death—a drama on an all-embracing scale. Cecil B. de Mille would have been proud of Roy Wiggin's production.

As the number of totems accumulated, the day of the performance drew near. I had arranged that the performance should take place at six p.m.; dinner would be served to the performers afterwards. Despite a delayed start, Roy Wiggin's new corroboree was a triumph. His brilliant totems are now in the Australian National Maritime Museum in Sydney. As objects that draw their inspiration from the sea, they could not find a better home.

∾

Each winter in Broome, there is a festival that lasts about a week. These fairs are jolly events, attracting large numbers of people—concerts, exhibitions, parades and other events fill out the week's program. This festival is called the *Shinju Matsuri* or 'Shinju' for short. It was never a traditional event, rather the idea of Dr Reid's family, created to help the tourist boom that the Reids felt, quite rightly as it turned out, was about to hit Broome. At first, the festival was centred around the pearling industry; *Shinju Matsuri* is Japanese for 'Festival of the Pearl'. Timed to coincide with the end of the pearl harvest, the festival used to include a race between the various luggers belonging to the local pearling companies. The race was discontinued; some say it was discontinued because the wife of a visiting notable, having drunk too much beer, fell overboard. The fact that the pearling companies had given up their picturesque luggers, which were prohibitively expensive to maintain, in favour of modern craft, seems a more likely explanation for the demise of this elegant event. Soon after this, however, the pearling industry and its festival drifted apart. The pearlers got on with their pearling and Broome's tourist authority got on with its festival.

During the festival week, an evening market is set up on the town's oval with stalls selling food and 'local' handicrafts. As is the way in even the most remote of places, these local handicrafts are far from local; handicrafts that are, in fact, manufactured tourist rubbish. The festival is a multinational event, with Malays, Japanese and Chinese, as well as European Australians and indeed the Aboriginals who preceded them all in their arrival on Australian shores. One of the dealers at the evening market was a smart young lad of Aboriginal descent. His sales technique was lent a certain urgency by the discomfort of his broad feet, which were encased in narrow, pointed shoes imported from Italy. One year, he had the idea of selling what he called 'real Chinese jade'. The Chinese community in Broome is prominent, and, after conferring with his colleagues, a respected member of that community shuffled up to the Aboriginal lad. He pointed to the jade and said: 'This one Kimberley coloured stone.' At this, the crowd melted away. As the Chinese went back to his group, the lad ran after him and seized him by the shoulder and shouted, 'Listen, do I tell people what you put in your long soup?' Then he walked off with as much of a stride as his shoes would allow. Having considered the situation, the Chinese shuffled back to the lad's stall, and, striking an inscrutable pose, announced: 'This is pure Chinese jade. Absolutely pure.' What he knew, and what the lad knew but the crowd did not, was that the secret ingredient in his long soup was Actifed syrup, which normally serves as a well-known international cough mixture. The world being the way it is, they had reached a necessary accommodation with each other.

By tradition, one of the events at the festival was an art exhibition. Local painters exhibited their work, a judge decided who was to come first, second and third, and small prizes were presented. Shortly after I arrived in Broome, I was asked to judge this exhibition. The year before, I had mounted a show of Sidney Nolan's early work in the town's library. The paintings, all from the late 1940s and early 1950s, came from my own collection and that of the University of Western Australia. All of these paintings, and there were about twenty of them, depicted the outback and the buildings of its small towns. As a result of this exhibition, opened by Sidney Nolan and the Shire president, Dr Reid, the committee of the *Shinju Matsuri* had come to the conclusion that I knew something about art. It was the tradition that the work winning the first prize was bought by the Shire and hung in the Shire's offices. For the previous two years at least, and possibly three—my memory fails me on this point—the wife of a Kimberley station owner, a pastoralist, had won the prize. Her paintings were talented but academic, high quality narrative pictures of station life and landscape. On the day of the judging, I spent several hours looking at all the works on show which, as you might expect, were a motley group. Some good, some bad, some talented, others lacking both expertise and talent. Only one painting, however, stood out. It was a dark and moody picture, a painting of near genius. A painting of the landscape in its abstract form, torn from the landscape. It was clearly streets ahead of all the others; in fact, streets ahead of any painting that I had seen at that date in the North-West. The first prize went to the gloomy land-scape, the second to the station owner's wife, and I went home to have lunch.

By mid-afternoon, the Shire president and town clerk were, metaphorically speaking, knocking on my door. When calling on a person in Broome, it seemed the habit just to walk straight into his garden and not finding him there, to walk into his house. Would I change my mind about the first prize? 'Why?' I asked. 'Well, people have complained. It does not have a frame.' To my undying shame, after a short discussion, I swapped the order of the first and second paintings. It was a small thing, or so it seemed at the time; why should I care who won a local art competition? If the locals felt so strongly about a painting not having a frame, why should I explain that most of the great paintings of the previous twenty years did not have frames and that the sculptures of the same period were more often than not without bases?

That night my shame was compounded, for as I sat with Romilly and half a dozen friends in Mrs Wing's Chinese restaurant, the eventual winner of the Broome Shire art prize approached and presented me with a bottle of wine in recognition of my appreciation of her talent. This tale of weakness on my part would have passed from even the deepest recesses of my memory had it not been for the fact that the picture I had demoted was by a certain Jimmy Pike—an Aboriginal painter of colossal talent. Unbeknown to me at the time of the art competition, Jimmy Pike was serving a sentence in Broome jail for murder. Now generally considered one of Australia's most important painters, Jimmy Pike is a man for whose work I have a deep respect. In fact, I would go further and state that I regard his work as outstanding among both Aboriginal and European painters in Australia. One of the few Australian artists who has an international reputation, his work is found in many important collections including several State galleries and the National Gallery in Canberra. His work is also represented in many private collections in Europe and America, and he has exhibited in Japan, France and Britain. During the last years of the 1980s, Jimmy Pike used from time to time to visit my zoo to sell me paintings. He has also recently had a highly successful show at the Rebecca Hossack Gallery in London.

Jimmy Pike spent his earliest years living a traditional Aboriginal nomadic existence in the Great Sandy Desert. As a teenager in the early 1950s, he and his family joined one of the last migrations out of the desert to the European settlements in the north. Settled on a cattle station near Fitzroy Crossing, Jimmy learned the trade of a stockman, only beginning to make prints and to paint while serving his sentence for murder in 1980. Released in 1986, he returned to the desert and set up camp with Pat Lowe, an English-born writer of considerable ability. Their life together has been recorded by Lowe in a series of extraordinary books including *Jilji Life in the Great Sandy Desert*, and the surreal work, *Jimmy and Pat Meet the Queen*, where Jimmy takes the Queen on a tour of his desert country and explains to her the problems that beset the issue of land rights.

7

In the late 1980s and early 1990s, the momentous events in Eastern Europe and the black comedy of people collecting lumps of the Berlin Wall seemed very remote to me as I walked down Cable Beach, the most north-westerly point of Australia, where people collect old bottles and remarkable seashells instead. Early most mornings, I would walk down Cable Beach with a man who, in the vernacular, would be described as 'my mate Snowy'. Short, stocky, fair-haired and blue-eyed, Snowy County was born in Melbourne. Rough and tough as Australians come, he made his way around Australia working in mining camps and construction sites, eventually finding his way to Broome. His tales of those days are truly horrendous: of 'bullfighting', where men get down on all fours and, racing towards each other, crack heads; of parties where all the guests arrive with a bottle whose contents are poured into a dustbin, stirred and then drunk; of fights and other escapades in camps where he worked.

Snowy makes Crocodile Dundee look like a suburban Sydney car salesman. Snowy County is a pearling master or, rather, the part-owner of a pearl farm that produces the very large and beautiful pearls that are sometimes seen around the necks of the world's most beautiful women, pearls of gem quality. But for every thousand pearls produced, there are only two or three that the pearling master will describe as 'gem'. Whether they are baroque, grey, pink, golden or white, with a deep, deep, lustre, rarely is a cultured pearl from Western Australia smaller than ten millimetres in diameter; the largest is the size of a damson. Some years ago, when Snowy was starting his pearl farm at Deep Water Point, he regularly drove the three hours down the track to Broome for supplies. On one occasion, the back of the truck was full of cardboard boxes containing the plastic baskets used in pearl culture. Sitting beside him was a young Japanese diver who was chain-smoking and casting the cigarette butts out of the window. 'It's hot today,' Snowy remarked. 'Very hot,' replied the diver, taking off his shirt. 'Bloody hot,' said Snowy, taking off his shirt as well. 'Very, very hot,' replied the Japanese, taking off his trousers. Now Snowy is used to hot weather but, before long, both he and the diver were bumping along in their underpants. It was a rough track, in fact, it is flattery to describe it as a track, and as Snowy slowed approaching a particularly deep ditch, the cab was engulfed in a sheet of flame. The pair of them jumped out and ran into the bush— or rather what was left of the bush after a fire the previous week. Shortly after Snowy had explained to the diver, in language that tended towards the crude, that it is not a good idea to throw lighted cigarettes out of a moving vehicle, the truck exploded.

Having got that off his chest, Snowy addressed their problem, which was that they were twenty kilometres from their camp, on a road that only they used, with no water, no hats, no shoes and only two pairs of underpants between them. Snowy took off his pants, tore them into strips and tied them to his feet. The diver did the same and they began to trudge through the bush. The temperature was 46 degrees centigrade, and after about eight kilometres, the diver lay down in a saltpan to die—Snowy's best efforts couldn't move him. So Snowy walked on, sometimes over rocks that were so hot that you could fry eggs on them—and then grill the bacon in their reflected heat. Eventually, Snowy reached the camp, put his head in a water trough and then called for help: 'There's a bloke out there on his back in a saltpan. Throw some water over him and bring him in.' After an experience like this, nothing could make the price of even the most beautiful of pearls seem more irrelevant.

Snowy was first my companion and my guide; later, my friend; and, after a while, my business partner. In all these roles, his behaviour was impeccable which, I may say, is not a tribute that I can pay to most of the people who played in those roles during the 40 years that I visited Australia. Snowy is the most congenial of men; he has a tolerance of the failings of others that would make a saint feel proud.

That I am an erratic driver Snowy has remarked on from time to time, and I suppose that I would be completely incompetent in the bush alone. However, with great patience, Snowy taught me the rudiments of driving, living and behaving in the bush. On our first journey together in the outback, I did not really understand how life operated in the bush. It was almost midday when I got my vehicle bogged down in a riverbed—I had not listened to Snowy's advice on how to cross seemingly dry rivers. Snowy and Charlie Diesel set to work with a winch and, using the second vehicle, pulled the bogged truck out as I set to work on lunch. Oliver Ford, our close friend and travelling companion, who even in those days suffered from weak lungs, sat panting in the heat under a tree with Romilly. In time, I finished my lunch and Snowy his task. 'Well,' say I, 'let's get on,' and off we drove. Snowy never murmured a complaint at missing his lunch. It was only that night as we camped that he explained that it might be wise if we shared some of the tasks and also shared our lunches.

৵৹

After Snowy settled in Broome, he became the Shire foreman and assistant to the Reid family at the time that Dr Reid was the Shire president. The Reids always had some cunning plan or other, which was likely to benefit only their family, and Snowy was often carried along in their general enthusiasm. It was all understandable, because the Reids moved as a clan and wherever they were, that is where the fun was to be had. Snowy joined with Rod Reid and Peter Kinney in a venture to establish the pearl farm at Deep Water Point, a place a great distance from human habitation on King Sound. The peninsula of Deep Water Point is a couple of kilometres long, rocky with rough bush and pandanus palms growing on it. Together they carved that farm out of the bush, breaking a track through the tangle of untouched vegetation, laying a pipeline for water over miles of uneven country and building accommodation for their work force at the pearl farm. Peter and Beverley Kinney were local Broome people who ran a very successful clothing store; Beverley was of Aboriginal–Chinese descent. When I arrived in town, the Reid's main plan seemed to be that they would sell me as many of their holdings as possible at prices advantageous to them and then decamp to Cairns. This plan, as it happens, suited me rather well. Snowy, however, became a victim of their desire to sell. Snowy's friend Peter Kinney had died of cancer and Beverley, his widow, had taken over his shares in the pearl farm at Deep Water Point. Rod Reid wanted to get out and, as Beverley was clearly not going to buy Rod Reid's shares, that left Snowy as the only avenue for Rod Reid's exit.

It was a hot Saturday and I had lunched well under the branches of the vast mango tree that provided the roof to my open-air dining room. Snowy wandered into my garden and joined me. I offered him a drink and put a freshly opened bottle of wine between us. We talked of many things and slowly the afternoon passed into early evening, empty wine bottles accumulating on my dining table. Then Snowy told me of his problem—he had at lunchtime given Rod Reid a cheque in payment for his shares in the pearl farm. As a result, on that Saturday evening, Snowy was the proud owner of two-thirds of a pearl farm, knowing that on Monday when his cheque was presented, he did not have the funds to cover it. Would I like to buy Rod Reid's shares from him? Filled with enthusiasm and wine, I answered, 'Yes.' The money only needed to be in Snowy's account by Monday morning. On Sunday, I rang my lawyer, John Adams, who said that I was mad. Later on, John bought a minority share and did very well out of it, but no matter. At the time, both Snowy and myself were considered a pair of mugs, lumbered with a pearl farm that was going nowhere—even Beverley Kinney must have had her doubts about the venture because a short time after my initial purchase, she sold me most of her shares.

There was a problem with the pearl farm, but it was one that was easily overcome. Nick Paspaley, whom I knew slightly as I had bought pearls from him in Darwin, was coming as my guest to lunch during the America's Cup races in Perth. Few people know more about running pearl farms than Nick Paspaley, and few people in the pearling industry measure up to the level of efficiency and integrity he has achieved. He was the obvious choice to run our farm and happily he agreed to take on its management. For a number of years, things went smoothly and profits rolled in. Self-confidence is, however, a dangerous friend. The farm ran so easily, its results we regarded as a triumph: 'Surely it is easy to run a pearl farm,' we told each other. Then one year the crop failed and, as is the way with pearl farms as the crops tend to go in pairs, the crop failed the next year as well. These twin failures hit me at financially the worst possible moment. John Adams, who had for years looked after my affairs, left for the Supreme Court to take up the post of Master, and Russell Chapman, my accountant, took over John's role. There were many differences between Russell

Chapman and John Adams, and this is neither the place nor the time to rehearse them. Suffice to say that while John ran the pearl farm, he never had any desire to be a pearl farmer—he was wedded to the law. Russell Chapman, an accountant, was different; his desire to be a pearl farmer became increasingly obvious. Under his management, the pearl farm did not run easily. Snowy County was unjustly removed from its day-to-day management. I discovered that, although I had 58 per cent of the pearl farm's shares, I had no more say in how it was run than the other partners who mostly had 3 per cent each. At John Adams's suggestion, I had sold shareholdings to these people for an injection of cash into the company of $25 000 each. In most years, the dividend that they each received exceeded $100 000 and the capital value of their holdings multiplied many, many times. Most of them contributed nothing of any consequence to the running of the farm; indeed, it is fair to say that the majority of them regarded it as a fine place to take a holiday. In the final event, after a deal of coming and going, in 1996 I sold them my shares. The behaviour of those friends and acquaintances in the last years of our partnership in the pearl farm was, if they ever take time and think about it, of a standard that was less than acceptable.

Snowy County, however, behaved with honour, dignity and generosity, and showed not the slightest trace of greed throughout that whole unpleasant period. The pearl farm made a difference to Snowy; it changed him from a man of simple means to an extremely rich man and he deserved every penny of that profit. Snowy moved from a shed to a fine house on Broome's Pearlers Hill—then nearby to the 'old Male house', named for its previous owners, which he has restored so that it has become the finest residence in Broome. Snowy, however, is not changed by wealth—he is still the same kind, companionable person that I knew when we first travelled in the outback. Always a traveller, Snowy visited London and stayed for a time with his friend in a guesthouse that my family owned, not a hundred yards from the Houses of Parliament. One night, returning home by taxi, they were opening the front door when the taxi driver, believing them to be a pair of burglars, called out, 'What are you two up to? Blokes like you don't live in a house like that.' If they are Snowy County, they do.

Many of my guests who came to stay while I lived in Broome found difficulty in coming to terms with the difference between the safety of the township and the dangers of the bush, as do most people who visit the North-West. Albert Roux, the proprietor of Le Gavroche Restaurant in London's West End, master chef and patron of a whole generation of young chefs, who have run restaurants in places as disparate as Yorkshire in England and Sydney in Australia, was among the most delightful of my visitors. Despite the fact that he was on holiday, he was generous with his time, cooking bouillabaisse for 25 of my guests, the soup made from the fish that he had caught that day. Apart from being a great chef, Albert is an accomplished fisherman. I sent Albert and his wife Monique on a trip into the outback with David and Lita Young. At the time, Lord Young was Secretary of State for Trade and Industry in the British Government. The culture shock of the bush threw them a little at first, but by the second night Albert was cooking crocodile steaks over a camp fire. They told me that these were delicious, and I can well believe that to have been the case, although the quality of that particular meal would have owed more to the expertise of the chef rather than the natural taste of the meal's ingredients.

Lord Young and his wife came back from their jaunt in the outback filled with confidence, not realising, I suppose, that their trouble-free travel in the bush was due to the skill of those who looked after them. A few days later, they set off alone in a four-wheel drive along Cable Beach, a safe enough place in all conscience. We expected them home at about six-thirty and when they had not returned by eight-thirty, I was beginning to get worried. A search party was in the process of being organised when the couple appeared, covered in mud from head to foot. It seems that, encouraged by the beauty of the scenery, they had driven to the far end of the beach where their four-wheel drive became bogged down. Inexperienced in handling such vehicles, their efforts to drive out of trouble only made matters worse. Soon the tide was on the turn, a tide that comes in at the speed of a galloping horse. The afternoon was hot and their efforts to dig the vehicle out became desperate. Luckily, a local, driving from the settlement at Coconut Wells to Broome by way of the beach, helped them out. That this man passed by was a chance in a thousand; had he come an hour earlier they would not have been there, and an hour later he could not have passed for the tide. The Youngs would have been faced with walking home through some pretty rough bush, while my four-wheel drive rotted under five metres of salt water. Despite this unfortunate incident, the Youngs seemed to enjoy their stay in Broome. Later, back in Britain, for some time they spoke a lot about their adventures.

My eldest daughter Jane, staying in Broome, set out with a friend to go north to the mission at Beagle Bay. The road up on the Friday was busy. Many people in Broome go camping at weekends and the coastline from Broome up Cape Leveque has dozens of popular places to stop. My daughter and her friend decided to return to Broome on the Sunday afternoon. Soon after they set out on their return trip, their four-wheel drive broke down. They had committed the cardinal sin of travel in the outback: they had not told anyone when they were leaving, where they were going or when they might be expected back. The road had been busy on the drive up Cape Leveque, so logic dictated that those cars that had driven up the Cape must return down its only road. However, they had not realised that the next day, the Monday, was a bank holiday, and so most cars would be returning on that day. It was then that they made another mistake: they left their vehicle and started walking, expecting to get a lift, but no cars came. The weather was stiflingly hot, so they drank some of the Coca-Cola that they had brought, instead of water, and ate some of the salted peanuts, which was the only form of food they had with them. They got hotter and thirstier and still no cars came. In the north, you must never leave your vehicle, however unpromising your circumstances; it is the only place that anyone will ever find you. Those used to the bush will take oil from the vehicle's sump and paint a cross or a circle on the vehicle's roof; lay tarpaulins around the vehicle; light a fire with the spare tyre to make smoke—anything to attract attention from aircraft that may be looking for you. Conserve your energy, conserve your water supply, sit and wait—those are the rules. Luckily for my daughter, she and her friend were in the end picked up by a passing car. They were, however, seriously dehydrated by this time and had the car not passed, they might well have perished.

Another couple who almost came to grief in the bush were my guests, Nicholas Barker, a painter, poet and excellent furniture designer who trades under the name of Alvis Vega, and his wife, Liza Bruce, a highly talented fashion designer who is also extremely beautiful. Neither Liza nor her husband is stupid: they have both spent time in New Mexico and are familiar with empty spaces. Nicholas was born and brought up in East Africa during the Mau Mau emergency and is familiar with the bush. They allowed themselves to be persuaded by my gardener, Ronnie, to set out on a drive to Coconut Wells. Even in those days, the road or track to

Coconut Wells was frequently used and was by local standards of rather good quality. Perhaps that was the reason why their four-wheel drive got out of control—Nicholas had found the driving easy, perhaps too easy. Suddenly, the vehicle began to slide on the sand and turned upside down. Nicholas and Liza were relatively unhurt; Ronnie has had trouble with his back ever since. A moment of overconfidence could have ended three lives. Such an accident could have happened, of course, on a suburban road near Sydney or Melbourne, but there the facilities are easily available to bring help. In the bush, however, it's just a matter of waiting until someone comes along.

∾

When I bought my home in Broome, I already had a garden for it in my mind. I dreamt of that garden, working in Perth; I thought about that garden, travelling by aeroplane, busily setting out the plans of it in my mind. Cardboard match covers were used as sketch pads, paper napkins became plans and plant lists. The idea of a tropical garden had me in its grasp. Turning through notebooks and old files long put aside as I researched this book, I came across a description of my gardener's dream, written in the year that I bought my house on the corner of Broome's Louis and Herbert Streets. I include it here not to show what I achieved, rather to give the spirit of what I intended to achieve. It went thus:

> Take red sand, hot winters, plants . . . Add water and mix—in weeks you have a subtropical garden. This region of Western Australia (the North-West) gives reality to the phrase 'instant gardening'. Clumps of strelitzia and canna lilies spread, blooming within days of planting; palm trees grow well over two metres in one year, mostly between December and February. Speed is everything in the tropical heat. The philosophy of gardening by extraction really counts.

88

The garden clippers give way to the crosscut saw. Paths are overrun, clumps merge, the violent colours of heat spring up where they are least expected. Carefully considered colour schemes can be destroyed in a week, while masterpieces, those brilliant accidents of gardening which we see creeping up on us in Britain, appear and vanish in a month. Bougainvillea, a delicate plant in the British hothouse or lightening the landscape of the French Riviera, grows thorns of savage temper and dreadful accuracy when fighting a bi-monthly pruning, curling great ropes grow into nearby trees. Their gentle colour has a violence which is almost invisible against the midday sun but reappears in the early evening in bright colours that match the sunset.

After the excitement of frangipanis, baobabs and African tulip trees, a monotony sets in. Gardening is done, the thing is made, flowers are perpetually in bloom—always this great mass of green. For a gardener from Hampshire—who takes for granted four to five hundred varieties of old-fashioned shrub roses, bulbs that flower in ranks from March until December, each different, and a hundred and thirty varieties of snowdrops together—what is there to do in this hot climate that happily kills most of the plants we know?

At Broome, I would start with ferns planted in clumps—different shades of green, different textures of green, different shapes of green. There are tree ferns, staghorn fern and elkhorn fern, with their stately fronds; calf's foot ferns, bird's nest ferns, club ferns, moss ferns, *Paraceterach muelleri*, *Lindsaea microphylla*, *Asplenium simplicifrons*. I planted upward of thirty different varieties of ferns in the ground. All them have to be planted in deep shade under the mango trees, which are part of a subtropical orchard: pawpaws, bush lemons, rambutans, custard apples, guavas, passionfruit, lychees, peach mangoes and pomelos.

There's a clump of bananas, colossal growers which drink gallons of water, and a palm garden hedged with Darwin palms, coconut palms (plant these away from people, the falling coconut can be deadly), the miniature date palm, travellers' palm, *Livistona muelleri*, *Liculnalea orandis*. The water garden is to have the blue, night-scented waterlily, the water hibiscus with a red flower the size of a cherub's trumpet, water lettuce, *Pistia stratiotes*, *Lotus nelumbium*, and several varieties of flax. Water irises could also be tried but they probably would not survive the climate in Broome. The water hyacinth *Eichornia crassipes* would grow wonderfully, but there would be little thanks to the gardener who introduced it to this part of the North-West, for further up the coast, inland from Wyndham, the waterways are clogged with it.

Around the house there are to be gardenias five feet high and covered with blossom; lilies, the Singapore lily, *Agapanthus africanus*; and ginger plants, Kahili ginger, torch ginger, shell ginger. Around the water, swathes of bamboo, and frangipani trees, the evergreen native, the deciduous pink and the yellow tamarind tree, Cape lilacs, hedges of oleander, hibiscus and bougainvillea. Smaller in scale are the plastic plants, two or three varieties, all brightly coloured and just like their name.

Candlestick plants (*Plectranthus certendahlii*), so often seen in florists' jungles, look quite different massed in a garden without their plastic pots and instructions on how to water tied to the stalks. *Monstera* curls and grows into the trees, useful in the shade. A thicket of heliconias, mixed in colour—if only it were possible to buy the jade vine in Australia, a plant that really fulfils a tropical expectation, pendulums of turquoise parrots' beaks. Perhaps in time a plant will be imported; it would certainly grow at Broome.

In the summer, winds come with the rain, six feet of it in over two months, so the garden needs protection and, as the house is set back fifty feet from the road on two sides, the verges have to be planted with a thick hedge of Australian natives, with wild-sounding names like waratah, wattle and bush oleander. These are all extremely hardy and will withstand wind and drought. Among them is the boab, the symbol of the region, a great, fat, bottle-shaped tree with nuts much prized by the Aboriginals for carving, and equally prized when carved and sold to the tourists. For water, there is reticulation for ten months of the year from a bore in the garden for two months' rain. All these plants must have water, lots of water.

The road itself has to be lined with frangipanis, planted in 40-gallon oil drums with the bottoms knocked out. These drums speed growth and protect the plants from the multitude of dogs and careless drivers (Broome is infested with both). Then there is a rock garden. The rocks barely need plants: the shapes would put new life into many a sculptor, coloured in red—and such a red. What to plant in this rock garden? Cacti, orchids, *Paphiopedilum* from Thailand, a group of *Angraecoids*.

Of course, there are the orchids—in the ground (*Lycaste stanhopea*); on trees (*Cattleya oncidia*); dendrobiums, particularly the Australian native, *Dendrobium speciosum*, with its long tongue of white bloom; and in tree stumps, *Cymbidium suave* and the black orchid, *Cymbidium canaliculatum*. These last are two of the three cymbidiums that will flower in the heat. The third is *Cymbidium madidum* but I have not been able to find it yet. Everywhere there are orchids . . . and then there are the bromeliads. Did I suggest that a subtropical garden could become boring? Surely I never wrote such a thing.

I fought the land around my house to build the garden of my dreams. I acquired fine orchids, *Cattleya* and *Dendrobium* in France, and native species in Sydney and Perth. Transported to Broome, I planted them in pots, fixed them to trees, even planted them in the earth. Water was the problem, not the quantity of the water, but the quality of that water. Still I persevered. I improved the water, but Broome is a seaside town and, in those days, without a great deal of foliage. I believe many of my orchids were killed by salt and wind. There was a gardener of sorts, hired to look after them while I was away. He had no feeling for orchids, nor much else; he knew the jargon but there was not a trace of green in his fingers. I did better with the ferns; they grew well for a while. The palm trees were a triumph—they grew so quickly that it was not long before I had to remove them, for they were too large or the white ants had got them. In fact, it began to occur to me, after about seven years of failed gardening, that I was growing the vegetable equivalent of caviar and feeding this delectable and expensive stuff to the local insect population.

I gave up on my efforts to create a tropical garden and settled for a yard with a few fine trees. The idea was still with me, however, and I did grow orchids with considerable success at my zoo, where I had skilled staff who were regular in attendance when I was not there. My dream of Broome as a garden became a reality; despite the failure of my dream garden in Broome, the town is now conscious of trees. At first, I planted boab trees in Broome, brought from the bush. There was considerable disturbance about this idea; the people of Derby were certainly upset. Derby was the boab town, Broome had the beach, so why did they need to steal the boabs? Well, it wasn't Broome that stole the boabs, it was me; and in any case, I did not steal them, I merely moved them a few miles and very fine they look in Broome, now that they have grown into stout trees with plenty of foliage. The problem with planting trees in the township of Broome, during the early 1980s, was that an element of the population used to tear the branches off them. Any horticulturist knows that it is better to transport a tree when it's young. Young trees improve at a far greater rate when they are moved than mature trees which lie dormant for some years after transplanting. It is, however, a lot harder to pull the branches off a mature tree than a young one and damn nigh impossible to pull branches off a full-grown boab tree.

~

In those days in Broome, there was a small group of people who opposed almost everything that I did on principle. I was the successor to the Reid family, Public Enemy Number One. The Reids were very commercially minded and often sought to change the status quo to their own advantage. And, as far as these people were concerned, I was the same. It is true that I was in favour of development but not the sort of development that the Reids had in mind. I was cast in a role similar to a famous gunfighter who had come to town. The local would-be politicians of the Left needed to try their hand at destroying me to enhance their own reputations—they needed to outdraw me in order to win fame. The irony of all this was it never occurred to me, nor, I suspect, to them, that such a game was being played. In the end, it was the pilots' strike and the overwhelming recession of 1989 that put an end to my activities, not the machinations of the Labor Left. As happens from time to time, the airline pilots in Australia were looking for better pay and conditions. Normally, this matter would have been resolved without too much trouble. However, Bob Hawke, the prime minister at the time, had other ideas. This was a splendid opportunity for him to discipline a white-collar union, and he grabbed it with both hands. The pilots struck and the Federal Government stayed firm on its original position. Emergency aid was made available by the Government to Perth and other State capitals. No provision, however, was made to help those who lived and worked in the North-West.

As for the political situation in Broome, much as the place may seem to change, in reality the situation stays the same. The small group that opposed me still clamours after power, a prospect that they do not fully understand, for power is given by the people and, when they have a mind, taken away by the people. An almost invariable rule in politics is: if you desperately want something, you seldom get it. The people mistrust those who try too hard and so, in the end, it is the people who withhold office, the prize for which ambitious politicians strive. So it is in all democracies, so it is in Broome.

Accustomed to living in a town where anyone who has a few bucks sets about multiplying them, usually at the expense of the community, these people were naturally suspicious of my activities. Try as I might to explain that my motives were to make the place that I had chosen to live in better, rather than worse, it made no difference. Understandably so, because my motives were not only beyond their experience but also beyond possibility of belief. As an Irish diplomat once said to me as we were drinking in the bar of London's Garrick Club: 'Innocence is a difficult position for a person to improve on'. How true these words are—trying to convince this small but eloquent group that I meant their town well was a fruitless task.

An outlet for this group's opinions was *The Broome News*. The Reids had run one of the previous editors out of town. However, as I could see no reason to be hostile to this journal, I provided it with subsidised accommodation.

Criticism I can take. I believe in a free press and a diversity of opinion: a catch-phrase that has always appealed to me is, 'To irritate is to stimulate'. However, *The Broome News* printed hair-raising stories of my activities, to the point that I began to believe that I was a masochist, helping these people to attack me. In the end, I resolved to fight them—I had tried helping them. I had supported their Botanical Garden Society, always a critic of mine, and I had housed their journal, *The Broome News*. Finally, I had to recourse to law in order to put a stop to some of the wilder rumours that circulated about my activities. How much more productive it would all have been if we could have worked together. As I look back on these arguments, I see quite clearly that these people were well-intentioned: they were not competitors, trying to sabotage my projects, merely people who judged what I would do in the light of what others had done before me. There is, I suppose, a similar scenario in many Australian boom towns—a dominant force trying to bring about development and a group of concerned citizens trying to maintain the status quo.

In the end, those in favour of development tend to win, for the simple reason that development brings jobs and jobs bring prosperity. Both jobs and prosperity are believed by most people to be beneficial. This is true, but only up to a point, for towns, both large and small, are about people, and when the town changes so the people change. While the town may be the better for change, there is now doubt in my mind as to whether the people are really better off, other than in a material sense. With growth and size comes crime; with wealth comes poverty; with business activity, sealed roads and neat municipal gardens and parks. Hand-in-hand with these obvious advantages come traffic and air pollution. The streets become dangerous places, homes have to be secured. People lose the privilege of knowing all the people that they meet in the streets; they live among strangers. Had the people who opposed my ideas for the development of Broome thought all these things through, or were they just playing the game of cutting down the tall poppy? Certainly I was motivated by the certainty that Broome would never remain the same paradise I found on my first visit. The growth of tourism in Australia and the newly created access to the town, limited as it was both by road and air, would see to that.

⚜

After years of combat, my opponents finally won. In the event, their victory was of great benefit to me. By their victory, I refer to their success at frustrating my efforts to build an airport, which, had I succeeded in constructing, would have opened in the face of the largest financial downturn in Australia's history. While both my opponents and I can take some comfort at the outcome of our battles, the failure to provide the Kimberley with an international airport will in time be seen as an act of treachery perpetrated by a timid Government and the project's opponents.

8

I had not been long in Broome before I discovered that Australia was giving away land—well, almost giving it away. All you had to do to receive a ten-acre block, slightly over four hectares, was to tell the Government what you wanted to do with it. If no-one else wanted the land for a similar purpose, then you paid $10 000 and the land was yours. Well, almost yours, for you were contracted to develop the land. Development in the early 1980s in Broome meant that the land had to be improved; improvements constituted erecting a fence around it and building a shed on it. Only then would the Government give you the freehold and you could do what you liked with the land, within the local planning laws. Laws which seemed to me, at least, to be extremely flexible and largely decided upon in the Pearlers Rest Bar at the Roebuck Hotel.

The snag was that this land was at Cable Beach, six kilometres from town, adjacent to the magnificent beach but, at that time, a long way from the population of Broome. Many years later, however, this initial disadvantage became the land's greatest advantage. I decided that I had better have some of this land; I qualified for a grant because I was a resident of Broome. I have always enjoyed keeping animals, so I would start a zoo. As it turned out, getting the land was the easy part. The fight with the bureaucracy of Western Australia to obtain a licence for a zoo was far more difficult.

It was the first of many fights that were to follow in the next twelve years.

My first experience with the wildlife authorities of Western Australia did not fill me with a deal of optimism in the matter of getting the licences that I needed to operate a zoo. The first Christmas that Romilly and I spent in Broome was a strange affair for us. Christmas in our minds was a time of chilly weather and family gatherings. Here, we were on our own, the weather was stinking hot and there was not a member of our family within 10 000 miles. Christmas lunch was spent at the Mangrove Hotel, in those days a low building with a central block of concrete walls with iron girders supporting its corrugated iron roof. Parts of this hotel had been purchased when the British closed down the rocket ranges at Woomera, then transported to Broome and added to the hotel's two wings; bedroom wings with about five rooms in each of them, wings that contained bedrooms of the lowest order. It was in the Mangrove Hotel that the Reid family celebrated their Christmas and we were their guests. We all assembled at about twelve o'clock, drank a lot of beer and then sat down to lunch along with about 50 other locals, who had paid to join the banquet. If Romilly and I had any nostalgia for a traditional British Christmas, that nostalgia was about to be sated in full. First, a course of melon filled with a sweet wine. Then turkey, fully trimmed, followed by ham with parsley sauce. Then plum pudding with a white sauce, something between custard and brandy butter. Mince pies and cheese followed. None of it had been cooked in quite the right way; it all lay heavy on our stomachs. The Reids, however, were generous hosts and whenever they gathered there was plenty of fun, so, in spite of the uninspiring food, we enjoyed ourselves.

At home on the corner of Louis and Herbert Streets, we stretched out in the sun beside our pool. The heat of the afternoon was incredible and soon I was dozing fitfully. 'Are you Mr McAlpine?' a voice enquired. I awoke with a jolt and there standing beside me was a fine-looking young man in a white shirt, shorts and long white cotton socks. 'I am from the wildlife department,' he announced with some glee. 'You have broken the law.' The delight in his voice was barely suppressed. I was a little confused, and asked him what on earth I had done that broke the law. 'It's the parrots,' he replied. True; I had, while in Sydney some months before, entered a pet shop and bought a pair of sulphur-crested cockatoos. I had arranged for these birds to be sent to Broome just after my arrival a week or so before Christmas. This operation had all gone according to plan. The only fault in the whole thing was that nobody had told me that I needed a licence to keep a parrot—or any other bird, for that matter. 'What are you going to do about these parrots?' the young man asked. 'Get a licence, I suppose,' I replied. That was not good enough for this enthusiastic civil servant who had taken the trouble to dress up on Christmas Day for, it seems, the sole purpose of dressing me down. I was treated to a half-hour lecture on wildlife licensing—a strange performance, I believe, because the birds that I owned were only a pair of pet shop parrots who sat in a birdcage exchanging bird calls with a couple of hundred of their cousins infesting the trees of my garden and eating the mangoes that were just on the point of being picked.

Exhausted by the heat and enthusiasm for his authority, the young man eventually left, muttering threats of dire punishment about to descend on my head after the Christmas holiday, when his colleagues in Perth returned to work. He was clearly destined for high office in his department, having caught an offender parrot-handed, so to speak. For my part, I rang my friend John Roberts. 'What's all this about parrot licences?' 'I haven't the first idea,' he replied.

'I'll ring Ray and ask.' The Ray in question was Ray O'Connor, premier of Western Australia. In those days, John was as ignorant of the protocol for owning birds as I was. Today, he owns one of the finest collections of birds in Western Australia, with many breeding successes to his credit.

Later, I discovered that in Western Australia there is virtually no activity the mind can conceive of that does not need a licence. As well as needing a licence to keep parrots, a licence is needed to export them from one state to another. The exporting of birds from Australia is, however, strictly forbidden, indeed, smuggling specimens of Australian flora or fauna can bring a fine of up to $200 000. Once I observed the law in action at Perth airport. A seemingly innocent man with a scruffy leather case was queuing to check in his luggage for a flight with Qantas when a hand fell on his shoulder and a voice ordered him to open the case. The tone of voice left no doubt that the man was a criminal, and so he was, for inside his case were at least 50 parrots, each with its head and tail sticking out of a cardboard tube. 'How was he spotted?' I asked the Qantas clerk. 'Somebody squawked,' he replied drily.

॰ৈ৹

The matter of the parrots passed over and life went on in Broome at a rather different pace from that set by the wildlife official. In the evenings, Romilly and I sat on Gantheaume Point smoking and watching the sunset. The sun, a great red ball, dropped below the horizon and, as the dusk began to gather, it seemed that all was over. Then, quite suddenly, the world seemed to catch fire. The sky turned red and the rocks at Gantheaume Point added that colour to their own bright red. Even the sea began to glow and as the redness left, the sky turned first yellow and then the deepest black. On a particular night of a particular month, when the tide was just right, we watched the stairway to the moon on Roebuck Bay. As the moon came over the horizon, every ripple on the mudflats across the bay became a step in that stairway. Nature in the North-West is bold and strong, sunlight sucking the colour out of everything, and darkness, or at least dusk, making the colours of the bush grow again. Often we would sit on the veranda of our home and watch the electric storms in the distance light up the night sky. These storms made the world's greatest firework display. Often people spoke of rain. 'It'll be an early wet this year', but in the early 1980s, the rain never came, unlike a few years ago when Broome had over 50 inches in twenty-four hours. 'The frogs are croaking, the wet will be early this year', and still the wet never really came.

Tales of Roebuck Plain flooded, the township of Broome waterlogged, and still no wet. One year, the weather just became hotter and hotter. It was as if we were all in a pressure cooker. Then the wind got up and soon the buildings were shaking, palm trees tried to imitate croquet hoops and the heat just seemed to increase. Then rain, a burst of rain, that rattled the tin roof of the house and flooded the garden. Then it was all over. We had been on the edge of a cyclone. The pindan, the semi-arid country of the region, sucked up the moisture like the most effective blotting paper. The township of Broome was green again, the red dust washing from the leaves of its trees and plants, the air cool, fresh and wonderful.

৵৻৶

In time, I was given my grant of land, ten hectares, and I was in the zoo business. Why would anyone want to open a zoo in Broome, all the officials asked? There are so few people in Broome to visit a zoo, surely anyone who opens one must be mad, these same officials thought. My line of approach was rather different: Broome has exactly the right climate for most of the birds that I wished to keep. To mollify the officials of Western Australia's wildlife department, I hired a curator from Perth Zoo to run the establishment in Broome. A pleasant-enough person, this man was an expert on snakes. At first, the birds that I wished to keep were the common local parrots, the mammals, banteng oxen, donkeys, water buffalo, camels and dingoes. Much later, I discovered that the Broome climate is perfect for the endangered antelopes of North Africa, such as the addax and the scimitar-horned oryx, which bred in Broome like the proverbial rabbit.

As was, of course, inevitable, after a while we found that the first ten hectares were too small for my purpose and more space was needed. As the zoo grew, so my plans for what the zoo might become grew. And those plans grew at a speed that was disproportionate to the reality of the situation. Another ten hectares or so were acquired from the Government. Still the zoo grew and still the plans multiplied. New and more exotic animals, new cages, vast aviaries and large paddocks. Lakes and ponds, forests and deserts—these ideas streamed from my imagination. I needed another 30 hectares; the animals needed space and I needed more animals; a railway, I imagined, would run around this zoo. The authorities in Perth allocated me the land, for by now my zoo was a great success. Often reported in the media and well-thought of by zoo authorities across Australia, the zoo was also a considerable tourist attraction and source of employment in Broome.

The land became mine, but at a price. The token payment that I had made when I acquired the initial lot changed into a realistic payment for my second lot, and for my third and largest lot, the price had increased beyond all expectation. By that time, the land at Cable Beach was no longer considered a rural subdivision distant from Broome, rather prime land for tourist development. The price of my new lot was over half a million dollars, a price rise influenced by the area's new affluence—an affluence caused largely by myself, for I had taken the Reid family's old caravan park, complete with its acres of septic tank, and turned it into an extremely attractive international hotel. While I was the victim of my own success, the scale of my zoo was the result of nothing more or less than my own folly. However, the narrative moves forward with too great a pace.

The first ten hectares of land that the zoo occupied was just behind the sand dunes that edged Cable Beach. Opposite my zoo was the Reid's caravan park, which could best be described as squalid. My zoo, grandly named the Pearl Coast Zoological Gardens, was, however, far from grand, just two parallel lines of cages and half a dozen paddocks. At least I had started, and possessed a licence to own and display animals, the only such licence for over 1200 kilometres in any direction. To extend the collection was, indeed, another matter. It was only after a lot of argument that I acquired permission to own a dozen or so black buck and a pair of dingoes. Black buck come from India but are to be found in a feral state in the Hamersley Range, dingoes almost every-where in Australia. The precautions that had to be taken under the terms of my licence to make sure that the dingoes did not escape made the average high-security jail seem like an open prison. Sure enough, however, the dingoes did escape. When questioned, no-one knew how they had got out. It seemed to me, however, that their escape had the assis-tance of humans. In the event, they ate a couple of my black buck and were recaptured while still at lunch. Their capture was no hard task, as my zoo manager was in the habit of taking them for a walk on a lead every afternoon. These dingoes were as tame as any pair of dogs walking with their owner in a city park.

At about this time, there was a lot of talk about Lindy Chamberlain, who was accused of murdering her baby. She had been convicted and sentenced to jail. Her defence had largely centred around the plea that a large male dingo had committed the crime. The jury did not believe her story, as a blood-stained coat, a vital piece of evidence, was missing. Dingoes do not attack children and certainly would not kill a child, experts testified at her trial. The incident took place at Uluru (Ayers Rock) where the dingoes are quite used to human contact. Many of them are fed by tourists and have lost any fear of mankind. Some years later, the bloodstained coat was found at the foot of the Rock, the sentence over-turned, and Lindy Chamberlain set free. I was relieved when she was released from jail, for I had always been convinced that the dingo was the guilty party. At the time, many people thought the whole incident quite bizarre and the controversy about the role of the dingo still causes considerable argument whenever the subject comes up. Many strange things, how-ever, have happened at Uluru.

I can only record that my dingoes, while tame as house-trained poodles, became manic when they saw small children. Animals that would take sausages from my hand and then lick that hand afterwards, would, when young children approached their enclosure, snap and bark, tearing at the earth and the wire fence with their teeth and claws. At first, I did not believe the father who told me that his baby girl had been frightened out of her wits by animals that were tame when he approached them, but became intensely hostile as soon as she joined him. The reaction of my dingoes came as a surprise to me but it seemed to support Lindy Chamber-lain's story. I thought no more about this until I read an article in an English newspaper about some British tourists who had been attacked by a dingo only a few metres from a camp site on Fraser Island, off the coast of Queensland. It seems that the dingo attacked without provocation. Dingo attacks on Fraser Island are no longer rare and tourists are routinely advised to be careful around them. If such dingo attacks could have been presented as evidence for the defence in the Lindy Chamberlain case, I doubt very much that the jury would have returned a guilty verdict.

There can be little doubt that the most dangerous of all wild animals are those that have lost the fear of mankind. From time to time in northern Australia, there are crocodile attacks. In 1971, when crocodile numbers were down to about 5000, hunting them was banned. While a protected species, the great crocodiles of the North had little to fear from humans, each year becoming an ever-increasing threat as tourism brought more and more people to the immensely beautiful lagoons, inlets and coastal rivers that are their territory. By 1999, the crocodile population had reached over 60 000, and the Northern Territory decided to lift the hunting ban and allow the first legal crocodile hunt to take place.

ↂ

Zoo-keeping is a learning curve; there is no expert who knows it all. When in the world of zoos and zoo-keeping, always expect the unexpected. As I set out my zoo, I made the enclosures, both for mammals and birds, far larger than was necessary. People who come to zoos do not understand that animals and birds are largely territorial, seldom moving outside of their own territory. I made the cages and enclosures in my zoo larger than they needed to be, not for the sake of the animals but to make people feel better about visiting the zoo. The downside of this was even when the number and variety of my mammals increased, I used to get complaints from people who had walked around the whole place without seeing any animals. The same, of course, was true for the birds, whose cages were filled with natural foliage. To see animals and birds in these conditions, you need to stand and watch until your eyes get used to the natural camouflage of the enclosure's inhabitants.

At first, I worked in my zoo, setting up cages and creating landscapes with rocks and trees. I enjoyed the physical work and was delighted with my small collection of animals and birds. Each evening at sunset, I would walk around the enclosures looking at all the creatures, many of whom were hand-tame. I fed many of the birds with the bird food from a bag that I carried. Soon, however, the collecting instinct took over. More bird cages were built to house a growing collection of birds. The feral donkeys went and scimitar-horned oryx came. These wonderful animals with, as their name suggests, horns shaped like Arabian sabres, were bred at Marwell Park Zoo in England. John Knowles, the proprietor of that zoo, then became my consultant, guide and conscience in all matters zoological. He visited Broome on several occasions and, between visits, we were in constant contact by telephone.

By this time, my first manager had left, and Ross Gardiner, formerly employed by the Western Australian Government department responsible for wildlife, had replaced him. Ross was not an expert on snakes or, for that matter, much else, but he had a wide knowledge of wildlife and considerable natural charm. In time, we did have snakes in the zoo. Not just the occasional trespasser, such as the python which slipped through the wire of a birdcage, ate the occupant, then found its bloated body prevented it getting out and so became a prisoner. Such snakes were either released in the wild about sixteen kilometres away from potential dinners in my zoo or consigned to the zoo's collection. Only once in all my years in the outback did I come across a snake in the wild. On that occasion, both the snake, a two-metre king brown, and myself were taking a walk. The king brown was wriggling its way up a path and I was meandering down the same path. Neither of us was taking much notice of the world in general, so we were really only a few metres apart when we noticed each other. I might have been expected to stand alert, my stick raised ready to strike, the snake to coil itself, equally ready for action—in the event, both the snake and myself turned tail and ran like hell. A snake that found its way among the audience at Broome's Sun Pictures was less lucky than the snake of my passing acquaintance, for this unfortunate python was delivered to my zoo with both its head and its tail sticking out of the same end of a short length of scaffold tubing. The rest of its body, some two metres of it, formed the loop that stuck out of the tube's other end.

It's easy enough to catch a python. They bite but their bite does not kill. In the roof of my house at the corner of Louis and Herbert Streets on Broome's Pearlers Hill, I had a python. This snake served a useful purpose, keeping the building clear of rats. Once a week or so, the python would catch a rat, usually in the early hours of the morning, and a struggle would ensue. The snake would wrap itself around the hapless rat and would crash and bang against the corrugated iron roof as it twisted and turned in its attempts to consume the rat. After a quarter of an hour's racket, all would go quiet. Visitors were frightened out of their wits by the disturbance above their beds. It is hard to tell really which was the more shocking—falling coconuts that hit the tin roof with an explosion, or the rattle of the feeding snake.

The consequences of playing around with poisonous snakes can, however, be severe. If you are foolish enough to interfere with them, they are certainly capable of doing you a deal of harm. Swan lager, the locals believe, is a great help when bitten by a king brown. You must, of course, have two cans of it: you drink the first and if you have time to drink the second, you will probably survive. A welder working at the zoo was engaged in cutting up piping into equal lengths when he saw a king brown about three metres long scuttle into a pipe, having been disturbed. Hoping to catch the snake for my collection, he tied a sack over the end nearest the snake's head, then he warmed up the end of the pipe at its tail with a blowtorch. The snake moved into the sack, so the welder tied the sack's neck with wire and picked it up. Unfortunately, there was a hole in the bottom of the sack and a very angry snake lost no time in passing through this hole and biting the man on the ankle on the way out. In moments, his leg turned black. Luckily there was help nearby and the hospital only five minutes away by car. He was two weeks in that hospital, suffering considerable pain in both his leg and his head. Without the hospital and expert attention being nearby, the welder would not have survived.

Broome is not a place known for snakes, in fact, they are almost a rarity around the town. On the other hand, around Go Go Station, situated on the southern outskirts of Fitzroy Crossing, a hamlet on the Fitzroy River, it is a different matter. During the dry at Fitzroy Crossing, they pile beer cans around the trunk of a tree. In the wet, the pile of empty cans, which by this time has reached the higher branches, is washed away by the flooding waters of the river. Not much else happened in Fitzroy Crossing in the days when I first went there, except regular fights when the hotel was closing for the night. On the occasion that Romilly and I stayed at Go Go Station, we were told that they shot eight king browns that day around the station homestead. The daughter of the station manager told us that the day before she had killed two king browns with the one shot. 'How did you do that?' I asked. Like all newcomers, I was eager for information, especially when that information involved animals as romantic and dangerous as snakes. 'They were copulating,' the girl replied.

After a year or two, the amiable Ross Gardiner left to engage in the tourist industry, a job for which he is well suited. If I were to take a trip into the outback, I cannot think of a more entertaining guide to show me its wonders. His position as manager was taken by Graham Taylor, an aviculturist from the Queensland–New South Wales border. Graham brought with him an assistant, Eddie Pszkit, a man who had a way with birds. With this team, I set out on what was to become the largest and most sophisticated expansion of my zoo.

Administrative offices and residential accommodation for the zoo's staff and their families were built, as well as a veterinary clinic and separate kitchens for the preparation of animal and bird food. A breeding complex and a whole series of new aviaries were constructed. One of the largest aviaries, over 100 metres in diameter and 50 metres high, had timber walkways, a considerable waterfall and a rainforest. It also had a microclimate that was over ten degrees cooler than outside. It was truly spectacular, and housed a collection of pigeons: the bleeding-heart pigeon, the Torres Strait pigeon, and the white-fronted ground dove. The Pearl Coast Zoo had the largest collection of macaws in Australia. There was also a collection of finches—Cuban finches, blue-faced parrot finches, long-tailed grass finches and star finches—and a good selection of waterfowl. In the grounds of the zoo, I built a lake with a surface area of over 13 000 square metres and, with it, a series of smaller lakes, ponds and waterways. Bustards and brolga cranes walked at will. Over 15 000 trees were planted in the zoo and goodness knows how many shrubs and plants. A dozen sorts of pigeons, finches and parrots perched in the trees, insectivores and honeyeaters—and the ugliest bird in the world, the tawny frogmouth. My parrot collection expanded until I had almost all the Australian species and most of the varieties and subspecies. The lake in particular was a great success. As the country around Broome is dry for most of the year, with few waterholes, wild birds flocked to my zoo—I used to say that seventy per cent of my stock were volunteers. Even the kangaroos and wallabies tried to break in rather than break out. Raised timber walkways were built throughout the zoo so that tourists could cross it without disturbing the animals.

Graham Taylor, who had a remarkable talent for putting together a most amazing collection of birds, spent many hours on the telephone being passed from breeder to breeder on the rumour of a rare species. In time, he managed to acquire a trio of palm cockatoos. Palm cockatoos are not uncommon among the rainforests of Queensland, but are virtually non-existent in captivity. These birds, however, were still of breeding age, so it was a considerable excitement to us when one of the hens laid an egg. We placed this egg in an incubator and reared the offspring to about six weeks, when it died. A few weeks later, the male bird also died. About three weeks after the death of the male, the female laid another egg. This egg was again placed in the incubator and while we were waiting for it to hatch, the female also died. In time, the egg hatched and we reared the chick by hand, again to about six weeks, when it, too, died. These birds were worth $20 000 each so there was a considerable financial loss to be taken into account. That, however, was a small thing by comparison with having such a spectacular success snatched from you not once but twice. The parents were old, it was a gamble anyway, one that no reasonable person could have expected to have come off, but those who breed animals and birds are not reasonable people. The last of the trio of palm cockatoos travelled with Graham Taylor to his home in northern New South Wales. Graham and the palm cockatoo had become quite attached to each other. Graham would put out his tongue and the bird would scratch the tip of it with its extremely large and powerful beak.

Breeding at the Pearl Coast Zoo was not always a tragedy. One of the most exciting moments for me, when I arrived in

Broome, was to visit the breeding complex. In the nursery could be found literally dozens of small chicks, all in different stages of development—some naked, some nearly fully fledged. Eddie Pszkit's wife would be feeding these chicks from a dozen different mixtures, using a narrow spoon to drop food into their extended crops. The greatest triumph that Graham Taylor and Eddie Pszkit had at my zoo was to breed the red-browed fig-parrot. Found in the coastal rainforest of the Queensland tropics this parrot is one of three subspecies of fig parrot in Australia. The breeding of the red-browed fig-parrot at the Pearl Coast Zoo produced valuable information that may have helped save the very rare Coxen's fig-parrot that was threatened with extinction at that time. Graham and Eddie could get these parrots to lay eggs, then the birds would sit and hatch them, only for the chicks to die after a few weeks. Even when they were hand-reared, the chicks died. Hand-rearing a chick the size of a small fingernail is no easy matter, but it was not the feeding that was the problem, it was the food. Aviculturists believed that these parrots eat the small figs from a variety of figtree usually found in the Queensland rainforests. They are often seen feeding on these trees and they gobbled up that tree's fruit when fed in captivity. It was, however, not the fruit that the birds were after, rather the larvae that grew inside the fruit. The solution to rearing the young was simple: add protein to their food. After this, we bred several fig-parrots, both in the nest and by hand-rearing.

Pelicans flew into the zoo's lakes and even jabiru storks, along with thousands of migrating birds. Eight million of them come from Northern Europe, leaving a European winter to join in an Australian summer. They land on the beaches of Broome and then move inland to the seasonal deposits of water. In the sky above the zoo, black, whistling and Brahminy kites could be seen, and ospreys were regular visitors. Among the injured birds and animals brought to the zoo were a pair of osprey chicks. They were reared by the zoo's staff, and for a season would swoop out of the sky to take the food held out for them. After that season, they moved on. Birds came and birds went; always there was something wonderful to see. Both white and glossy ibis made their home at the zoo. Royal spoonbills came, along with great egrets, Pacific heron and straw-necked ibis. Lesser frigatebirds, their red chests inflated, wheeled in the sky and, swooping, took fresh water from the lakes. Eyton tree ducks, black duck, white-eyed duck and grey teal all came in the season. Marsh sandpipers, sharp-tailed sandpipers, common sandpipers, green shanks, grey-tailed tattler, bar-tailed godwit, black-tailed godwit and the black-fronted dotterel, all waded in the marshes at the edge of the lakes. In these marshes lived reptiles and lizards, amphibians, burrowing frogs and two species of tree frogs—desert tree frogs, green tree frogs.

All came as volunteers to my zoo. The only species that did not come in great numbers was humans. Sadly, the visitors to the town of Broome, of whom there were each year increasing numbers, did not share my enthusiasm for animals. New plans were hatched to attract the tourists. A large complex was to be built to house primates. Tourists love primates—they can stand and watch an ape for hours on end. They don't, however, seem to get the same pleasure out of watching a brolga crane or a spotted bowerbird—tourists are curious creatures. Some of the varieties of marmosets from South America were installed; cheetah arrived and settled into their fine enclosure. Our ostriches bred, but once again we had trouble with the offspring. Searching for food in the pindan, the earth of the Kimberley, the young ostriches used to swallow a considerable quantity of this earth, which went solid in their intestines and destroyed their digestive systems. The Australian cassowary is a fine-looking bird but a poor display for the tourist; it tends to hide in the thick bush of the rainforest enclosure. A bird that is both formidable and highly dangerous in the wild, the cassowary must be handled with great care. Cassowaries are short-sighted, attacking when they hear a sound rustling through the bush, pushing trees aside with their heads that are protected by a huge helmet or lump of bone. These birds have a savage kick and their claws are capable of tearing out a human's stomach.

John Knowles supervised the selection of the mammals and their transport. An expert in the field of conserving endangered species of mammal, he took particular trouble to make sure that we not only imported mammals that would thrive in the climate of Broome but also prepared the correct habitats for them before they arrived. He has earned my undying admiration for the patience he demonstrated in his dealings with the officialdom of both Canberra and Perth. A Boeing 707 was hired to fly in addax, red lechway, sitatunga, nyala, nilgai, greater kudu, gemsbok, Grevy's zebras and Congo buffalo. Banteng cattle, Asiatic water buffalo, black buck, rusa deer and hog deer were acquired from within Australia, as were various varieties of kangaroo and wallaby. One of the rarest species of Australian wallaby, the nail-tailed wallaby, was indigenous to the land where the zoo was built. The climate of Broome was perfect for them and they bred well. My zoo was at last becoming an ark, where breeding stock of the some of the world's rarest antelopes could live in isolation away from disease and, more importantly, poachers and warfare.

The zoos of the Australian capital cities were generous with both their advice and their stock. Melbourne Zoo sent us a pair of pygmy hippos on breeding loan. The RAAF flew them for me to Broome. Unfortunately, someone with a curious sense of humour told the military personnel concerned with this operation that the hippos ate cream buns, and a large quantity of cream buns was included on the aircraft's manifests. News of these cream buns reached the ears of a parliamentarian in Canberra, who made a considerable fuss about the whole affair. His efforts to cause trouble, however, came to nothing. Not only was the RAAF engaged in an exercise of conservation by moving these hippos, they had good reason for apparently doing me a favour.

During the war, a Spitfire had crash-landed on some mudflats near Walcott Inlet, some three hundred kilometres north-east of Broome. The RAAF wished to return it to Melbourne where it would be restored and put on public display, since Spitfires these days are even rarer than pygmy hippos. The RAAF's problem was how to get the Spitfire from the mudflats to a point where a low loader could transport it to an airfield. John Adams and I had the answer: we owned the only landing craft in north-west Australia. We did a deal—the RAAF delivered my hippos, we lent them our landing craft, and the aircraft that brought the hippo took away the Spitfire.

Some years earlier the transporting of a tapir from Melbourne to Broome had not gone as smoothly. Ross Gardiner and his assistant had been despatched to Melbourne to collect the tapir. The animal was loaded into a crate made by the Melbourne Zoo's carpenters and the crate put on the back of a trailer. It was about a three-day journey from Melbourne to Broome, travelling mostly by track, via Alice Springs and the Tanami Track. For the first two days, all went well. Then the tapir decided to break out of the crate—whether the crate was badly made or the tapir too strong for it will never be known, nor, indeed, will the reason why it took it into its head to escape. A tapir cannot be allowed to roam the Australian bush; despite its chances of meeting a mate and breeding being somewhat remote, the officials in Canberra just would not stand for it. Ross Gardiner had no alternative but to shoot the tapir and bury it. The zoo's staff and I had waited with great anxiety for the much-delayed arrival of the tapir and it was with considerable sadness that we learned from Ross Gardiner that the animal had been killed. Whether you run a farm or a zoo, the old adage, 'Where you have livestock, you have dead stock' is equally true. It did not seem to matter whether that dead stock was large and rare or small and common, the sense of failure was always the same.

One of the most attractive Australian mammals is the wombat. This cuddly creature has never achieved the same popularity as the koala. The wombat's habitat, a deep hole in the ground, is probably the reason for this. It is a lot easier to feel well-disposed towards a cuddly animal that spends its time sitting in a tree munching eucalyptus leaves than to an animal that spends most of the day deep underground. The wombat, however, has a better nature by far than the koala, which is inclined to scratch and bite when handled, quite apart from covering the unwary handler in foul-smelling urine. At my zoo, I had a pair of wombats—at least, I thought I had a pair of wombats. Their cage was carefully constructed. It was a large cage roughly 30 metres square, with full-grown boab trees in which resided a flock of Torres Strait pigeons. The floor of the enclosure had been excavated to the depth of over a metre and heavy steel mesh laid all over it, cut carefully around the roots of the boab trees. The earth was then put back, and a pond, a large waterfall and a stream built. The overall effect was most attractive. The pigeons flew around the aviary and rested in the spreading branches of the boab trees. A boab is a fine tree for putting in an aviary, and it transplants well even when full grown. Indeed, where boabs have stood in the way of road construction and have been uprooted, thrown into the bush and left lying on their sides, they have been known to take root and to continue growing in a horizontal position. Boab trees also have the advantage that they seldom grow over eight metres in height.

The wombats arrived and were introduced to their cage. At first, they sat around and sometimes played with each other, then they began to dig. We were all very pleased about this, as digging showed that the animals were really settling in. Then for days on end we did not see the wombats. The daily, or rather nightly, ration of food was still disappearing and I was coming to the conclusion that the only way we could see the wombats during the day would be to build a tunnel for humans beside the tunnel that the wombats had built and put observation panels between the two. Before I embarked on what would no doubt have been a most costly exercise, I thought we should see where the wombat tunnel ended. A fire was lit at the tunnel's mouth and the smoke was sucked straight down the hole, which clearly meant that the tunnel had another entrance. Nowhere could we see smoke in the park, so one of my staff climbed on to the roof of the cage, which was about ten metres high. He saw smoke all right—a plume of smoke much as a campfire might make on a still day rose to the heavens about half a mile away. My wombats had escaped; they were long gone and we had been feeding an empty cage for some months. Their food, I suppose, was taken by rats and mice but the wombats were never seen again.

❧

We used to get a number of calls to help birds in distress. This other function of the zoo, as an animal first-aid post, was one of the most exciting aspects of the whole venture. On one particular day, Des Higgins telephoned from Waterbank Station just outside Broome. The weather was dry and his waterholes were drying up. At one waterhole, there was a mass of ducks stuck in the mud. Graham Taylor immediately sent out some of his keepers to help. In the waterhole, there were about fifteen or twenty centimetres of slush and then just mud. The feathers of the ducks were all coated in mud and they could barely move, let alone fly. The problem, however, was easily solved by a good washing. To their surprise, the men who went out to help the ducks noticed that what water remained in the waterhole was boiling with the movement of fish. They thought that the fish would be mullet, which are common in the waterholes of the North-West. So, having brought the ducks back to the zoo for the necessary remedial work on their plumage, the staff returned with their fishing nets. The fish, however, were not mullet as expected, but rather good-sized barramundi. Twenty or 30 of these barramundi were subsequently released in the zoo's lake where they grew and also bred. At feeding time, they were summoned to the pavilion on the walkway in the centre of the lake by someone banging a metal bucket. The sight of these barramundi being fed, each fish now weighing about nine kilos, was quite spectacular. All went well with the barramundi until a wet when a small crocodile escaped from the nearby crocodile park and found its way into the lake. There was considerable consternation when a visitor to the zoo, Nick Paspaley, the pearl farmer, spotted this young crocodile, which was growing rapidly on a diet of barramundi. That crocodile, I am bound to record, took quite a deal of catching. No-one was particularly keen to get into the water in case the small crocodile's big brother was somewhere about.

⚭

Looking back, I sometimes ask myself which bird was my favourite, and which mammal. Each time, the answer is different. In the end, I suppose, it is the eclectus parrot, a variety where the female wears the smart red clothing and the male a simple green jacket. I love these parrots because of their size, their dignity and their humour. And which mammal? The answer is simple—it has to be the scimitar-horned oryx. Whether they are standing, racing across a paddock, or sparring with heads down and horns locked, they are things of beauty, elegant and, oh, so terribly grand.

9

It was the pilots' strike and the subsequent recession that brought my zoo to an end. I had dreamt too much and brought too many of those dreams to fruition. The time came and it all had to end. It was sad to end it, but the story would have been far sadder had the zoo never been built in the first place. My ambition to set up an ark to save a number of endangered species may well have failed but, even so, every effort in the fight to save the wildlife of our planet is worth something in the overall scheme of things. While my ambition was thwarted, the fate of living creatures remains one of my paramount interests. When I think of the Pearl Coast Zoo, I smile. Although I failed to create something of lasting value, what I did create gave value to the lives of those involved in its creation. A quotation taken from the last pages of Lord Haldane's memoirs sums up his personal philosophy, and seems appropriate to my situation on the closing of the Pearl Coast Zoo. Haldane, a considerable figure from the first half of this century, a statesman, philosopher, minister of war and Lord Chancellor of Britain, wrote:

The best that ordinary mortals can hope for is the result which will probably come from sustained work directed by as full a reflection as is possible. This result may be affected adversely by circumstances, by illness, by misfortune or by death. But if we have striven to think

119

and to do work based on thought, then we have at least the sense of having striven, with such faculties as we have possessed devoted to the striving. And that is in itself a cause of happiness, going beyond the possession of any definite gain.

As for the animals whose existence I tried to safeguard, my efforts were but a drop in a vast ocean of need.

At the time that my zoo in Broome opened, there were disturbances and civil wars in Africa, and the Middle East, a place not unfamiliar with warfare, was a tinderbox waiting to be ignited. For centuries past, man has fought over its fertile valleys and deserts, has built monuments and then destroyed them. Towns and cities have been consumed by warfare and rebuilt in the image of the conqueror. Great cities have been destroyed by earthquakes, peoples destroyed by famine and pestilence. In the heart of this region lies Basra, the site of the Garden of Eden, the site of the beginning, perhaps, of life on earth. What is certain, however, is that the valleys of the Euphrates and Tigris rivers meet here, valleys that are the flight path for millions of migrating birds, birds that journey from Europe far into Africa, birds that travel each year from Russia to northern Australia, birds as diverse as the white stork and the small warbler. While man is ingenious enough to rebuild and improve upon destroyed architecture, and his hands are supple enough to replace broken artefacts, he has, however, no means of replacing a lost variety of bird or beast.

The desert area of Iraq is of particular importance in nature, as it is the meeting point of European and Arabian species. The brown bear, seldom found now in Europe, the Arabian wolf, and many other interesting and beautiful animals and birds can be found here. One of the ironies of the destructive attack upon Kuwait by Saddam Hussein was the disastrous consequence of the action necessary to remove him. This area, where allied troops fought Saddam Hussein's army, was one of the few places in the world making great efforts to repair some of the ravages of the twentieth century by restoring locally extinct species to their original habitat. A small group of the extremely rare Sommering's gazelles, along with the animals in the Old Botanical Gardens of Kuwait City, were shot by Iraqi soldiers. However, the real tragedy is the loss of the plans by the Kuwaiti Government to establish a national park along the border with Iraq, a park where it intended to reintroduce the Houbara bustard and the Arabian gazelle, a desert reserve to which many of the species now extinct in this region would return. It must be hoped that when the rebuilding of this region begins, these plans will not be overlooked when the Kuwaitis construct new motorways, hospitals and schools. Reservoirs of these rare animals need to be established not only in Kuwait but around the world in places not given to regular wars.

In Saudi Arabia, the government has set up a centre for the conservation and breeding of many of the endangered species native to that country, with the intention of returning them to the wild. In this centre, there are well over 1000 of some of the world's rarest animals: sand gazelles, Arabian gazelles; the Saudi dorcas gazelle, extinct in its habitat; the Saudi wolf; and the Ruppell's fox, a small and rare sand fox. Then there is the Arabian oryx, the most beautiful of these creatures, an animal thought to be the mythical unicorn, for when seen in profile, its long, sweeping horns seem as one. It was an animal hunted for 3000 years by desert warriors, yet it survived. But no antelope, however agile, is equipped to withstand the advent of the automatic rifle, and the early 1960s saw its demise outside captivity. The research centre in Riyadh has prospered, and the number of these rare animals has increased. There are several zoos with important collections in Israel, and the Tel Aviv University Wildlife Research Centre has done much work for conservation, and still cares for many rare animals. In Oman, meanwhile, repatriation of desert antelopes has started. There is now a wild population of the Arabian oryx, the descendants of captive-bred animals returned to their habitat. Another population of this elegant animal is in Jordan, and there are plans for a reserve on the Jordanian–Saudi border. All of this work goes on in one of the world's most volatile regions.

These animals are in great danger. In the early 1960s, small groups of antelopes were caught and taken to zoos in America and Britain: the addax, short-legged, beige and corkscrew-horned, now thought to be extinct in the wild; the Dhana gazelle, long-legged and long-necked, of which less than a thousand remain; the scimitar-horned oryx, another antelope extinct in its natural habitat. The subsequent civil war in Chad and the famines that sprang from it, combined with high-powered military rifles, have proved the wisdom of this action. These zoos have become a Noah's Ark for these animals, places where they can be bred and studied. London Zoo is one of the organisations active in this field, and has an almost unique expertise in combining field work and research. Zoos are no longer animal prisons; in their modern form, they can be havens of safety. The scarce resource of these rare and extremely beautiful animals, spread among zoos on a planned basis, means that neither disease nor war will ever destroy them completely. Man being the aggressive beast that he is, it is unlikely that the war against Saddam or, for that matter, any other war, will end all wars. We had better take good care of our zoos so that they at least can take care of the world's birds and animals after terrible carnage, and play their vital role in the rehabilitation of our planet.

I believed that Australia had a vital role to play in the conservation of the wonderful antelopes that are endangered.

Sadly, we never managed to import either the Dhana gazelle or the Arabian oryx into Australia, but we did bring in the scimitar-horned oryx and the addax, both of which are extremely rare. They are now to be found in Australian zoos in considerable quantities. It was, I believe, the memories of my visits to Kenya and East Africa at the beginning of the 1970s that inspired me. In those days, black rhinos were plentiful while the white rhino was endangered and rare. Within ten years, the situation changed. By 1980, the exact opposite was the case—the white rhino was plentiful in zoos, breeding well and being returned to the wild, while the black rhino was in danger of becoming extinct. It was always my ambition to set up a breeding colony of black rhinos in Broome. In the event, this was not to be; this ambition, like so many of my ambitions, was to be unfulfilled.

It must be fairly obvious to anyone who has ever read a newspaper that a large part of the world's wildlife is in considerable danger. Just how bad this situation has become is not always apparent. All of us know of the dangers to the black rhinoceros in Africa and to the tiger on the Indian subcontinent. Fewer people may realise that there are today around 911 animal species on the critical danger list (this figure comes from the recently published Red List of the World Conservation Union). When you compare this figure with the 1265 species that have been lost in the past 400 years, it shows that the rate at which we are destroying the wildlife on our planet has speeded up to a point where it has become dangerous. The figures produced by the World Conservation Union are indeed frightening. In 1994, it appeared that 18 per cent of mammals were endangered. More complete figures now reveal the real figure to be 25 per cent. And it is not only animals that are in danger—23 730 species of higher plant life are threatened. If you include all plants, 13 per cent of the total number of species is in danger of disappearing.

Sadly, the main cause of the situation is not so much the changing climate of our planet but rather the changing habits of its human inhabitants. The clearing of forests and the polluting of rivers and seas are some of the causes. Surprisingly, the inhabitants of this planet most endangered are fish, reptiles and amphibians. There is always, however, the argument that our lives are not much the poorer for the loss of the world's dodos. Indeed, there are many who take the view that it is one thing to talk of conserving tigers, for instance, when you live in the leafy suburbs of a great city, but quite another if the tiger that someone else has conserved has just eaten your only goat. While most who read these statistics will be shocked and probably sympathetic to the plight of the animal world, few will actually do anything about it. These were the grand thoughts that were in my mind as I set up my modest zoo in Broome.

✧

In northern Australia, the ban on crocodile hunting changed the habits of the estuarine crocodile. This is a creature that can grow to nearly nine metres in length and move as fast on land as in water. It seems to have known about the ban that protected it, because now it has little fear of mankind. In truth, you can upset the balance of nature by conservation quite as easily as you can upset it by destruction. While the subject is immensely complex, it is not the first difficult problem mankind has had to face—with determined effort, the Americans managed the inconceivable and put a man on the moon. Unfortunately, stemming ecological change does not offer the same international prestige as landing on our nearest planet. It is as if the great nations of the world were suburban businessmen proudly polishing their cars on a Sunday morning in front of their houses, in full view of the neighbours. Unseen in their kitchen sinks, the unwashed dishes from Saturday night's party join the general dirt and deterioration of wild and careless living. People do not march in the streets on wildlife issues, yet they will sit glued to their televisions watching a documentary that shows how some branch of the animal kingdom is about to be extinguished. They will picket ports to stop the live export of domestic animals; the treatment of veal calves was one of the most emotive issues raised in Britain in the past five years and caused far greater interest than many of the terrible tragedies involving humans.

There is little public interest, however, in the fate of the Galapagos tortoise, despite the fact that this animal was one of the creatures that led Darwin to his theory of evolution. People are occasionally motivated to complain about zoos that mistreat animals, but fortunately, bad zoos are becoming fewer and good ones are at the forefront of animal conservation. In such environments, rhinos, tigers, bears, antelopes and wolves can be saved. It is in zoos that they are being bred with the idea of repatriating them to their original habitat. While all this is good, it is not the final answer—that lies with governments. Politicians, however, move slowly, and not at all unless they are pressed. Meanwhile, only wildlife organisations can explain to the people why they need to care. The following paragraphs are how I described the closing of my zoo in the first volume of my memoirs, *Once a Jolly Bagman.*

The Australian summer of 1989 was over. It had been wet, the trees and foliage of my zoo had grown well, all looked splendid. The winter, which is Broome's peak tourist season, looked as if it would produce a bumper crop of visitors. Then the Australian airline pilots went on strike. The winter season was lost, instead of 50 000 visitors, my zoo received a few hundred. Days went by and no-one came to look at my birds and animals and, what was worse, there was no way to send the surplus birds that we bred for sale to the aviculturists of eastern Australia. That year we successfully raised 700 endangered birds, plus many other common varieties. At their moment of triumph, Graham Taylor and Eddie Pszkit, his assistant, were faced with a desperate situation that was neither their fault, nor within their capacity to correct.

Graham and Eddie performed the closing of the zoo as efficiently as they had built it up. No bird or animal was put down; all were placed either with other zoos or collectors. It was a great sadness to me to see the zoo that I had physically worked on in the early days, and certainly spent all my free moments planning, come to a close. Despite the fact that I would far rather have succeeded in what most people believed to be a mad venture, I do not regret it for one moment, because in a small way my zoo helped to change the attitude to zoos and captive animals all over Australia, and the rare antelopes and zebras I imported have become foundation stock whose progeny will breed for generations to come.

10

Shortly after I started my zoo in Broome, I decided to build a hotel, not the usual sort of hotel found in the North-West, something rather different. It was my intention to create a hotel that had all the modern comforts, yet still played homage to the traditional style of building in Broome and its multicultural heritage. If it was to attract an international clientele, this hotel would need a particular touch of European chic.

A friend of Romilly's and mine was, by profession, an architect. She is a Greek, indeed, a very beautiful Greek, who goes by the name of Aphrodite Gallengha. Aphrodite had never worked in Australia before but, nevertheless, she jumped at the opportunity to take this commission. Together with Peter Arney, of Oldham Boas, Ednie-Brown, the architects who had carried out all my work in Perth, she set about designing my new hotel. Aphrodite was to do the conceptual design; Peter Arney and his colleagues were to carry out the detailed work. As a team, they worked well together, and the first stage of what is now the Intercontinental Cable Beach Resort was soon under way. My partner in this venture was an agency of the Western Australian Government. The hotel comprised a central block and about 50 cottages built on stumps with lattice walls, settled in a recently planted tropical garden complete with streams and lakes. To construct this garden, fully grown trees were moved onto the site and a team of gardeners set about planting them and literally thousands of plants. A large swimming pool and several tennis courts were also built. The hotel was opened by Peter Dowding, then the premier of Western Australia; the majority of the guests at the opening were Broome people. It was a magic evening, hot, balmy and lit with flares. It seemed as if the hotel had arrived by magic; there was nowhere like it within a thousand or more miles.

Before long, it became apparent that the hotel could not stay this size; it needed to become larger if it was to have a chance of making a profit. Three new wings of studio rooms were added and a further wing with luxury suites. Two more restaurants, several more tennis courts, a health club and another even larger swimming pool were also constructed. The décor of the hotel was provided by two talented women, Joan Bowers from Sydney, who imported artefacts and architectural elements from India, and Judy Barratt-Lennard, a Perth decorator of considerable taste and talent, who provided furniture and furnishings from Indonesia. At the same time, I set about acquiring a large collection of Australian paintings, mostly by local artists. In the hotel's cottages there are about a hundred crayon drawings by Joe Nangan, and in the suites, works by Sidney Nolan, Elizabeth Durack and Humphrey Price Jones. Aphrodite pulled all these disparate collections together, and we had a hotel of a most unusual and interesting design.

Business took a nasty turn with the pilots' strike and the Government agency was not half as delighted as it was on opening night. It was then that I took a decision that cost me dear. I gave them their money back regardless of the fact that our association had been short and the hotel was then worth a fraction of what it had cost. In a difficult situation is it is often easier to carry on alone than with a partner who is unhappy; it is, however, a folly to pay three times what half a hotel is worth when on the edge of a giant recession. The airport that had the Government's backing was never built. It is also folly to rely on governments, unless you have their signature on many bits of paper and, even then, the chances of them performing are not guaranteed.

The hotel, the zoo, the airport and other tourist ventures were all part of a carefully considered plan—the airport had been the linch pin of that plan. What had once been a serious business strategy, now had the feel of an incredible gamble. Customers in Broome were what I needed, more and more of them, yet Broome was a long way from the Australian market. Still struggling to get the existing airport made international in the face of a sponge of bureaucracy, I set out to publicise the hotel, which was then called the Cable Beach Club, and my zoo. In truth, the people who came loved both of them, but not nearly enough people came. This publicity campaign was greatly helped when the Variety Club of Australia planned to end its annual cross-Australia motor rally for classic cars in Broome. My family company decided to enter a car, a 1963 Humber Super Snipe. In order for this car to cope with the bush tracks from Burke to Broome, it needed some modifications. Sergeant-major Mike Hanlon arranged for volunteers from the Australian Army, Karratha 22 Construction Squadron, to provide a hundred hours of their spare time. A second Humber Super Snipe was acquired and its parts used to make one serviceable vehicle which was fitted with heavy-duty suspension and a fridge to keep the necessary refreshments cool. The finished vehicle was painted in garish colours. I already had two expert bush drivers and mechanics, Snowy County and Charlie Diesel; all I needed was a third. In London, I was dining with the prime minister, Margaret Thatcher, and her family, when I mentioned this project. In a moment, Carol Thatcher had volunteered her services as the third driver. Six months later, Carol, Snowy and Charlie set off along with 200 or so other entrants from Sydney's Bondi Beach, in pouring rain and great razzamatazz. The bash was a great success, enjoyed by all those who took part in it. As a result, the Cable Beach Club received a considerable amount of publicity, not only in the press but on television as well.

Achieving publicity, however, for a middle-sized, up-market hotel is not an easy matter. By far the best form of publicity for such an enterprise is by word of mouth, so I set about getting Sydney's society to visit Broome. To this end, I hired Primrose Dunlop, an expert in this field and a woman who knew everyone who was worth knowing. She did a splendid job and slowly the trickle of wealthy people coming from Sydney to visit the Cable Beach Club in Broome became a stream. Glen-Marie Frost and her husband, Bob, were also invited to visit Broome—Glen-Marie has always been a highly successful Australian publicist.

As a result of the publicity that it received, over the following years, Broome and the Cable Beach Club became host to a large number of celebrities. The recession, however, got deeper, interest rates rose remorselessly and, in the end, the Cable Beach Club and the company that owned it, Australian City Properties, were sold at about the same time that I closed my zoo. Some years later, I sold my house in Broome and left to live in Italy. My attitude to the Pearl Coast Zoo was one of deep commitment. I did not open that zoo casually, nor did I close it on a whim. I also had a deep commitment to, and enthusiasm for, my other ventures in Broome. Perhaps this piece, taken from notes in my library, explains my approach to people, places and possessions, rather better than anything else that I have written:

At ten o'clock on the 16th May 1990, Sotheby's will begin to auction the contents of my house, West Green, near

Hartley Witney in Hampshire. The accumulation of the last sixteen years of my life and a number of objects from the previous 25 years will disappear in almost a 1000 lots and two full days of selling.

The eighteenth-century furniture of the Grand Saloon, the minerals of the mineral room will be sold alongside the collection of over a hundred mocha ware mugs. These mugs, with white and blue bands of colour around them, were used in nineteenth-century pubs to drink beer. On all of them are the chocolate marks that give them their name—marks made by the craftsmen spitting their chewing tobacco at the damp glaze, strange marks in the shape of trees. Wives used to say to each other, when their husbands returned late and a little less than sober, 'He was very tired last night—he's been lifting too many trees.' The collection of garden implements from the sixteenth century to the modern, with its star attraction, a horse-drawn lawn mower complete with leather coverings for the horse's feet, to protect the lawn, will go. So too the shepherds' crooks in the hall, the stuffed birds in the master bathroom, all English birds. The bric-à-brac of my life, collected and hoarded, each individual piece of great importance to the collector.

The mugs, the minerals, the garden implements—they went somehow with the house and now I need a new home with a different feel, harder, emptier, sharper. I am a nomad from a nomadic stock, setting little store in possessions. Anxious in their pursuit, casual in their disposal, I love many things and hate quite as many. No work of art, however wonderful, is a substitute for its creator, or of more consequence than the meanest man that would destroy it. Why sell all? To rid oneself of the chore of making a choice, to make a different style of life, to win the freedom to choose again.

The collections gone, dispersed. What is left? Snow-drops in the garden, over a hundred different varieties, a collection; hellebores, carpets of them in profusion, and roses, old garden roses, perhaps 400 varieties—the record of all these plants and their planting was lost in a fire. There are follies by Quinlan Terry, some built, some, as in all interesting gardens, only on paper, and others only in the mind. And the garden itself, shaped and cared for by a human being, by chance called Mr Mann—sadly, now dead. A garden, I hope, in the spirit of the first owner of West Green, a certain General Hawley, a man who fixed the motto: 'Do as you feel inclined' above his door. Hawley used to visit his friend across the common. One night, after they had dined well, Hawley picked up what he believed to be a lantern for his walk home in the dark. Out in the cold night air, he was pursued by a terrible screaming; the faster he ran, the worse the screaming. Fearing the devil meant to collect his soul that night, he ran faster and even faster—until he fell into a ditch where he stayed till morning. He woke to find that he was clutching his friend's caged parrot.

A garden with the ghost of Hawley's dog; a garden haunted, so word would have it, by Highland pipers come to be revenged on Hawley, who led the cavalry at Culloden. They are as likely to be playing Hawley on as opposing his charge, for more Scots fought on the side of the English than on the side of the Scots in that battle. There are even tales of buried treasure. Many people have lunched there: drunk well, I know; eaten well, I hope; enjoyed West Green and its contents, some more than others. I remember a man who came to lunch. He held the party enchanted by his words; he made two jokes and all the room laughed and laughed. He made a third and there was silence. I mentioned this to him later and, far from embarrassment, he expressed delight. For he had, he said, an audience capable of discernment and it is the bad jokes that one should remember—failure is somehow funnier. It is often that your true friends are not the most brilliant people that you meet and it is often a triviality rather than a great event that changes your life.

After Sotheby's have knocked down the last lot and the marquee is gone, the garden swept, there will still stand the obelisk that commemorates the life and work of Mr Mann, the gardener. It bears his portrait in stone, my prize-winning goose between his legs, his hand on the obelisk with his back to the garden and all it might have been, thinking perhaps of what might be. Do I regret leaving? I suppose that I do have a regret at leaving West Green—it is that I should have picked the snowdrops last year.

A few days after that auction, my home was blown apart by a terrorist bomb. I feel today much the same way about the demise of my zoo as I felt about leaving West Green. In all my life I have been blessed with a multitude of advantages, and the greatest of these go hand-in-hand—an incurable curiosity and a never-ending optimism.

III

Travels in the North-West

11

As I was spending much of my time in the small township of Broome, it was inevitable that I should succumb to an urge to travel, an urge which has been with me since I was a small boy, an urge that I inherited from my father, a man who was endlessly boarding ships and aircraft to visit faraway places, a man who would jump on a train just for the pleasure of travelling. Many of my journeys in the North-West have been described in *Once a Jolly Bagman*. Here I shall fill in a few gaps in some of those travels and describe others in far greater detail.

One day in 1982, half a day's journey out of Broome, Romilly, Oliver Ford and I were driving along the main road to Port Hedland just short of Sandfire and we turned left into the bush. Shortly after the turn-off, we came across a bunch of cattle being driven by men on horseback. The cattle were moving at a leisurely pace in the afternoon sun; it seemed such a peaceful sight that we stopped to watch them for twenty minutes or so. Men and horses moving as one gave credence to the centaur of Greek mythology. Later that night, we stayed at the Ironclad Hotel in Marble Bar. This town has some fine old administrative buildings from the turn of the century; they are red brick and fort-like in appearance. Marble Bar also has the greatest range of temperature of any town in Australia; freezing cold in the winter to baking hot in mid-summer. Happily, we were there in the spring when the temperature was about as pleasant as you could imagine. The town—though the place is barely worthy of the designation 'town'—is named after a reef of spar that runs across a series of small waterholes. This reef was thought by the early settlers to be marble when, in fact, it was the much rarer material, spar. We, in the fashion of ignorant Europeans, expected to find in the Ironclad Hotel, a long bar topped in marble with a couple of dozen dour outback characters drinking at it. How wrong could we have been. We found the inhabitants of Marble Bar to be, in general, extremely friendly, ready to offer information on the place and its history, and eager to tell us about the delights that we would encounter on our journey south.

Some years later, I recommended to John Kasmin, the London art dealer, that he visit Marble Bar. His description of what he found varies from mine, largely because he spent most of the night drinking in the bar of the Ironclad Hotel which, incidentally, is named after the first ironclad warships, not the fact that it is built of corrugated iron. Kasmin sat and drank and watched two others drinking, a man and a woman. The man kept knocking the woman off her chair. Each time she climbed back onto her chair, he knocked her off again. Kasmin, believing that such behaviour was disgraceful, tried to bring it to the attention of his neighbour at the bar. 'I'm deaf in this ear,' the man replied, 'and even if I wasn't, I wouldn't want to hear anything that you have to say.' Kasmin, a creature of continental Europe, likes to affect the attire of a French lorry driver when travelling. He stuck out like a sore thumb among the drinkers in the Ironclad Hotel.

Another half day on and we were in desolate country. The countryside around Newman has the feeling of a wasteland—burned landscape, burned trees, burning sun and rocks. Newman itself is a mining town, a town in a brown wasteland. It is as if someone has put a glass dome over the whole place, for it has rows of detached houses with green lawns and cars parked in their driveways. With its supermarket and urban shopping centre, airconditioning and ice-cream parlours, Newman could have easily been removed in its entirety from suburban Perth. Beside the track we came across the carcass of a sheep. Perched on the dead animal's head was an eagle tearing at the sheep's brains with its beak, the skull held firmly in its claws. For several hours' travelling, we saw neither man nor beast, only birds of prey circling in the savage blue sky. We stayed that night in Meekatharra, a town about which Malcolm Fraser's wife made some disparaging remarks while campaigning with her husband, the then prime minister. These remarks were picked up by the local press and the poor woman had to return and make a public apology. Meekatharra is not much of a town; it has an airport and a railway station, the end of the line from Perth. It is a town for shipping cattle and sheep.

⁓

As we became more experienced in the art of travelling in the outback, we avoided the small hotels of the townships that we passed through, sleeping instead in canvas swags. No tents, no shelter—just the stars above us which, in nights spent in the desert, were stars as I have never seen them before. They started on one horizon and cluttered the night sky across to the other horizon. Among them was an almost continuous parade of shooting stars. I was always so excited I did not sleep more than an hour or two each night. My wife Romilly always said that she would never share a swag with a man who kept his boots on. However, despite missing the pleasure of having Romilly near me at night, I judged it safer to sleep in my boots in case I needed to get up in a hurry which, indeed, was the case on that first night on the Tanami Track, when the heavens opened and rain came down in sheets. When we travelled, I took a heavy calibre rifle with me, mostly in case we got lost and needed to shoot something to eat. After our first journey, we had become more cautious and took Snowy County and his mate Charlie Diesel with us as guides. The desert around the Tanami Track is flat, lacking even sand hills. It is not desert in the accepted sense of the word, as the earth is red pindan. Pindan, the earth of north-western Australia, is as hard as rock in the sun, but in the wet its mud is like quicksand. The scrub that grows in this land is straggly and, at first sight, seems easy enough to drive through—in reality, it is easy enough to get lost in.

Always an early riser, I usually woke before first light in the bush. Snowy, who barely slept, was already dressed and joined me in breaking sticks rather noisily in an attempt to wake the others. Failing to achieve this, we would usually build up the fire, cough a bit, drop billy cans and then make tea with as much noise as was possible.

In this manner we would have the whole group awake by first light, usually shortly after four-thirty. I liked to be under way by five and get a good four hours' driving in before breakfast. On our trips, I drove the Toyota Land Cruiser with Romilly and our other companions, while Snowy and Charlie Diesel took it in turns to drive a Toyota truck. Charlie Diesel's real name is Helquist; the 'Diesel' part is a Broome name, earned in the years he lived there by his ability to fix almost any defect in the engines that powered the pearling luggers of the 1970s. Charlie is a genius when it comes to diesel engines, a talent that he demonstrated like some great magician. On one occasion when one of our trucks broke down, he gathered us around the vehicle, opened the bonnet, gave the engine a considerable tap with a hammer, then signalled to Snowy to start the vehicle up. The truck worked perfectly and we had no more trouble for the rest of the journey.

Charlie Diesel's home was Melbourne, where nowadays he

runs a highly successful business erecting and repairing the cranes used in the construction of the city's skyscrapers. Travelling with us across Australia was, for Charlie, a break from his business life.

Often when I was crossing Australia, either by truck or by air, I visited Alice Springs. On my last visit there in 1996, I found the town was rather different. The land around Alice Springs had the green tinge about it that a rainy season brings. I looked out as my Ansett flight made a long, low approach to the airport. I had not been to 'The Alice' for nearly five years. It seemed that nothing much had changed: there were no new houses to be seen as we flew towards the airport, no new roads. All appeared much as before, the low hills that hide the town, the satellite tracking station with its white domes and dishes bright in the sunshine. Only when I climbed down the aircraft's steps did I begin to think I had come to the wrong place. A sign said 'International Airport', and that is exactly what I saw. Gone was the collection of tin buildings stitched together that passed for a terminal. In front of me was a modern airport building—there was no longer a grubby bar with grubby customers where sweat and stubble mixed with ice-cold beer: the flies had gone as well. The cafeteria could seat a hundred and needed to, for planes arrived every few minutes instead of once or twice a day. Like most airports these days, the terminal at Alice Springs has become a shopping mall. Gone are all those men with jaws like set squares and hands like shovels, with floppy hats and a pocket knife at their belts. Gone are the women in their ill-fitting dresses and straw hats. The days when the population of 'The Alice' came to the airport for a beer and to wonder at the miracle of flight are long over. Today, the airport population at Alice Springs mainly consists of pushy German tourists and excited Japanese on a quick flip around Australia. The Germans study maps of the outback and straighten the creases in their canvas shorts and bush jackets, sending ordinary mortals reeling as they turn and strike them with their backpacks. These Germans are as well-equipped for a day in Alice, en route to Uluru, as if they were setting out for several months in the outback; indeed, they are far better equipped for the outback than are the men and women who have lived there all their lives. The Japanese at Alice's airport spend their time and their money buying clothes and Aboriginal artefacts, didgeridoos as long as themselves and paintings by the desert painters. As for the Aboriginals, apart from those who sell their products, they seem to have disappeared, blending in with the other denizens of the outback who now all wear ties and suits.

The airport at Alice is not the only aspect of Australia that has changed. Across the Tanami Desert along the Tanami Track, past Rabbit Flat on the way to Hall's Creek, you will, if you make a detour to the north, come to Turkey Creek. It is not much of a place compared to the standard set by the terminal at Alice Springs—just red earth and tin huts. But Turkey Creek, for all its lack of modern facilities, is the home of Australia's most exciting school of painting. It first came to fame when Rover Thomas, one of its citizens, represented Australia at the Venice Biennale. His friend Paddy Tjamati was another of Turkey Creek's painters who broke away from the idea of simply reproducing tribal patterns on canvas. These two artists painted the landscape of their country on dismembered tea chests. The works were used in the Krilkrill, a variation of the corroboree. Since the days of Paddy Tjamati and Rover Thomas's early efforts, a great deal of attention has been paid to the work of the painters from Turkey Creek. The painters of Turkey Creek are, however, not the only painters in that part of the Western Australian outback. A few years ago, a group of painters from Fitzroy Crossing exhibited their work in a Perth gallery, artists with wonderful names like Stumpy Brown and Jimmy Bent, Butcher Cheval and Peanut Ford. Their work was received with great acclaim and now fetches good money in the world's sales rooms. These artists from the small bush townships paint their country, its myths and its reality; they paint with great passion and perfect simplicity. In the words of Honey Pulikati, as she describes one of her paintings: 'This is a river behind the station at Yungngora in the rain time. After the rain, the water lies around in purra [billabongs]; we catch fish in these small waterholes, as the waterholes dry up they get caught—they cannot get back to the river.' It's all a bit like that for her people.

❧

On another trip, Romilly, Oliver and I were driving the 2400 kilometres from Perth to Broome by the inland route through Meekatharra, Nullagine and Marble Bar. We stopped in the near-ghost town of Cue with its wonderful Victorian buildings, the gold all gone and most of the people with it; the bandstand in the main street long without musicians. On that trip we were novices and we nearly perished. It is a strange fact about travelling in the north-west of Australia, a land of low scrub that comes right to the edge of the track, but you see no animal life, or rather you rarely see animals and birds. We had travelled for two days and not seen a kangaroo; indeed, Oliver Ford began to doubt their existence. I felt I had let him down badly in this matter, for I had told him that the whole place was stuffed with kangaroos. So when a group of emus crossed the track, on an impulse, I turned off into the bush after them. We chased the emus in our Toyota Land Cruiser for a few minutes but we soon lost them, then, in an effort to return to the track, we could not find that either. Oliver was the tallest among us by some measure, so

143

he climbed on top of the vehicle, but he could see nothing, just bush. The path we had made through the bush, a wide track it had seemed, was now invisible, the saplings back in place, the ground rock-hard, no tyre marks could be found; we were truly lost. We searched and searched and in time happily we discovered that we were only a few metres from our original road.

∽∾

In 1983, a party of us travelled from Cairns to Cape York. Romilly, her father Tom, Snowy, Charlie Diesel, Oliver Ford and I, along with Stephen Fay and Olga Polizzi, travelled by truck and four-wheel drive, fully loaded with equipment. As we set out from Cairns, a rough town in those days, a place with one modern hotel, an airport and little else of significance, we communicated between the two vehicles by two-way radio. The night in Cairns had been uneventful, just one fight in the local hotel, but that was almost over when we arrived. We stayed in Cairns's new international hotel, a small barren place with few other customers, recently opened. How it has all changed. Cairns is now a large thriving town filled with tourists and those who serve the needs of tourism. We drove along the coast road, a sealed road edged on one side with the sea, a brown sea, not the bright blue sea to which we were used, and on the other with cane fields, mountains in the distance as their backdrop. We were in no hurry, stopping first at the Hartley Creek crocodile farm, then at a bird park. The bird park had a fine collection of local birds—the small, red-browed fig-parrots were of particular interest to me.

Soon we came to Port Douglas. I had heard of plans to build a spectacular hotel there and was interested in seeing the place. Many years later, in the mid-1990s, I returned to Port Douglas. The hotel had fulfilled its cycle: it was built, received great applause for its beauty and subsequent success, became the subject of a scandal, was sold once and now was for sale again.

Years ago, when I first visited Port Douglas in Queensland, Port Douglas was not there. At least, not in the sense that it is today. There was a church and a graveyard filled with the names of British pioneers—names that came from places as different as Cornwall and Scotland. The Central Hotel, a fine Queensland building, stood on Macrossan Street, notable in those days for two monuments, one to the pioneers who settled Port Douglas, another to the local men who died in the First World War. It took a minute to see all that was worth seeing and I drove on excited by the prospect of the Daintree Rainforest and Cape York.

On my return to Port Douglas since, it had changed out of all recognition. Even the church has left the graveyard and it now sits on the foreshore beside the marina and the shopping centre that boasts shops with names like Louis Vuitton, Ralph Lauren and Loewe. The Mirage Hotel has been built with vast blue lagoons that double as swimming pools. A small railway runs past the town's resorts to a station complete with turntable at the marina. The marina is the *raison d'être* for the commercial explosion that has taken place. From here thousands of tourists are transported by high-speed catamarans out to the platforms on the Great Barrier Reef where they putter around in glass-bottomed boats, snorkel and dive on that extraordinary mass of gloriously coloured corals, teeming with fish of all sizes.

The place is a spectacle, Port Douglas's passport to fame and prosperity. A prosperity almost entirely due to the fact that it is the closest part of Australia to the Barrier Reef. Great palm trees line the roads around the town, palm trees with massed ferns growing up their trunks, manicured golf courses abound, lawns and hedgerows are neatly clipped. The whole effect is of a model town, but a town that could be anywhere where the weather is hot and water plentiful. A Japanese restaurant seems to have been removed from Japan, a Chinese restaurant from China. A restaurant called the Nautilus in Murphy Street, where the food is delicious and the atmosphere seductive, with coal braziers to warm you as you dine in the open air, could have been taken from the Bahamas or Florida or, for that matter, Los Angeles.

In Macrossan Street near the Pioneer Memorial is Club Tropical, a modern building disguised as a cave whose bar offers a drink called a 'Comfortably Numb'. Club Tropical also serves a 'Bushman's Breakfast', which is a very large plate of bacon, scrambled eggs and snags, as they call sausages in this part of the world. I felt quite numb after working my way through this confection. I am afraid that, judged by the standards of Club Tropical breakfasts, I am a pretty pathetic bushman. Opposite Club Tropical and its exotic décor is the Iron Bar Restaurant, a bush restaurant conveniently placed for those who might otherwise travel the bush for years without finding such a place. Their specialties included the 'Bob and Dolly Dyer's Seafood Platter', 'Pig Iron Bob's Steak Royal', 'Squizzy Taylor's Bank Rolled Chuck' and the 'Bradman Steak'. I asked what form the 'Bradman Steak' took, only to be told that it was a very large one. 'Skase's Crab Bounty', also on the menu, appears to be a reference to the fact that Mr Skase built the Mirage Hotel and left in a hurry, leaving large debts behind—the 'C' of Crab is perhaps meant to be a 'G'.

Far more delightful than all the other delights of Port Douglas is the Sunday market. Like all the weekend markets that abound in Australia, this one sells the same goods as the tourist shops of Australia on week days. But, hidden among the dross of tourist clutter and handicrafts, there are a few real gems. The stalls that sell orchids, for instance; these rare and wonderful plants are there in plentiful supply. Many on

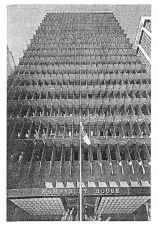

Hamersley House, Perth

The Parmelia, Perth

The fully restored Bishops House, Perth

Cable Beach Club, Broome

The Pearl Coast Zoological Gardens, Broome

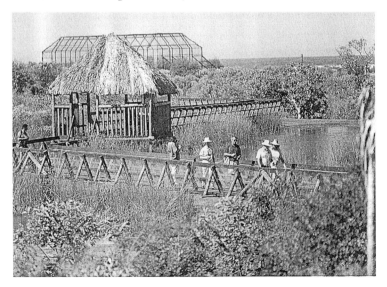

Dancing with a brolga crane at my Pearl Coast Zoological Gardens

My wife Romilly, by the McAlpine Oval in Broome

Albert Roux, putting the finishing touches to a wonderful lunch, in my kitchen at Broome

The dining room under the mangoes at Broome. Romilly is on my left and my daughter Skye is in the foreground on the left.

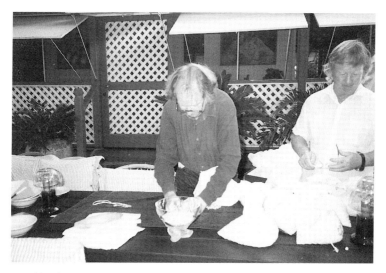

Myself and Snowy County with the pearl harvest

Myself, John Adams, John Roberts and Dennis Cully at the America's Cup Ball

Margaret Olley dancing, after a
dinner party at Joan Bowers' house

The last remaining trick from a youthful
repertoire as a conjuror

Myself and Margaret Olley at Joan Bowers' house

Myself and Romilly at Margaret Olley's house

Myself and Joan Bowers at Margaret Olley's house

Dining with John Olsen and Joan Bowers before John's retrospective at the National Gallery in Melbourne

Dining with John Roberts

offer were species from the forests of northern Queensland. The fruit stalls sell exotic fruit like sapota or chocolate pudding fruit—which really does taste just like chocolate pudding. The governor's plum was for sale, too, a bitter fruit with the highest content of vitamin C known to mankind, while the most exotic item was wattle seed ice-cream.

As I left, I watched an Aboriginal playing a didgeridoo the size of an Alpenhorn. Didgeridoos are now sold all over Australia; even some of the Aborigines of Western Australia, who have no culture of playing these instruments, sell them, only they don't bother to hollow them out. However, the aspect of this demi-paradise built by Australian men and Japanese money that interested me the most was the proliferation of government agencies offering counselling.

In 1983, we wasted little time in Port Douglas. At this time, I was convinced that Broome in Western Australia was to be the recipient of the tourist boom. I was wrong, of course; Broome in those days was totally isolated, served only by internal flights. Cairns and the towns of the east coast are served by both a railway and good roads; Broome merely by a long, empty road. It is the railway that makes the difference; masses of people can get to a place cheaply by railway. Now that the coastline of New South Wales and Queensland is fully developed, the railways are finding a new role. The Eastern & Oriental Express—whose sister company runs luxury trains from London to Venice, then on to Bucharest and, finally, to Istanbul, as well as a similar but even more luxurious train from Singapore to Bangkok—now runs a luxury service from Sydney to Cairns and on into the rainforest. Travelling by the luxurious trains of the Eastern & Oriental Express is a far easier way of seeing the countryside than travelling by truck and four-wheel drive in a cloud of grey bull dust.

Our next stop was Cooktown, a place where under different circumstances I might have stayed and never moved again. A town filled with giant mango trees, a town built on a gentle slope to the sea. Its single-storey and double-storey houses have corrugated iron roofs and sit on stumps; lattice-work abounds. In Cooktown, there was a small museum of local history and artefacts. I have never returned and I have no idea what the place is like today, but then it was to us a place of pure magic. We should have lingered there but I insisted that we needed to make our way to a place where we could make camp overnight, for I did not want to have to spend a night in the rainforest. It was all a bit ridiculous really, because a better camping site than Cooktown would have been hard to imagine. However, as we were still at the beginning of a journey destined to take us more than three weeks, I felt that we had to press on through the Daintree rainforest. As we travelled by ferry across the Daintree River, we searched the waters in the hope of seeing the cousin of the giant crocodiles that we had seen performing in the croc farm outside Cairns. There we had seen apparently coma-tose crocodiles come to life and jump four metres in the air to take a proffered chicken. Flat empty waters break into turmoil as a crocodile six metres long is disturbed and springs to attack—the cause of his disturbance usually a long bamboo pole.

The going was hard once in the rainforest. Badly built tracks, deep ruts and mud slides had made travelling almost impossible but we pressed on until we came to Weipa in the mining country. In the event, we never did get to the top of Cape York; rather, we turned round and came down the other side of the peninsula, making our way around the Gulf until we came to Arnhem Land. At the Roper River crossing, we were supposed to pick up our permit to enter Arnhem Land, but as the permit had not left Katherine, we had to go there to get it. Arnhem Land is set aside for Aboriginal use only. It has a high degree of self-determination in how it conducts its affairs. The use of permits prevents this attractive and romantic place being overrun by tourists—in this way, the Aboriginals who live there are able to carry on their traditional lifestyles without unwanted interruptions and interference.

Back in Western Australia, the Bungle Bungles, situated just south of Lake Argyle, look like the curled rope beehives of the nineteenth century, but on a magnificent scale. When I first visited the Bungle Bungles it was like coming across a deserted city, rising out from endless kilometres of scrub. Travelling in the bush is often a series of long, lonely drives with only nature for company that comes to an end as the sun drops. To stand in the bush on a rise, looking out to see nothing, to hear nothing but to feel as if every rock and plant is watching, listening, waiting for you to speak—no wonder people fear this beautiful place.

༄

The towns of the bush are isolated from the general run of life, populated with inhabitants who specialise in the unusual. Towns like Wyndham, hot as hell in the summer, cool and perfect in the winter. Road signs that promise paradise when all they deliver is hell. A hot, hard place is northern Australia, a place that is now only part tamed by airconditioning and mobile phones. Towns with grand names are more likely to be no more than a cluster of houses, a hotel and a shop or two. Somewhere north of Tobermory, we stopped for fuel and a meal. A youth, perhaps in his early twenties, filled our vehicles with petrol. He smoked as he did his work. We, for our part, stood well back and prayed silently, wondering how many more trucks he would fill with petrol while smoking before an untimely end came to him. When he had finished, I asked the youth a question about an art deco building the other side of the dusty track. 'That building, has it been closed long? 'About twenty years,' he replied. 'Closed because business was bad?' I asked. 'No, business was good, they just moved away.' Down what passed as a street was a hotel. 'Can we get a meal here?' I asked. 'If you wait a few minutes,' came the reply. We waited some 30 minutes in a bar filled with workers from the Main Roads Department. As a bell began to toll, these men raced for what passed as a dining room, a shed with wooden trestle tables and benches. Post-haste we followed and secured six places on benches at a crude table. The waitress, a giant of a woman with a bristling moustache, advanced towards us. We were a great curiosity to her. 'What would youse be doin' 'ere?' she enquired. 'We've come for dinner,' I replied. The waitress's expression was one of pure contempt. 'There's boiled cabbage and beef,' she announced. The Main Roads men were getting restless; we were clearly getting between them and their evening meal. 'Can I see the menu, please,' I innocently enquired. Before the giant could speak again, Charlie Diesel whispered, 'Run for the trucks.' Snowy, Romilly, Oliver and my father-in-law were already in the street. I followed them as fast as I could into the trucks and we were away. A few miles on we stopped, and I asked, 'What was all that about?' 'She thought that you were taking the piss out of her. At best, she would have beaten you up, more likely the whole mob of them would have set on us. They have to live with that monster; upset her and they don't eat.' It is true that as we left I had noticed the Main Roads men come pouring out of the canteen like a swarm of angry wasps.

༺ঔ༻

Among all the dangers in the outback, the waitresses in small towns are the most fearful. In the north, the people rise early and get on with the day. We arrived in Derby at about 5.30 a.m. and walked into the local hotel, not the smart new brick construction with a swimming pool and an abundant supply of air hostesses, rather the atmospheric hotel just down the road. 'What do youse want?' Once again, it was a waitress. Once again it did not occur to her that we might be visiting her restaurant in search of food. 'Can we get break- fast here?' I enquired. 'Are youse off the street?' she replied. In time, I discovered that this meant that we had not spent the night in the hotel. There was only one other couple eating breakfast. I walked over to a table by the window. 'Youse can't sit there.' 'Well, where can I sit?' 'Over with them. I'm not dirtying a table just for youse.' And so it went on. Small town after small town—friendly people, hostile waitresses. Is this just me, I wondered, or is it a phenomenon of rural Australia that I have discovered? Far better to eat Snowy County's main roads stew at a campsite, to sleep under the stars, wash in streams when you can find them, and share a basin of precious water when you cannot, than to suffer the taunts of these outback dictators and eat their foul food.

⁂

After a heavy storm the night before, we were driving down the Tanami Track in 1983 on the way from Broome to Sydney. It continued to rain constantly that day and we were bogged down several times. Further on down the Track, we helped tow a low loader with a V8 bulldozer on it out of the red mud of the pindan by hitching both our vehicles together. It was a spectacular sight to see these two small vehicles pull this great lorry and its even heavier load out of the pindan. When the low loader moved, it came away like a cork out of a bottle of champagne. A night in Alice, four days and nights in the Simpson Desert and the Channel Country and we reached Bourke.

After Bourke, the driving was boring, the weather wet and cold. Mid-morning, we stopped to visit the zoo at Dubbo, which had been completed not long before we arrived there, and a fine zoo it is, built to accommodate some of the larger mammals from Taronga Park Zoo in Sydney. These great beasts—hippos, rhinos, elephants, giraffes and the rest—can be seen in their large paddocks from a series of small car parks as you move around the zoo in your motor vehicle. The place was all very new when we arrived there; lots of concrete and some tiny trees. Now, I suppose it has matured, the trees grown high and the concrete hidden. The rain fell around us with a solid consistency; the animals sought shelter as best they could. The weather was cold and, try as they might to reproduce Africa, the planners of Dubbo Zoo had produced a landscape which the weather changed into one not so very different from that of northern Europe.

While I was interested in the zoo's layout and its animals, the whole thing seemed terribly unsatisfactory by comparison with the hot red earth and sunshine of my zoo in the North-West. Dubbo itself is not an exciting town and when it rains, it is not a place that encourages you to linger. We sought somewhere to eat breakfast, without much success, so we carried on to the Blue Mountains, with its high peaks, forested slopes and chalets that seem to come from the turn of the century. On hairpin bends, we looked down into deep valleys with small farms resting in their folds. Farms that had post-and-rail paddocks, with horses and cows. Once again, there was something terribly European about the whole place. I had not come all this way to visit Switzerland or Liechtenstein. I did not care a lot for the Blue Mountains. I am a desert man, not a man of the mountains. I have always suffered from vertigo; I really disliked the narrow curling roads that wound their way through these mountains and I abhor panoramic views. Too much all at once is never good, has always been my thinking. Driving through the suburbs of Sydney, two trucks in convoy recently arrived from the deep bush, we felt so superior to the automatons who drove to and from their work each day amid dreams of golf and sailing. We, after a week, were men and women of the stars and sands, the camp fires and the bush. At the Wentworth Hotel, the doorman greeted us as if we had just arrived in a stretched white Mercedes and our laden trucks were hastily despatched to the hotel's garage.

୶ಲ

Sadly, this was the last trip that we made with Oliver Ford. He died on 17 October 1992, killed by emphysema. He died suddenly while standing in the Great Hall of his home at Lacock—in his later years, he was hard to entice from there. Virtually retired from his business, he devoted his time to his garden, and a remarkable garden it was. Oliver had a certain touch with gardens. His reluctance to travel may well have misled those who knew him only in his last years, for he was in fact a great traveller, not by any means a tourist, but a real traveller who undertook long journeys. He was the most congenial of travelling companions, filled with humour, seldom grumbling, although he in fact disliked foreign food, preferring steak and chips to curry and the other concoctions of the Orient.

In Singapore once, after four days of Chinese food—I am addicted to Chinese cooking—I asked Oliver where he wished to dine. He chose a Japanese restaurant, one special-ising in *teppan yaki*. I was a bit surprised at this, but he ordered only chopped steak and quietly bemoaned the missing chips. One night we visited the old Bugis Street. This street was pure theatre. It was filled with tourists who in their turn became part of the spectacle that tourists came to watch. These were the days of the Vietnam War. There were soldiers and sailors who, as the evening grew late, drank and sang; local musicians and vendors came, as the audience, lubricated by Singapore beer, became generous with their money. Then began the parade of the transvestites—soon they were all muddled up. Sailors, tourists, and transvestites, all on the

153

most friendly of terms. Oliver and I were watching all this when a transvestite sat on his lap. 'I am a pretend Mary Poppins,' this exotic creature announced, though how he came to that conclusion eludes me, for a more far-fetched version of that demure creature would be hard to find. Oliver protested, the transvestite kissed him on his bald head and set off to find new pickings. The soldiers and sailors were all drunk, the tourists began to go home, the pimps became more insistent, fights broke out, bottles and glasses smashed. We headed for our hotel. As we climbed from the trishaw, Oliver, offering to pay, found his wallet had gone. Pretend Mary Poppins had not been quite as innocent as she wished us to believe.

Oliver Ford was direct about his life: 'Camp as a row of tents,' he often used to say, and to a female client who boasted of her Queen Anne dining-room chairs: 'My dear, I have more chance of being Queen Anne than those chairs.' But this was the stuff of London. I also knew him in the Australian outback where there is red dust and bogged vehicles. When I remember Oliver, it is not fine curtains and grand houses I think of, but the Tanami Track, the banks of the Diamantina River and the Simpson Desert, sleeping on the sand in a swag under the stars, more stars than in all the heavens put together. He was to my wife Romilly and I, a good friend.

⹂

It's strange driving in the outback, you see long stretches of bush that all seem the same but, in fact, change every quarter of an hour that you drive. The change is subtle but definite. There are areas of what seem like total dereliction, then areas of immense beauty, beauty on a scale unequalled anywhere in the world. It is no surprise that Aboriginals believe that God is in the land. Gorges with pools of water, dark and seemingly bottomless, rock walls that climb into an endlessly blue sky. No cathedral constructed by mankind has this dignity, nor this beauty.

When travelling in northern Australia, it is nature that wins the day, the nature of Australia, the world's oldest continent—the strange paradox is that people the world over refer to Australia as a new continent. Its people are so direct they make Americans appear tactful. I am, if nothing else, a collector, I will go to great lengths in putting together a collection. On the face of it, the Australian outback would not seem a promising place for collectors, but the reverse is true. One of the choicest of my collections is to be found there. It consists of the work of man and of nature, combined to form a culture unique to this continent. But before elaborating, let me dispose of some of the more familiar Australian collections that I am not referring to here.

Australiana, for instance. This means acquiring an object—any object—that has a kangaroo or an emu on it: jugs, tins, odds and ends. This is not collecting, it is accumulating. Nor do I mean Aboriginal art, though a tradition that is several thousand years old has produced objects that range from the incredibly beautiful to the mundane. I do not even mean the great painters, like Arthur Streeton of the early twentieth century, or those other twentieth-century Australian masters, Sidney Nolan and John Olsen.

The collection I admire the most was put together by God. I am thinking of the big pieces, not of the smaller natural objects—the incredible range of shells on the coastline; the amazing fossils, sometimes opalised to produce objects that would do credit to a Renaissance court jeweller; the birds; and the pearls of unequalled size and lustre. The collection I am thinking of—the masterpieces of nature that enrich this continent—contains no objects that can be held in the hand or placed in a cabinet: the vastness of the Simpson Desert; the waterfalls on the Prince Regent River; Uluru, carved by the wind and rain to a shape that, from the air, looks like a great red sleeping dog; and the Bungle Bungles, those recently discovered domes that rise from the earth like papal crowns, bejewelled with the bright green hanging gardens caught in their crevasses.

In the gorges in the Kimberley you stand alone yet always sense someone else's presence. It could be an Aboriginal behind the bush, or God—you take your pick. In the Wittenoom Gorge in the Hamersley Range are high rock faces that leave an impression to compare with Indian temples or Gothic cathedrals. These works of art were created by the heaving of the seabed and the chiselling of the wind. The collector stands in awe of their greatness and wonders whether any gilt-framed canvas will ever seem the same again, whether any man can reproduce such great beauty. Reproductions, however, like the memory, fade.

Photographs in tourist brochures are delightful, but they fail to tell the truth about this hard land in northern Australia, where drought and famine are commonplace and there is seldom a feast. A place where there is either no rain or too much rain. When rivers flood, water spreads for hundreds of kilometres, it is a beautiful but inhospitable place. For the first white men to cross the continent, coping with nature meant cheating death.

12

I did not only travel in the north by truck, I had journeys by boat and aeroplane as well. I often made boat trips from Broome among the humpback whales that migrate along the coastline, watching from a few metres away as these extraordinary animals rose out of the water and then sank back, heading for the depths. Turning again, they broke the water's surface, rising out of it like missiles, only to fall back again, sending spray in great quantities all over our small boat. I used to go fishing, but after a while I had no desire to continue for we caught too many fish, sometimes as many as 60 or 70 in a morning. Once while we fished, my daughter Victoria was both holding a line and reading a book. She caught three large red emperor fish on the same line, almost without realising it. Later on, while we ate lunch, she swam in the picture-postcard sea beside our boat. Lunch finished, I threw my line over the side and caught a sizeable fish. After a considerable struggle, I brought aboard a cod whose body must have been the size of Victoria's. I write 'must have been', for the body had been taken by a shark and only the head was left. Flying over the islands east of One Arm Point, I watched a vast shark lying in the tide race, moving lazily from side to side in order to catch the fish that were forced towards it by the tide.

༄

When I first arrived in Broome, Siggi Halter was among the people to whom I was introduced. Siggi was the local charter pilot in Broome. Siggi flew me over large parts of Western Australia and the Northern Territory. On one of these flights we flew to the Bungle Bungles; it was not possible, however, to land near the Bungles. This was the first time that I had seen these curious mountains and I was deeply impressed by the scale of the whole place. They seemed to stretch for miles. As a result of my cursory visit, I was left with a strong urge to return to the Bungle Bungles. We flew on to the Argyle diamond mine. I had never seen a diamond mine before, not least from the air, and I was a bit disappointed with the experience. The hole was impressive mostly for its size, which I suppose is a great deal bigger these days as the mine was then only just getting started.

Lake Argyle, however, was another matter. Siggi began to take the plane down until we were less than 30 metres from the ground when we crossed the southern shore of the lake. The land on the run-up to the lake was swamp-land. Flocks of birds, many of them pelicans, rose into the air as we passed over them. Still Siggi allowed the plane to lose height until we nearly touched the surface of the water. It was an exhilarating experience: the bright sunlight, red hot above and cool water rushing past below. The edge of this artificial lake was trimmed with dead trees rotting in the water that had killed them. Many of the trees were stained white from the excrement of the birds that used them as a lookout in the never-ending hunt for fish. As with the Bungle Bungles and so many of Australia's natural curiosities, it is the scale of Lake Argyle that is so impressive. One other matter sets Lake Argyle apart from all the rest and that is the fact that the lake is man-made—man-made and eight times the size of Sydney Harbour. It is a waterhole that will one day help to dramatically change the north-west of Australia. A few years later, I was taken on a boat ride across Lake Argyle and had a close look at its islands and the rare rock wallabies that live on them. Siggi lifted the nose of our aircraft and we shot over the narrow dam that holds back Argyle's waters. Up into the sky and round the township of Kununurra we circled, coming in to land at its suburban airport.

The next time that I visited the Bungle Bungles, we were able to land. Once again, Siggi flew me there and on arrival wo dodged between mountain caps. These mountains were boils on the ocean floor milllions of years ago. Forced up by volcanic activity, they now form a curious mountain range, with palm trees growing where their roots can find water, making small rainforests among these mountains in the desert. We landed nearby and walked or clambered as best we could in the heat amongst the inhospitable rocks. There are now tourist facilities at the Bungle Bungles, but when I first went there it was a wild and savage place, where an explorer with a camera had caught on film what seemed to be shots of the long-extinct Tasmanian Tiger as it ran between the rocks.

Often, animals, in particular birds, are believed to be extinct and are then found again. Such birds are the night parrot and the paradise parrot which is, as its name implies, one of the world's most beautiful parrots; both were believed to have been lost to the world. While travellers tell with certainty of places where the night parrot can be found, only rumours keep occurring that tell of the paradise parrot. Indeed, one rumour suggests that an aviculturalist from Queensland knows where the paradise parrot is to be found in the wild, while others suggest that certain aviculturalists have this bird in their collections.

೧೪

Once, in London, I was invited to lunch by the Royal Geographic Society. Their premises, near the Albert Memorial, are truly wonderful, filled with the memorabilia of exploration. Lunch was already served as we sat at the small round table, about six of us. I finished my first course, a salad of some sort, and, as my plate was removed, I noticed beneath it a small brass plate. It read: 'Upon this table in the house of his friend John Arrowsmith FRGS, David Livingstone worked out the geographical records of his missionary travels in Africa'. The subject of our discussion over lunch was a projected expedition to explore the Kimberley around the Prince Regent River and the Mitchell Plateau, an area to the north-east of Broome. The next year, in 1985, a team of 40 scientists arrived at what they described as the last great, unexplored wilderness in the world. While every day flora and fauna disappear from our planet, it is also true that every day new flora and fauna are discovered. This expedition discovered a great number of new insects and many new forms of plant life. While the Prince Regent River is sometimes visited by tourists who take their boats right up to the waterfalls, it was once the site of a tragic accident. A party of young people swam ashore; two men climbed the falls while the girls stayed behind on the rocks. As the tide came in, so did a crocodile. One of the girls, Ginger Meadows, a young American model, was taken by that crocodile.

Mitchell Plateau, on the other hand, has very few visitors despite there being an airstrip there. Once I sent a small party of guests to this remote place for a picnic, Siggi Halter flying them there in a light plane. As they ate their lunch, a helicopter arrived carrying a survey party from an oil company. 'What are you lot doing here?' they asked my English guests. 'Just having a picnic,' one of them, Dame Shirley Oxenbury, replied. 'Do you always come to places like this for your picnics?' the surveyors enquired. 'Oh, yes,' replied Dame Shirley. No-one lives within hundreds of kilometres of their picnic spot.

꧁꧂

The Ord River leads from Lake Argyle to the sea, some sixty kilometres from the dam, and empties its water into the Joseph Bonaparte Gulf. The town of Wyndham sits on the estuary that feeds that gulf. At low tide, the great mudflats of the estuary are empty, empty, that is, except for crocodiles; at high tide, the swirling waters are filled with danger. I had been to visit a man in Wyndham who bred finches, and I often bought stock for my zoo from him. This man kept a 5-metre crocodile as a pet in a mud hole in his garden. There is not much to see in Wyndham—the town sits broken into three parts: 12-mile, 6-mile and Wyndham, in the shadow of a great red rock. At the time I first went there it boasted a meatworks and a racetrack. Crocodiles lay on the mudflats around the meatworks; seen from the jetty, they looked like so many maggots lying on a rotting carcass. Today, the meatworks has closed and the town has a crocodile farm instead.

Once, I travelled down the Ord River in a tin punt driven by a small outboard motor. I had been to see Carlton Hill Station and my companion was Susan Bradley, the flamboyant shire president from Kununurra whose husband, David, was the local vet who also owned that station. Susan thought that I might like a trip on the river, some barramundi fishing and a night in the bush. There can be no doubt that I enjoyed myself thoroughly as we moved at a leisurely pace down the Ord River. The banks of the river were low, the depth of the water shallow and the width of the river not great. Bushes grew along the banks and as we passed the Bradleys' station, we could see the cattle grazing in the distance. The sun shone and it was an idyllic lazy afternoon. We fished for barramundi and caught several of a good eating size. As for crocodiles, we saw only a few and those that we saw seemed for all the world to be sound asleep. When we climbed into the punt, I had noticed that the boatman carried an automatic shotgun and a box of cartridges loaded with buckshot. After an hour or so, I concluded that he was just of a cautious nature. That night, we dined on grilled barramundi, slept well on the riverbank, and in the morning returned the way we had come. I asked the boatman about the crocodiles. He told me that he had seldom had any trouble with them until the week before, when he was filling a large metal billy can with water from the river and a crocodile sprang from nowhere taking the can instead of his hand and his arm.

Some months later, I had cause to be in Kununurra looking for a site to build a hotel. Hiring a helicopter, I travelled the length of the Ord River. Given the advantage of height over the clear water of the river, I could see what lay below the surface. The whole river was swarming with crocodiles, mostly of the extremely large variety. There they were lying on the river's bottom, waiting for a meal to come their way. As I remembered that pleasant afternoon with Susan Bradley, the memories sent shivers down my spine. When all looks so peaceful, it is easy not to take the crocodiles seriously. I took them so seriously, however, that when I bought a site at Kununurra—as part of my strategy to build a chain of hotels between Exmouth and Darwin—I chose a caravan site on the upper stretch of the river, where there are supposed to be no crocodiles. Heaven alone knows why this should be the case, unless the presence of so many people has driven them away. My wife Romilly and our friend Lucy Nelson, a tall, svelte blonde, swam there and came to no harm. Happily, they had not seen the crocodiles in the lower part of the river.

Crocodiles were, however, always on my mind when we travelled in the outback. Always cautious, I asked a station hand who sold me fuel on a trip from Broome to Darwin by the Gibb River Road—which is in reality a stony track: 'Are there any crocodiles in Bell Gorge?' He replied with considerable contempt for my obvious temerity, 'No.' And then he added, 'Well, only Johnson River crocs.' These are small crocodiles about a metre long. 'Will they bite me?' I asked. 'Only if you step on them,' and then, 'I would bite you if you stepped on me.' Never take chances with crocodiles in the north of Australia, there is no such thing as a harmless crocodile. The extraordinary thing about people and crocodiles is that people seldom realise the risk they take with these animals. While flying in a helicopter, I have often seen a family lying in the sun or fishing on a riverbank while behind a nearby bush is a crocodile. Such families always seem oblivious to the crocodile's existence. The curator of birds at San Diego Zoo once told me that he had tried keeping birds and crocodiles together. Over a period of a week, most of the birds vanished, so he kept watch to discover what was happening. It was not long before he saw a crocodile rise out of the water to take a bird in flight four metres above it.

When I flew up the Prince Regent River a few feet above its surface, it was the same. The crocodiles, some of an immense size, could be seen as they slept below the greenish water. Or did they sleep? The saltwater crocodile is a mammal unchanged for forty million years, the finest killing machine that God ever invented. I asked Siggi whether it was safe to fly so low. 'No worries,' he replied. 'I've done a lot of this in the jets of the German air force.' The jets of the German air force, I pondered, are specially equipped for low flying, whereas in a Cessna you do it by eye. We flew among the thousand islands of the Buccaneer Archipelago. One of these islands is quite spectacular: in its middle it has a considerable lake with two inflows for water from the sea. As the tide rises, water rushes in through these narrow channels until the lake is filled. When the tide drops, which it does in a matter of minutes, the lake begins to empty, squirting water out through the narrow channels. These waterspouts shoot high above the water level of the sea and extend about a hundred metres from the island on either side. The Buccaneer Archipelago must, with its whirlpools and waterspouts, be one of the most beautiful pieces of ocean anywhere in the world. A thousand or so islands dotted in a bright blue sea, whose water is so clear that, from the air, its giant fish are easily visible.

On one return journey, we stopped at Karratha for fuel. While the plane was being refuelled, my companion, Clodagh Waddington, and I took a car into town, or rather to the dock where we were shown heaps of rocks with carvings of fish. What was different about these rocks from other rocks that we had seen with fish and snakes carved on them, was that an attempt had been made to terrace some of them. Only remnants of this terracing remained but terracing it appeared to be, nevertheless. Our guide regarded this terracing as highly significant for, despite being unable to date it apart from the fact that it was very old, this terracing proved that the Aboriginals at some period had taken an interest in gardening or agriculture. Some years later, when I visited an island in Collier Bay, we found pits filled with stones which were used by the Aboriginals to grow yams. The stones collected the moisture from the air and watered the yams which grew longer as they tried to reach the water at the bottom of the pit. When the yams were fully grown, being planted in stones made it all the easier to pull them out of the ground.

಄

Darwin is a city that I have always enjoyed. When I first visited it in 1980, it was a strange mixture of modernisation and the culture of the Australian outback. Houses built of timber and corrugated iron that were spared by the terrible cyclone, Cyclone Tracy, that devastated Darwin on Christmas Day 1974, rubbed shoulders with modern office blocks and hotels. Trucks just out of the bush jostled in the traffic with the latest models from Mercedes-Benz. The outback trucks, which have extensions from their exhaust pipes fixed to their driving cabs which allow them to cross fairly deep rivers, always seemed to carry a jumble of baggage, with dogs sitting atop, swags and other equipment piled on the flat body behind the driver. In Darwin, you could walk out from a modern hotel fitted out to a very high standard and into the local hotel bar with characters as rough and ready as they come. Once walking down the mall in Darwin, with my middle daughter Victoria, I came across a character who threatened to fight anyone who came his way. Luckily, someone had knocked him over by the time we came near. The shops of Darwin sold useful goods as well as fancy stuff, very fancy stuff. My youngest daughter Skye was about five when I first took her to Darwin. Skye fell in love with a bridesmaid's dress that must have been intended to be worn during a Greek wedding. For a few dollars, I bought this exotic confection for her. Happily, in time she grew out of this extravagant dress and now has developed a sharp eye and good taste in the matter of fashion. Usually when I was in Darwin, I called on the shop that sold Aboriginal arts and crafts, never leaving it without a pile of packages to be sent home to Broome.

෴

In the early 1980s, my friend Barry Sharp and I visited a number of places in the Kimberley. Barry's shop had changed dramatically since the day that I first visited Broome. Gone was the old butcher's shop; Paspaley's Pearl shop stands there now, as smart a shop as you would find in the main shopping streets of any of the world's capitals. In fact, today in Broome there are a number of jewellery shops selling diamonds from the Argyle mine and pearls from the coast around Broome, set together to the highest professional standards. In fact, it is no romantic exaggeration to state that the pearls available for sale today in Broome are better than those in any other place except, perhaps, Paspaley Jewellers shop in Sydney, where you can find at least their equal. Barry and Kerry Sharp's emporium of the mid-1980s, however, was not as

165

grand as the Broome jewellery shops of today. It was, never-theless, a fascinating place. Kerry's collection of shells had grown since we first met and now were carefully displayed in smart showcases. A stonefish, one of the most deadly fish in the North-West, rested in an aquarium waiting in vain for some creature to step on it as a preliminary to becoming its lunch. Sea snakes curled and twisted in their own aquarium, surrounded by baskets of shells and trays of souvenirs made from shell. Hung on the walls were skulls of sharks, their large and deadly teeth bared for all to see, along with Abor-iginal artefacts, the shells of turtles and sawfish snouts. Needless to say, Barry also sold pearls. He also had a number of mother-of-pearl pubic shields, which were hung around the waist on hair belts by the Aboriginals during some of their ceremonies. They were mostly carved with geometric patterns. Some, however, were not used in ceremonies and were carved with fish and sea-going mammals. 'Butcher' Joe Nangan carved a number of these pubic shields, as did a gentleman called Sampi.

Once I saw a pubic shield carved with the image of a motor car that would now be a rare vintage item and, in the days that the shell was carved, must indeed have been an even rarer sight in the Kimberley. These early innovative shell carvings, that depicted the artefacts of the civilised east of Australia on the traditional ceremonial equipment of the north-western Aboriginals, interested me very much indeed. Asking Barry Sharp if he had seen such carvings, I was delighted when he replied in the affirmative. He had seen a mother-of-pearl shell with an aeroplane carved on it; a bi-plane, probably from the 1920s. The next day we set off for One Arm Point and the Lombadina Mission where this wondrous pearl shell was reputed to be found. One Arm Point is near the tip of Cape Leveque, a place of rocks and boiling water as the seas race between small islands. On our way to One Arm Point, our light plane passed over a promontory into the sea that surrounds the Buccaneer Archipelago. Below us was a beach with sand as white as the paper used in this book. We flew low over a creek where a giant crocodile, at least six metres long, lay visible beneath the shallow water. Not far from the coast, we saw a school of whales which seemed to be playing rather than travelling. As we approached the rough landing strip at One Arm Point, I could see the lighthouse and a few habitations that are now used to house tourists who visit the place.

Our landing was bumpy but safe, and soon we were met by a truck whose Aboriginal driver greeted Barry like the friend that he is to the Bardi people, who live nearby. After a short but rough drive, we arrived at the settlement. Barry introduced me to the Aboriginal who owned the mother-of-pearl shell and, after considerable discussion, he offered to show it to us. We followed him to his home, a corrugated iron building raised off the ground on short metal posts. Most of two sides of this building consisted of glass louvres, although much of this glass was broken and the rest so caked with dirt that you could see neither in nor out. The Aboriginal owner asked us to wait while he went inside to fetch his famous possession. It was then that the strangest thing happened. As Barry and I watched, a long arm came out from between the glass louvres and moved towards the ground, then its hand dug around in the loose earth below the building. Finding what was sought, the arm, the hand and a carved mother-of-pearl shell were retracted through the window into the house. In a moment or two, the owner of the pearl shell joined us and, unwrapping a piece of old newspaper, he produced a brand-new, carved pearl shell. True enough, the shell did have a carving of an old bi-plane on it, but it was not the shell that I sought. As a matter of politeness, I bought that shell and several others that its owner had carved.

The mother-of-pearl shells that I bought at Lombadina were different from the carved shells that I had bought at La Grange Mission, where the carver told me that each of the geometric patterns used in carved mother-of-pearl shells was a 'key'. (A sign of identification is what I believe he meant.) In any event, he was quite clear that each pattern was the property of one man and that no-one except that man's heirs must carve that pattern. Generally, carved mother-of-pearl shells come from the coastal regions of the North-West and are then traded to tribes living more towards the centre of Australia. The tribes who buy these shells believe that carved pearl shells have the power to bring rain; scrapings from the shells are thrown into the air during rain-making ceremonies. As a result, the carved pearl shells that you might find in Alice Springs, for instance, are much smaller and of far greater religious significance than those found in and around Broome, where they are used merely in dance ceremonies and for trade.

∽

Carved mother-of-pearl shell is also used in love magic and is regarded as having a powerful effect. While, to a person of European descent, all of this may seem strange and quite barbaric, it is worth remembering that Doge Dandilo, a thirteenth-century Doge of Venice, used to eat each day scrapings from a narwhal's horn. He and his contemporaries believed both that this horn came from a unicorn and that to eat it guaranteed long life. Doge Dandilo led his Venetian troops at the sacking of Constantinople—at the time he was well into his nineties and blind, yet he was still first over that city's walls. This was an exploit that must have been due to something, but I doubt if it was eating the scrapings of a narwhal's horn. His successors to the position of Doge, no doubt impressed by the effects of this horn on Dandilo, decided to try the same diet. The city's government, however, fearing for the complete destruction of their rare and immensely valuable 'unicorn's horn', banned the practice. The much-scraped narwhal's horn can be seen today in a small room, up a narrow staircase to the right, just inside the main entrance to St Mark's Cathedral.

❧

Shortly after our visit to One Arm Point, Barry Sharp and I travelled to Kalumburu to visit Father Chris, then the priest at the mission. Kalumburu in its day was a model of what a mission should look like. It had a fine herd of pedigree Brahman cattle and bred fine horses as a result of a gift of a stallion from brother monks in Spain. The mission buildings were laid out in an orderly fashion and its approach was along an avenue of massive mango trees. The place was clean and its gardens produced a whole range of vegetables. In the late 1970s, however, the Government disapproved of the church running these missions, believing instead that the State should take over the running of them and that the education the monks provided should become part of the State education system. The natural discipline that the Catholic religion gave these missions deteriorated into the unruly mould of so many State-run organisations where bureaucracy has killed initiative.

Chris Saunders at Kalumburu, along with the priests at other missions, now played the role of parish priests, responsible only for souls; the fabric of the place was looked after by the civil servants. Despite the change at Kalumburu, Father Chris did a remarkable job and became much admired for his work. Barry Sharp and I arrived by plane with Siggi Halter at its controls. It was a lovely afternoon. I had never met Chris Saunders before. Tall, physically fit, with a strong but gentle face, he is a man of natural authority. He was at the landing strip to greet us as we walked from the plane, offering us tea, which we accepted with enthusiasm. We sat and talked. Barry obviously knew Chris well and clearly had a great respect for him. In time, I was shown around the mission, and I bought two small examples of the art works that the local Aboriginals had made—Wadigji figures, the strange painted images that are almost human in appearance, people from outer space, with helmeted heads showing only eyes, their mouths entirely missing. In the centre of the mission there were a number of round concrete tanks about six metres in diameter. In these were kept small crocodiles, which I imagine had been hatched from eggs found in the river estuary nearby. The crocodile is a strange creature. I once watched one hatch; slowly it bit its way through the leathery skin of its egg. The egg was held by Malcolm Douglas, a considerable expert on crocodiles and the owner of the crocodile parks in Broome. Malcolm told me that the first instinct of a new-born crocodile is to attack whatever comes its way. True to his words, the crocodile, with only its head out of the shell, sank its teeth into his finger. Time passed quickly at Kalumburu, and at the end of a congenial afternoon, Barry Sharp, Siggi Halter and I all flew back to Broome. We crossed low over Walcott Inlet, the surrounding stretch of countryside an area with which I was to become deeply involved.

A few years later, in 1996, Father Chris became Bishop of Broome. His appointment was greeted with great joy by the people of the Kimberley. His diocese is an area of two million square kilometres with only 29 000 souls in it. Over 2000 people turned up for the ceremony in Broome. The service that marked the episcopal ordination of the Most Reverend Christopher Alan Saunders, DD, Bishop of Broome, was for me both a sad and happy occasion—sad to see the departure of Bishop Jobst, happy because the new bishop was Christopher Saunders. The new bishop's predecessor in the Diocese of Broome was a man of considerable standing, relentless in his fight to improve conditions in the Kimberley for Aboriginals and whites alike. Bishop Jobst was a fine, handsome man with steel-grey hair and piercing blue eyes, and a back as straight as an iron fencing picket. Many tales are told of Bishop Jobst—whether these tales are true in their entirety is a matter of conjecture, but they give the feel of the man, if nothing else. On one occasion, while visiting the minister of education in Perth, he made a forceful case for more funds to help with Catholic education. The minister had determined to say 'No'. Bishop Jobst, however, had in his mind that the only answer that was acceptable was 'Yes'. The meeting dragged on and on, the bishop giving no ground. After some time, the minister announced that he had to leave in order to catch a plane. The bishop replied that he would accompany him. I suppose that the minister put up with his arguments as they drove to the airport, imagining that he would be rid of this troublesome priest when he boarded the plane. When that moment arrived, however, the bishop went on board the aircraft with the minister and took the seat beside him. Such was the fame of Bishop Jobst that none of the flight crew batted an eyelid at this behaviour.

Bishop Jobst, I believe, along with Charles Court and a few others, was one of the great advocates for the people of the North-West and the Kimberley at a time when they and their country were regarded by most politicians in Perth as a regrettable nuisance. The Bishop's exploits with aeroplanes were almost as notorious as his art of lobbying politicians. It was his habit to start his aircraft in its hanger, then let the throttle in to take off from a standing start. Once, impatient at idle aircraft staff, who were delaying his take-off by lingering when they were supposed to be fuelling his plane, he took off anyway, coming down out of fuel in the bush somewhere short of his destination. On another occasion, he asked two nuns who were his passengers to hold the throttle while he swung the propeller. Perhaps they were unclear about how they were to hold the throttle or maybe there was just a misunderstanding. In any event, the plane and the nuns went off without him. Mercifully, they crashed at the end of the landing strip and no-one was hurt. Flying with the bishop, Barry Sharp told me, was like accompanying the pilot of a Stuka bomber on a dive-bombing mission. The bishop would approach an airfield and then point the plane's nose towards the ground. Their seemingly endless dive would terminate in a sudden levelling of the plane and a hectic landing.

৶

Bishop Jobst is a fine and good man, who often visited my house in Broome and Romilly and I became very fond of him. On one occasion, over lunch in Broome, he asked if we had ever met the Pope. The answer was 'No'. Bishop Jobst then asked if we would like to meet the Pope; the answer, of course was 'Yes'. Romilly and I thought no more about this conversation until a month or so later, when the invitation for a private audience arrived from His Holiness. That spring, Tom Stephens, the upper house member in the Western Australian Parliament for Broome and the Kimberley set out from Australia and joined us in Rome for this great occasion. The weather was perfect as we presented ourselves to the Swiss Guard at the Vatican's Gate. We were passed from hand to hand along the intricate maze of the Vatican corridors; each guide who took charge of us was rather grander than his predecessor. Finally, a tall and extremely elegant Italian in a tailcoat, white tie and with a heavy gold medal hanging around his neck, took us in a lift to a large and sparsely furnished waiting room. We sat on straight-backed chairs and watched television, which seemed totally out of keeping with the dignity of the room. After a few minutes, the gentleman in the tails turned off the television and a group of Papal officials entered. They ignored us and began a discussion about how the Pope should pronounce my name. Romilly, who is fluent in Italian, explained their conversation to Tom Stephens and myself. It went like this: 'McAlpini', 'No, Alpini' . . . 'Perhaps Alpino'. Then a bishop who had not spoken before said, 'He will just have to sort it out for himself.' The Pope, who spoke perfect English, had no trouble at all with my name. It was a wonderful experience to meet this man who has done so much towards the destruction of communism. I came away with a feeling that he was tired and old, but he had given his life to God and, while it might well have been the inclination of another to retire, His Holiness knew that he had to continue in his arduous task until his end. I felt that I was in the presence of a goodness that I had never come across before. As we walked from the Vatican, we barely spoke: all three of us were greatly moved by the experience of that morning.

We lunched in a restaurant, Piperno's, in the heart of Rome's old Jewish district. We ate simply and then returned to the Vatican where we met an Australian priest who took us below the crypt where the popes are buried, into the Roman graveyard where we saw St Peter's tomb. Legend had always identified the spot; nobody, however, knew for sure if it was the true tomb of St Peter. The tomb was excavated during the Second World War. The Church, believing that the war would mask the outcry if, in fact, it turned out to be the tomb of an unknown man or woman, took the opportunity to carry out the exhumation. In the event, the skeleton was male and matched both the known characteristics of St Peter and the manner of his death. Despite St Peter's having been built long after the graveyard was covered over, the tomb is exactly beneath the hole in the centre of the Cathedral's dome. Again, it was a moving experience, being so close to the roots of a great religion. Later, as we came out of St

Peter's, we visited the tourist shops and, like the millions of pilgrims who come every year, we bought our souvenirs.

৵

It was on one of my trips in the Kimberley that I was first seriously affected by the disease that was to require me to have heart surgery. There had been problems before. I passed out on a plane on the last stage of my return from a visit to China, and I had passed out during the opera at Glyndebourne. Carried from the auditorium, I was laid out on the floor of the foyer and for some reason the first aid attendant had taken my trousers off before going to get help. Just after I had come round, a flood of people who had been watching the opera joined me. I felt rather silly lying on the floor wearing a black dinner jacket, a bow tie and no trousers. Doctors had told me that there was nothing much wrong with me except I was overweight. Then one Sunday night, after a long and heavy lunch in the country, I had travelled to London. At about eleven thirty that evening, after I had been asleep for about an hour, I awoke feeling sick and suffering from what at first I took to be indigestion. In time, I decided that it was my heart. Romilly disagreed with me, saying I had drunk and eaten too well which, of course, was also true. The next day the doctor confirmed her opinion, adding that I had a hiatus hernia. At a London clinic, I had tests for this hernia, which confirmed my doctor's opinion. A packet of pills was the cure. I left his office much relieved.

In time, I left as usual to spend the English summer of 1987 in Australia. I did not feel well as we drove from Broome to Darwin through the Kimberley. Along the Gibb River Road, which was barely a track, are a number of small lakes and waterfalls in rocky country inaccessible by motor vehicle. We—my two eldest daughters, two girlfriends of theirs, Romilly, Snowy, Charlie Diesel and myself—decided to walk to one of these lakes, called Bell Gorge. That morning we had breakfasted in Derby just after six, in an outback hotel with outback staff and outback food. In this type of hotel, it was, as I have written, quite normal to be asked to share a table to save dirtying another tablecloth. There were enough of us on this occasion, however, to warrant a table to ourselves. I ate a plate of kidneys and bacon covered in brown sauce, fried bread, potatoes, beans and tomatoes, toast and marmalade, all washed down with a mug of coffee. The sun was hot as we walked to Bell Gorge down a steep slope, climbing over rocks until we reached the water. The girls stripped off their clothes and stood under the waterfalls; Snowy and Charlie swam in the clear water of the small lake; I sat on a rock feeling short of breath and sick.

For some days my left arm had ached. I believed that the pain came from my posture at meals, that my chair was too low or my table too high. As we set out to climb back to our vehicles, I lagged behind. I felt pain in my chest and was violently sick. Snowy came back and helped me. We all put my illness down to a heavy breakfast and the hot sun. I drove on and two days later, after two nights sleeping in the bush, we reached Darwin.

When we returned to Broome it was to a political battle over my idea of building an airport. A public meeting was called and I had an overwhelming majority of 1200 to six, or something of that order. A petition in favour of the airport was circulated, and was signed by over 2000 of Broome's inhabitants. Then it was back to London and to a difficult Conservative Party Conference at Blackpool.

At the Party Conference, I felt tired and ill. On the Monday after it, I visited my doctor who arranged for me to see a heart specialist the next day. Foolishly, I missed the appointment and it was the Wednesday afternoon before I met with the heart specialist. By Thursday, I was in the Wellington Hospital having an angiogram. The best artery that I had leading to my heart was working at 40 per cent of its capacity; the worst, at 10 per cent. 'Do not even get out of bed,' the heart specialist told me. 'I want to get a really good surgeon, and I want him to operate tomorrow. He will need to be fresh; this is going to be a long job.' I was, on the whole, rather relieved by this news. At least I knew what was wrong with me. The next day, Gareth Rees operated on my heart for eight-and-a-half hours. When I woke in the Intensive Care Unit of the Wellington Hospital, I asked how it had gone. 'Six bypasses,' he replied. 'Bloody heck,' I mumbled, and dozed off. The nurses kept waking me. I was desperately thirsty, so they gave me cubes of ice made from lime juice to suck, which I thought a wonderful invention. As I lay I could hear the voices of Romilly and Olga Polizzi, who both sat with me all night.

Romilly slept in my room when I was out of intensive care, and it was wonderfully reassuring to have her there. As it turned out, I had been very lucky, for my activities of the previous year had not been ideal for a person with a heart that was barely working. Later, my doctor told me that it was my lack of exercise that had saved me. 'Had you ever played squash or taken heavy exercise, you would have died of a heart attack.'

13

Pearls, diamonds and cattle are found in the Kimberley, the world's last great unexplored wilderness, now officially explored but, for all that, still a vast wilderness many times larger than the state of Texas. For many generations, the wealth there sprang from cattle. In the Kimberley, cattle stations can run anywhere from half a million hectares in size to literally millions of hectares, and the owners of the largest stations were kings. Their world was well-ordered: the Aboriginals who worked for them received no wages; on the other hand, the station owners provided food and accommodation for their workers' extended families. This they regarded as generous and I believe that they were sincere in this respect. They were, however, clearly without remorse for the fact that they had taken the land that provided their wealth from the very people who were the recipients of their apparent generosity. While it is clear that a number of station owners formed a real and often lasting relationship with the Aboriginals they employed, this was not always the case, particularly with the large cattle companies who were, in effect, absentee employers. They often became the object of considerable hatred. The lot of the Aboriginal was not a happy one, despite the facts that the white fellows brought them education and medicine. They also brought disease, alcohol and the notion of poverty. One cannot deny that this grievous state of affairs happened, however why should it be a bar to a civilised existence in which the Aboriginals play an equal part with their fellow Australians, who currently happen to be all shades of white and yellow?

✧

Today, cattle stations are close to becoming a liability. The station that my family owned was Roebuck Plains, just south of Broome with Roebuck Bay on its western side. The man who managed it for me, David Thom, was well-known for his knowledge of cattle and how to handle them. He set out to make Roebuck Plains into a model cattle station. The old hybrid stock were phased out and new pedigree Brahman cattle were imported from Queensland. The ancestors of these cattle originally came from India. They are successful in the Kimberley because they generally have a quiet temperament, unlike the local cattle, and their skin is nearly hairless, thus making them resistant to cattle ticks. Australians like big, red cows whereas the Brahman are a pale tan, white, brown, black or even a dusty shade of blue: a herd of cattle looks so much better if it is of one colour, so we set about dividing our herds into different groups, each of the same colour. The land was fenced, paddocks built with runways between them, to ease the handling of the cattle. Towards the end of the years that my family owned Roebuck Plains, the quality of the stock had risen and the place was prospering. Roebuck Plains, however, was not bought for its cattle or for its broad hectares. I needed a strip of land, just a few hundred hectares out of over 300 000 on that station to build an airport. It would be easier and, I believed, cheaper to buy the whole place rather than to try and negotiate an excision of land from another owner. Despite this, I wanted to make Roebuck Plains into a cattle station to be proud of and on my behalf David Thom succeeded in achieving that very thing. On the station was a dried-up lake called Eda. I am bound to say that when I drove across the station for the first time with the owner's agent, the whole place looked like a dust bowl, overstocked and under-watered. You would never have guessed that Lake Eda had ever existed, although the owner's agent claimed that he had been waterskiing on it during the wet season.

It was David Thom's careful management and the slow build-up of cattle numbers that turned the land from dust to soil-bearing grass. Among the first things to be done, when I took over the station, was to set about building proper accommodation for the station workers; the place was a mess. Indeed, the first cyclone would have taken it all away. At the same time, I decided to fence off Lake Eda and about 8000 hectares around it. It was always my intention one day to move the large mammals in the collection at my zoo from the township of Broome, leaving the zoo containing only parrots, small mammals and birds. In the space of about three years Lake Eda returned to its natural state. Without cattle, the lake held its water or the greater part of it for the whole year. The bush around the lake regenerated the place— in a word, it became a paradise. Now large groups of brolga cranes gather there, jabiru storks stand in the shallows and fish swim in the waters of Lake Eda. Water birds cover the lake in the dry, wading birds come there during the wet. On the coastline of Roebuck Bay that edges the station, there is a bird-watching post. When we pulled down the accommodation at the caravan park that is now the Cable Beach Intercontinental, I gave several of the cabins to the local bird-watching society. A few guests pay each year to watch the migration arrive and these cabins provide their accommodation. There is, however, no season in the Kimberley when conditions are not good for bird-watchers and certainly an evening spent at Lake Eda would be the high spot of such an expedition. The beauty of Roebuck Plains and Lake Eda is that they are only about twenty kilometres from the town of Broome. In the end, Roebuck Plains station was sold in 1994, along with the rest of my family's company, Australian City Properties. Now the great days of cattle over, the meat works in Wyndham and Broome are closed, and the age of the farmer in the Kimberley is just beginning.

The land around Kununurra is prosperous farming country. The road between Broome and the turn-off to Derby and the north is now populated with a series of agricultural holdings. These farms are producing a variety of fruits and vegetables. Their watermelons are formidable—heavy with juice and filled with flavour, they have to compete, however, in the markets of southern Western Australia when they should be sold in the north or exported to Singapore, Indonesia and Malaysia. It is only a matter of time before someone produces pineapples on that immensely fertile soil around Broome. The problem, however, is the distance from the perceived markets in the south, and a lack of speedy transport to the markets of the countries to the north. A modern airport would of course resolve this problem, an airport that could take the large freight-carrying aeroplanes.

⌀

Pearls are another source of wealth in Western Australia. In the waters of the Kimberley almost 80 per cent of the world's cultured pearls are grown. When in Darwin, I would visit Nick Paspaley, a leading master pearler and his family, on occasion buying pearls from him but more often just going to his office and looking at the truly wonderful pearls that he kept in a safe the size of a small room. In fact, Nick treated this safe like a room—hung with pictures, carpeted and complete with easy chairs, a table and a sofa—it was a delight to sit there and watch Nick pull out wondrous pearls from a cabinet.

On one occasion, I watched his year's crop being sorted. The pearls come in all shapes and sizes. There was a small

mountain of pearls ranging in colour from steel grey through
to gold in all its shades to white and palest pink. There were
baroque pearls and teardrops, button pearls and perfectly
round ones, literally sacks of them. Then Nick asked if we
would like to see a few pearls that he had put to one side.
Romilly and I entered his splendid safe, sat down and were
served cold drinks, then Nick drew a bag from the cabinet and
spilled the pearls onto a velvet tray. The quality was truly
incredible. 'Each of these pearls I have picked because I have
never seen its like before,' he said. One specimen brought to
mind the parable of the pearl of great price—*St Matthew*,
chapter 13; perhaps you will recall that parable. I have always
known that feeling: finding something for which I would sell
everything. It is the instinct by which a true collector can be
recognised. This pearl was pear-shaped and 15 millimetres in
diameter. Nick called its colour strawberry, but to me it
appeared at first to be coloured pale gold, and then changed
before my eyes into a pale pink. Every time I moved it between
my fingers, the colour changed. After studying this pearl for
some time, I asked if I could buy it. Nick took it, looked it
over and slipped it back into its bag before returning it to his
safe. 'How can you price a pearl like this? This pearl has no
price,' he said. Sadly, it was a case of no price, no deal.

My first visit to a pearl farm was in 1981 when Romilly
and I travelled up Cape Leveque to visit the Brown family, or
rather the brothers Brown and their respective families. The
Browns' father had come ashore there when, fishing for pearl
shell in the Buccaneer Archipelago, he spotted at once the
beauty of the place. With his eldest son, Lyndon, he set about
putting together a small cattle station and a pearl farm,
carved out of the bush. Their cattle were from Africa, big red
cows; as Lyndon had told me: 'Australians like big red cows.'
The Browns slashed the wattle on their small station and, as
a result, young shoots sprang up and the cattle ate a plant

that they would otherwise have avoided. Among the rough buildings of the Cygnet Bay pearl farm, buildings that looked as nothing but served their purpose, and were wonderfully situated to take advantage of every breeze, was a tennis court—the grass was bright green among the burnt bush, the surface as smooth as a marble tabletop.

The Browns were friends of Thea and David Hutchinson, the chemist in Broome, who had taken Romilly and I there to stay the weekend. Alison, the wife of Bruce Brown, the younger brother, was a schoolteacher, and a party of school-teachers and civil servants arrived after lunch on our first day at the farm. Lyndon Brown hated schoolteachers and civil servants alike and, what is more, said so. He and his wife stayed at home; the rest of us went to play rounders on a saltpan just down the coast. I hate any game that includes a ball except perhaps billiards, and I am none too keen on billiards, so it was not much of an afternoon for me. Next day it was tennis; things were beginning to look desperate as far as I was concerned. What on earth would we do next? Swimming, I supposed. I hate swimming and particularly I hate swimming from beaches, the sand gets between my toes and no amount of washing will get it all out. 'Can I possibly see some pearls?' I asked Bruce Brown. 'Sure,' he replied, and we went into his bedroom where he pulled several plastic buckets from under his bed. These buckets were covered with dishcloths and filled with pearls. 'Do you want to sell any of these pearls?' I asked. 'What else would I do with them?' he replied. Romilly and I chose about fifty baroque pearls of the sort that the pearl farmers call tornadoes. They have a band around their widest part and this band is replicated on each side of the pearl's centre in an ever-decreasing size. These tornado pearls, when of the best quality, are by far and away the most beautiful of the Australian pearls. For some time they were quite common; today, they barely appear at all.

Their absence is due, I believe, to the greater expertise that is now used in the growing of pearls. The casual attitude of the Browns to their pearls and to every manifestation of authority was, I found, quite refreshing. That night, Romilly and I wandered along the beach at sunset and all was perfect in a paradise that hides a multitude of dangers. The next day, we drove back down the sandy track to Broome leading our small convoy of two cars. The bush roads now held no terror for me and I was driving with a new confidence and I believed considerable skill, when the car skidded out of control and away into the bush. I was lucky that it did not turn over or hit a tree; I was also lucky that there was a car following to help me back onto the track.

The pearl farm at Deep Water Point that Snowy County, Rod Reid and Peter Kinney started, and which I owned most of during its formative stages, now prospers. That farm was a ramshackle affair to begin with. Soon, however, we improved the accommodation and now it is a fine-looking place. The theory of management that I have always applied is to give good accommodation to your employees and so be able to employ the best people available. Sometimes that theory works, sometimes it fails. The men and women who spent their weeks there bathed in the sea and played tennis on the court that had been built. Beverley Kinney, ever imaginative, had constructed her own home complete with an outdoor shower built among the rocks. Snowy had a manager's house built in the Broome style; later, he moved out and the farm manager took over this residence. Busy with my zoo, I only visited the place half-a-dozen times. Life on the pearl farm was hard work and the solitude broken only at weekends. During the year, the oyster shells, which were about the size of a small dinner plate, were taken each week from the sea and cleaned. The plant life that is attached to the oyster shell competes with the oyster for the food that floats past. Machines need to be maintained, boats cleaned and repaired: the work is arduous, tiring and really quite boring. Only when the pearl harvest was on, and the work was almost non-stop, was there any excitement about the place.

In the early days of the pearl farm, Snowy spotted a crocodile lurking in the water while the work on the pearls went on. A wary eye was kept out for this creature. Then, for a time, not much was seen of it. A few years later, it, or one very like it, was captured. Its legs were tied with rope and its mouth was bound with electric tape. Immobilised, the animal was put in the spare bedroom of the manager's house and a message sent to Malcolm Douglas in Broome, for he usually deals with recalcitrant crocodiles. That night, the crocodile freed itself and, jumping through a window high in the wall of the building and smashing the glass, took the window frame from the wall along with it on its dash to the sea. This crocodile, clearly not best pleased with humans, has moved further down the coast to a still-peaceful spot.

༄

When the pearl farm was just beginning, Snowy used to drive down from Deep Water Point in his truck, the pearl harvest in cotton sacks under his seat. He would arrive at about breakfast time and empty the sacks on my breakfast table. My guests were truly amazed at the heap of pearls amongst the platters of fresh fruit. Nowadays things are done differently. Snowy no longer runs the farm, and pearl robberies have become a regular occurrence on the Cape Leveque Peninsula. There are no more breakfast-time displays of casual affluence, rather a hurried trip with the pearl harvest to a bank's vault. At the time of writing, five Broome men are in the dock charged with the theft of between half a million and two million dollars' worth of pearls. The police allege that these men systematically raided a pearl farm 150 kilometres north of Broome in the Buccaneer Archipelago, and that about 1700 pearls were removed from the pearl shell at that farm. Their operation was carried out using a two-metre-long fibreglass boat. No pearls have, however, been recovered. In the light of this and other robberies from pearl farms, plans are in train for a squad of police to be set up to deal with the theft of pearls, similar to the squads that protect the gold-producing industry. Pearling in and around Broome has changed over the years from something akin to a profitable hobby to a multimillion-dollar industry, an industry that is one of the largest employers in north-west Australia.

Sadly, pearls are not the only things that thieves in the North-West see profit in stealing these days. Recently, two men have been charged with stealing dinosaurs' footprints. Cut from the rock about 38 kilometres north of Broome, these footprints are from a stegosaurus and are believed to be 130 million years old. The traditional owners of the area, where these footprints were, have not unreasonably asked the Western Australian Government to limit access to their land. No doubt this will be yet another firebrand thrown onto the smouldering issue of land rights in the North-West.

In truth, the only answer is for the Government to step up supervision of these remote and immensely beautiful areas to stop the criminal vandals who will plunder them. If the Government believes it worth the cost of protecting the pearling industry, an employer of much labour, then it should definitely spend the funds to protect the material wealth of a growing tourist industry in the North-West, an industry whose value will one day far outstrip that of pearling. Closing land is not the answer: the Kimberley is no longer the greatest unexplored wilderness in the world; it is part of a modern, industrialised continent with all the advantages and disadvantages of that status. Human footprints in rock have also disappeared from the Lombadina area, 180 kilometres north of Broome. These stolen footprints will, without a doubt, find their way onto the world market for fossils, a market which is of such a scale that the chances of either the five-toed stegosaurus footprints or the human footprints ever being recovered are somewhat remote. While Joseph Roe, the representative of the Goolarabooloo people, quite rightly, wrote to the State's Premier, Richard Court, this sorry affair is not, however, an Aboriginal matter. It is a matter that should deeply concern all Australians. Richard Court should act speedily to set up the necessary safeguards for valuable natural specimens located in remote parts of his State.

⁘

Diamonds are another great source of wealth in the Kimberley. So far, there is only the Argyle mine operating, which produces about one-third of the world's diamonds. There are, however, many aspiring diamond tycoons who search for, and seldom find, the fortunes that they seek. For many years, I have held the view that alluvial diamonds must be hiding in the prehistoric rubbish under the sea off Roebuck Plains, rubbish that was part of a river bed. Roebuck Plains was once such a river, a river vast in size that is now removed and become the Fitzroy River, its mouth a hundred metres wide in the dry, 160 kilometres wide in the wet, its waters having risen up to seventeen metres in past wets. My own experience of diamonds is somewhat limited. I did, however, discover in a casual conversation with a member of the Oppenheimer diamond family that they had spent literally hundreds of millions on searching for diamonds and only found them in any quantity once. Apparently, all their best mines have been found by independent prospectors. It was, therefore, with hope in my heart that I agreed to a proposition by Des Higgins, as independent a prospector as one is likely to come across in a long day's march.

Des Higgins was a gaunt man with a considerable gap between his front teeth. Ross Gardiner, the gentleman who once ran my zoo, was of the opinion that the gap was caused by drinking from a stubby of beer when his truck went over a bump while travelling at high speed. For myself, I prefer to believe that the gap in his front teeth was natural, a sign given to him at birth to show his luck with money and, I hoped, with diamonds. The Higgins family lived on Waterbank Station, which had the township of Broome along one of its boundaries. For years there was tension between the Higgins family and the Broome Shire Council. The town authorities coveted the Higgins's land and, to my certain knowledge, it has taken them over twenty years to lay their hands on it. The Higgins family is, to put it mildly, eccentric, a family who are their own men and women, a family that, like myself, has a strong distaste for bureaucrats and all things bureaucratic. What was theirs, they regarded as their own, and they didn't want others interfering with it or trying by bureaucratic means to take it from them. Mrs Higgins is a fine woman and a strong Catholic, much involved with the Church and charity. A naturally kind woman of strong principles, she and her family have had more than their share of tragedies. Des Higgins, a brilliant raconteur and entertaining companion, often used to call at my zoo for a beer. On one occasion, he told me of a skeleton he had found in the desert; the length of the skeleton was about three metres. Allowing for exaggeration and the natural lengthening of the body as it decomposes, this skeleton had undoubtedly been that of a very tall person. It is with some regret that I write of never having made the journey with Des to view these remarkable remains. Des Higgins, who sadly is now dead, spent much of his time in the bush, grading tracks for the Main Roads Department, going to places that few of the inhabitants of Broome had ever heard of, let alone visited.

One day, Des sat down on my veranda and, accepting a beer, began to explain that the reason for his visit was not just social. As he talked, he leant forward and tipped what looked like four small lumps of grizzled glass onto my table. 'Diamonds,' Des announced. He had found diamonds which, I am bound to say, came as no surprise to me at all. 'Where?' I asked, and Des began to explain. After five minutes, I was lost in the desert somewhere to the west of Halls Creek. The diamonds, however, were far away from there, hiding in the rubble of the rocky outcrops of the Caroline Ranges. During the next half an hour, Des and I did a deal: we would go fifty-fifty on the diamond mine and, in return, I would give Des a set of new tyres for his truck and enough petrol to get him back to the find. Then I would contact diamond companies and set about turning our claim into a fortune for both of us. The diamonds were, in fact, real diamonds. The mineralogist who looked at them was of the opinion, however, that they came from South Africa. This could be explained in part by the fact that Des had a previous partner in this deal, a man of dubious reputation who had been in litigation with others who claimed the land he regarded as his, and which now both Des and I regarded as ours. The diamond business, however, did not come to me with the same basket of luck that I had received when I bought a share of Snowy's pearl farm.

◦∫◦

While most people believe the name of Broome to be synony-mous with pearls, for many years when Broome was mentioned, people spoke of the place in terms of Diamond Jack and the stolen diamonds. During the war when the Japanese invaded Indonesia, the Dutch authorities put all the diamonds that they had control over in an aeroplane in order to get them to safety in Australia. This plane, piloted by a Russian, was shot down off the coast of Cape Leveque near Carnot Bay. None of those aboard were aware of the fortune that their aircraft carried, in the form of £250 000 in diamonds, packed in a parcel the size of a cigar box. By chance, Jack Palmer, a beachcomber, was passing in his lugger. While four members of the party on board died, the pilot and some of the plane's passengers made it ashore. The pilot despatched two of them to fetch help and, after another brush with the Japanese, help came in the form of two RAAF planes which dropped supplies. When the wreck of the plane was searched, no diamonds were found. Jack Palmer handed in some diamonds but nobody believed that he handed over all of them. For years afterwards, diamonds began to turn up in the Kimberley, and so began the legend of Diamond Jack. For myself, I have often imagined, as I walked along Cable Beach in the first light of the morning, that I would stub my toe on the largest pink diamond known to mankind.

Despite the fact that our diamond mine never materialised, I was well-disposed towards Des Higgins, although never a week went by without some person or other warning me about his character. The aspects of his character that others found so inconvenient, I greatly admired. He was a simple man: if you treated him well, he would treat you well in return. While he may well have been a simple man, towards the end of his life Des Higgins had the most memorable of experiences, an experience that was far from simple to explain in any rational sense. Staying in a motel at Kununurra, he woke after an hour or so of sleep. In the corner of his room was a blue light. Imagining it to be the television or some other electrical device, Des turned off all the switches in the room but still the bright blue light would not go away; in fact, it began to get brighter. Des was quite perplexed at this, so he got up and left the room. As he did so, the blue light began to fade. After smoking a few cigarettes on the motel's veranda, Des decided to go back to bed. As he entered the room, the light began to glow and steadily it increased its intensity until it was a startling bright blue. I am not sure how or why Des Higgins came to the conclusion that this light was a visitation by the Virgin Mary. Although not a religious man himself, he was clearly influenced by living with a wife who is deeply religious. Greatly impressed by what can only be explained as a vision, Des later visited each of the people with whom he had had disagreements in the past, making his apologies to his enemies. Shortly afterwards, he died at peace with his own conscience and returned to the fold of his God. Whatever you care to make of this strange light that Des Higgins saw, there is no doubt about its impact on him. A man who spent much of his time alone in the bush, it is no surprise that he reacted in the way that he did, for, if ever there was a country truly inhabited by God, it is the lonely wastelands of north-west Australia. It is a place where strange happenings seem not strange at all, a place where the bizarre and the unusual are quite in tune with the nature of the countryside and its people.

After some years of living in Broome, I began to long for a place in the bush that had less people around. Broome had become my place of business and I needed a retreat from that business. Walcott Inlet at Collier Bay seemed just the place and the land on one side of it, which was called the Charnley River station, became mine in the strangest of ways. In Broome, I had a lady who worked in my garden. She was a pleasant young woman, who in her own way kept my garden tidy and did her best to encourage the few remaining plants to grow. One morning at about 6.30 a.m., this lady asked if she could have a few words with me. It was my habit to rise early in Broome, to bathe and then to take a walk along Cable Beach. This woman caught me just after my bath and before my walk. Her request was quite frankly inconvenient. She, however, was in a considerable state of agitation about something, so I arranged to see her later in the morning. She got on with raking my yard, and I with my daily exercise.

Later, it transpired that her father owned a cattle station

of over 32 000 hectares in the Kimberley. His proposition appealed to me immediately. For some time, I had been in communication with the Lands Department looking for a small cattle station. Her father had exactly what I required, which was just as well as he desperately needed to sell his property. Later that day, the young woman brought her father to see me. He turned out to be an extremely pleasant man and we concluded a deal in a matter of minutes. He would sell me his cattle station at Walcott Inlet with any cattle that I could find on the property for $20 000. The station had, to all intents and purposes, been bought sight unseen. With Siggi Halter, I had flown over the property and noticed cattle on it but I was uncertain about its boundaries. Walcott Inlet itself formed one boundary and the Isdell and Charnley Rivers two more, but heaven knows where the fourth boundary was to be found. Situated approximately 300 kilometres north-east from Broome as the crow flies, it is one of the most beautiful pieces of land in the Kimberley, teeming with wildlife. The countryside is wild and wonderful; fresh water is plentiful in the rivers that provide two of the station's boundaries. Fish are plentiful at Walcott Inlet, and it is a place much prized by barramundi fishermen. Ducks nest there, migrating birds come and go as they please. It was exactly what I needed, a small cattle station with three boundaries that cattle either could not or would not cross. The fourth was rugged mountain land that in many parts was as good a barrier as a fence. To add to the advantages of this station, it backed onto a national park. The Charnley River Station was the perfect place for the experiment with my British White cattle.

That afternoon, I rang John Adams about my latest purchase. Surprisingly, he seemed rather enthusiastic and offered to take a half-share in my land. This pleased me, for a partner of Western Australian birth would make life much easier with the authorities. It was my intention to breed British White cattle on this station. The British White is one of the world's oldest breeds, it was brought to Britain by the Romans, and has several characteristics that would make it suitable for use in the Kimberley: the cattle are naturally polled, so they have no horns to damage fencing; they have virtually no hair, so they would not be troubled by ticks; and, while their coats are white, they have a black pigment in their skin that protects their teats, noses and the skin around their eyes from sunburn. In Britain, they will survive the winter on a bale or two of straw, fattening quickly when there is new grass available for them to eat. What is more, these animals are dual-purpose cattle: they produce enough milk to raise twin calves and are sometimes used as dairy cows. As beef cattle, they have a double thigh giving them extra kilos of prime steak. A butcher in England told me that he would pay an extra 50 pence a kilo on the carcass of a British White steer on account of the quality of its meat. Finally, these cattle were by nature extremely tame; even the bulls could be treated like big dogs. In the past, the British Whites had prospered in Kenya and, as I had a herd of these cattle in England, it was my intention to bring stock out to Australia and see how they managed on this remote station.

John Adams and I approached the Minister of Lands to have the station transferred into our names. We attended a lengthy interview where we were told that cattle could not survive on this station. So we produced photographs showing that quite clearly this was not the case. Then I explained my theory about the British Whites. The minister and his staff clearly believed that I was nuts. Indeed, anyone who opened a zoo in Broome and believed that town would grow to become a metropolis must in their eyes be nuts. So the bizarre nature of this new request came as no surprise to them. In the event, they gave me permission to take over the land. After all, John Adams and I had bought it legally and clearly intended to farm the place. For our part, we set about this venture with great enthusiasm, acquiring a landing craft to move cattle in and out of the station, and hiring a drover to muster what cattle he could and to shoot the rest so the station would be free of TB. Finally, we commissioned plans for a station homestead. Then came the rub—what had seemed the land's greatest advantage, its proximity to a national park, turned out to be its greatest disadvantage. Someone came up with the idea that this station should become part of that national park.

About six months after we had acquired the land, all hell broke out. The small group of activists in Broome who believed that the mantle of the Reid family had fallen firmly on my shoulders set about trying to stop me from carrying out my plans at Walcott Inlet. As mentioned earlier, *The Broome News* and the people who congregated around its flag certainly succeeded in irritating me; in fact, they stimulated my thoughts to such an extent that I achieved far more in Broome than had ever been in my mind when I first went there. The irony of this journal and its supporters' attacks on me was that, only some time after the attacks had abated, did I, for totally different reasons, leave the township of Broome. There was no plot, no cunning plan, no hidden agenda to my activities in Broome. These people and their journal were a nuisance, but no more of a nuisance than the sandflies that come with the spring tides in Broome.

On the matter of Walcott Inlet, the writers at *The Broome News*, and others, went too far, one of them stating on the local radio that I was involved in corruption. Faced with such charges, I had no choice but to sue. I won judgements in my favour on all the cases, and apologies were forthcoming. It was never my intention to earn money out of litigation, rather to clear my name. By this time, the West Australian Government was involved. The activists in Broome were insisting that Charnley River Station should be part of the nearby national park, a national park, incidentally, which the nation was not allowed to visit. The ecologists spoke of it as a lung, which is a curious thought when you consider that Australia, being approximately the size of North America, has a population of only eighteen million people. The whole place could be considered a lung under those circumstances. Without doubt, I can accept the principle of lungs in the world, but a land that is nearly all lung reduces this principle to the ridiculous. The people of Australia should be allowed to visit areas such as Walcott Inlet, for a nation must have in its makeup a degree of soul, and the country around Walcott Inlet is nothing else if it is not a place of the soul.

John Adams and I argued that Charnley River Station had been specifically excluded from that park when its boundaries were drawn up. The chairman of the commission had, by coincidence, been Phil Adams, the father of John Adams. The argument lasted several years, with John and I offering to pay and accommodate a manager to protect the Inlet, where poachers had been shooting crocodiles. The Government was adamant. Pressure from the Broome activists gave them no room to manoeuvre. I agreed to abandon my cattle-breeding project, and we offered to give up all except 40 hectares of land in return for permission to put a camp site for tents there so that tourists could visit the national park. This was unacceptable to the Government, for the last thing they wanted was for people to visit their newly extended national park.

In the end, the State Government bought Charnley River Station from John Adams and myself for twenty thousand dollars, the price that we had paid for the place. The venture had cost John and I four or five times that figure, quite apart from time that it wasted. I now predict that, without the shadow of a doubt, it will only be a few years before the Government of Western Australia will be begging a developer to bring tourism to Walcott Inlet and their national park. Not only will they be begging a tourism operator to go there but heavily subsidising that company's activities. It was, I think, the pure tedium of dealing with uncertain and weak governments in Australia that caused me to divert my energies elsewhere. This is written not in recrimination at plans unfulfilled, rather to record how I was dealt with, in the hope that those in authority and their successors might read these words and, realising how badly the North-West has been served, bring about a change in attitude which will allow the Kimberley to truly become a source of wealth for the whole State, rather than remaining a creature in receipt of subsidy.

IV

Politics and Politicians

14

When Margaret Thatcher came to Australia, she was in fact the first British prime minister to do so. But she never came to Broome; despite the fact that her private jet passed right over the town, she is too canny a politician to take the risk of visiting friends at the expense of the British taxpayer. She did, however, come to Perth, staying in my family company's property and private residence, the Bishop's House. She loved Perth and thoroughly enjoyed her fleeting visit to Australia. Her schedule was hectic; her stay in Perth was only for a day and a night. Early the next morning, I was waiting with some of her staff in the kitchen of Bishop's House for her to come down for breakfast. Suddenly there was a series of loud crashes. The security men sprang into action; it was, however, no emergency— simply the prime minister pulling a heavy suitcase down a flight of jarrah stairs.

While Margaret Thatcher was in Perth, I raised with her the matter of Yagan's head. My friend Ken Colbung, one of the most decent people that I came across in Western Australia, was at the time of Margaret Thatcher's visit searching for the whereabouts of this severed head. It was known to be in England but nobody seemed to know quite where. Just before Margaret Thatcher was entertained by the Western Australian Government on her one evening there, I arranged for Ken Colbung to have the opportunity of a few words with her about his search. Afterwards, she told me that in principle she was sympathetic to the idea of returning Yagan's head to Western Australia, where the rest of his body was buried, but she could not do much until the head was found. In 1995, more than four years after Margaret Thatcher left office, Yagan's head was discovered. The Conservative Government was still in power in Britain and, although I was not by any stretch of the imagination *persona grata* with the prime minister, John Major, I was definitely on speaking terms with several members of his cabinet. I set about trying to get Yagan's head repatriated, without, I may say, any success at all. After many unsuccessful private approaches, I decided to write of the British home secretary and the fact that I had found him reluctant to do anything about this matter. At the time, I was a columnist in the *European*, a newspaper which served as a perfect forum to liven up the debate. I took the matter into the public domain and I reproduce the piece that I wrote here:

It is seldom that a writer gets the opportunity to record a tale that involves a severed head and a British government minister, so I will not miss the opportunity. The severed head is that of Mr Yagan and the member of her majesty's government is Home Secretary, Michael Howard.

Yagan was born in Western Australia in 1810, twenty years after the British first colonised Australia. His father was Nyoongar chief Midgegooroo. An important leader of the Aboriginal community, Yagan soon came into conflict with the British authorities.

Despite the murder of his brother and execution of his father without trial, Yagan was generally well-disposed towards the settlers who had arrived in his land. He helped them find food on occasions when otherwise they would have starved. However, after a series of retaliatory attacks on the British following the slaying of various members of his tribe, a price was put on Yagan's head.

Bounty hunters captured Yagan but he escaped. He was then pardoned, but before long was again in trouble with the new arrivals. He was deemed outside the law and again a price was put on his head. Despite his troubled relationship with the authorities, he enjoyed cordial relations with the white settlers. He was murdered, however, while out hunting with two teenage settler friends, William and James Keates. While Yagan walked in front of the pair, they took the opportunity to shoot him in the back of his head and earned themselves a £30 reward [A$78].

That was not the end of the matter. Before he was decapitated, the decorated skin on Yagan's scalp was removed and turned into a belt. Later, his severed head was smoked for several weeks and then sold as an anthropological specimen.

Robert Dale, a British soldier, bought the head and took it back to Britain with him on 29 September 1833. Unable to sell the head at a profit, Dale donated it to the Liverpool Royal Institution, which later loaned it to Liverpool City Museum where it was displayed for some years.

By 1964, the public attitude towards exhibiting bits of other people's bodies in museums had changed and the Liverpool Museum sought permission to inter it in an unmarked grave. For many years, it remained undiscovered in a cemetery.

Ken Colbung, an articulate Western Australian Aboriginal leader, who is a descendant of Yagan, had for years searched to find his ancestor's head. Last year, Cressida Ford, a postgraduate archaeology student at Southampton University, located Yagan's head in an Everton cemetery. It was in a grave beneath the coffins of twenty stillborn babies.

The Home Office was approached and they set in motion the procedure for recovering Yagan's remains. This procedure involved asking all the parents of the twenty stillborn children their permission to dig up the grave. Some of the parents could not be found and others refused their permission. Colbung and his relatives were devastated by this news. They are still attempting to reunite Yagan's head and his body. This issue is of great significance to the Aborigines of south-west Australia, in particular, and to those of Australia in general. To the British Home Office, it does not seem a matter of any importance. They simply say that there is nothing to be done.

Some months ago, I wrote to the Home Secretary and a month or two later received a reply that contained the biggest load of nonsense I have read in years. Yagan was only one of many thousands of Aboriginal and Maori peoples whose heads were taken to Britain and sold as souvenirs. To their credit, many of the museums and institutions that held these heads have since returned them and reputable salesrooms nowadays no longer trade in human remains, although this was a regular practice until just a few years ago.

Usually the problem is finding the rightful owner of the heads to return them to. In this case, however, the ownership is clear. To take these heads in the first place was a barbarous act, but an act committed in a barbarous age. To keep Yagan's head in Britain today shows a total lack of sensitivity for the feelings of Yagan's people in an era when generally we are more attuned and sensitive to these issues. Yet, as far as the Home Secretary is concerned, nothing has changed. There can be no justification for keeping Yagan's head in Everton cemetery while his body lies in Western Australia.

While the removing of Yagan's head from Everton might upset a few British voters and there are no Aborigines voting in the next British general election, it is too much to hope that Howard will do anything about this issue. It seems that Ken Colbung will have to wait until there is a less ambitious and electorally sensitive head of the British Home Office for his ancestor's remains to be reunited.

Two years later, the Conservative Party was destroyed at the polls. Within a week, Ken Colbung came to London and helped the New Labour Government solve all the unsolvable problems of Yagan's head, which only goes to show that where there is a political will, there is always a way. Yagan's head was exhumed and returned to Western Australia in September 1997. In the event, there was a further dispute over its ownership, but this was finally resolved and Ken Colbung's mission completed.

Margaret Thatcher chose me to be the treasurer of her party in 1975. I was a Conservative by instinct and habit. I was never an activist, climbing my way up some party ladder. It was to join Margaret Thatcher's 'Long March' that I went to work in 32 Smith Square, the Conservative Party Headquarters. I am still, by instinct, a Conservative; the habit, however, has now been broken. I am more searching in my enquiries these days as to how the Conservative Party conducts itself. I feel that I have remained much the same in my views, but that the Party has crept away, like some husband slipping from his lover's bed in the early hours of morning to return to his wife. Margaret Thatcher's Long March culminated in 1979 when she became prime minister, with the Conservative Party being seduced back to conservatism from the near-socialist philosophy to which it had been married during the previous twenty-five years. While I am sad that the political ideas of Thatcherism are one by one first reviled and then discarded by those to whom they handed office, I have, however, few personal regrets.

Margaret Thatcher changed my life, as she did the lives of so many other people. I have, however, changed many of my views over the years. Many years ago, I gave up going to the Church of England and, after a long period in which religion played no part in my life, I started attending Catholic churches. I am now a regular churchgoer; I feel better when I have been to church. To me, birth, life and death all seem the greatest of miracles. I am still interested in politics and occasionally active, though most of the time I just write about politics. I write and travel, and am still blessed with an endless curiosity about people, places and things. I live in continental Europe; I revel in the beauty of that place and the vast quantity of man-made masterpieces there. I have, however, after years of looking at man-made beauty, come to believe that it is only human beings who are really important.

∽

Working in British politics and being closely associated with the prime minister, I expected to attract the attention of the terrorist IRA. Always on the alert at sensitive times such as elections, I sent my wife and daughter overseas. Each night I would sleep in one of three different hotels, choosing among them at random and making the decision only when I was in my car in the early hours of the morning. When my friend Airey Neave was murdered by the IRA, I was desperately sad. To me, however, they still seemed an abstract threat—that is, until the terrorist attack on the Conservative Conference taking place at Brighton in 1984. The second bomb attack that I was involved in took place in May 1990. I had left my home at West Green. I had for some years been a specific target on the IRA 'A' list, and West Green was vulnerable to attack. I suppose some instinct encouraged me to move; indeed, I also moved my London residence. A week or so later in my new London apartment, I woke to discover that the IRA had destroyed West Green.

Unpleasant as these two experiences were, they came as no surprise. An incident, however, that did surprise me was one that happened in Australia in the mid-1980s. I had bought for myself an old house in Peppermint Grove, Perth's smartest suburb, so-called because its streets are shaded by huge peppermint trees. This house sat on a double block and was just down the street from John Adams's home. It was my intention to knock down this poorly-designed house from the 1950s and build something better-looking. By chance, while I was waiting on the plans so that I could apply for permission for the work to be done, John set about extending his house. 'Could I and my family borrow your house for a few months?' Without hesitation I agreed, and the Adams family moved in—John, Liz and their son, complete with his nanny. Some weeks later, John and Liz left to visit Sydney for a weekend. On the Sunday night, someone put a fire bomb in the main bedroom and another under John's Mercedes-Benz that was parked in a lean-to at the side of the house. The place went up like a Roman candle. The nanny and child escaped out of a window. The police investigated the attack and could find no culprit. Perhaps, they said, it was a bomb meant for a doctor who lived opposite, who was often involved in acrimonious disputes over workers' compensation. If that was the case, no further attempt was made against him when his enemies discovered that they had bombed the wrong house. As far as I can discover, this attack on my house is the only incident of its kind ever to have happened in Peppermint Grove. Was it an attack by IRA sympathisers? Who knows, and, as far as I am concerned, who cares? I was not harmed nor, indeed, was anyone else. As for the house, it was due to be pulled down anyway. It is only fair to record, however, that I sold the empty block some time later, and that while I was in Perth, I continued to live in the city.

15

Australia is so distant from Europe that in Britain they tend to think of it, if they think about Australia at all, as just an unusual place to visit. A continent of breaking surf with handsome men and women who spend a great deal of their time cavorting in that surf. A land of sheep and cattle, deserts and jungles, populated by that exotic race, the Aboriginals. Seldom do we Europeans remember that Australia is a vast continent strategically placed on the Pacific Rim—an area that despite recent setbacks is destined to become the epicentre of prosperity in the next millennium.

As for their politics, the generality of Europeans know nothing at all about the politics of Australia. When it is explained to them, Europeans find the political system of Australia as incomprehensible as those who are not Italian find the politics of Italy, or those who are not British find the politics of Britain. It takes a considerable effort to explain to Europeans the complexities of a system where the Liberals are really Conservatives, the Country Party is interested in more than country matters, and the Labor Party has spent much of the last ten years trying to jump over the backs of the Liberals to occupy their policies—which they have, in fact, generally succeeded in doing. While I tend towards Labor in Australia, in truth, I would be in a quandary if I had the vote there, as to how I should cast it. The two parties both embrace free enterprise; their policies are so close that, at times, it is hard to tell them apart. While I disagree with particular policies in Australia, I seldom disagree with the overall thrust of either party. A good deal of what Paul Keating achieved, I am sure John Howard, now prime minister, agrees with, for it was John Howard's efforts as leader of the conservative opposition that largely set the agenda of politics that forced Paul Keating and his party to the right.

Paul Keating was a man who had great success at the hustings and who served Australia both as treasurer and then prime minister. I knew him well. I particularly admired this cultured man's use of language in a parliament that is the antithesis of culture.

Paul Keating is on record as having often addressed parliamentary rivals in less than complimentary terms. He is a fine practitioner of the art of verbal violence. Some of the phrases and words that he uses to describe opponents are: 'piss-ants', 'harlots', 'sleazebags', 'perfumed gigolos', 'dummies', 'scumbags', 'gutless spivs'. He even called one opposition member who returned to a portfolio that he had some years before given up, 'a dog returning to eat its own vomit'. Paul Keating turned parliamentary abuse into an art form. In his private life, Paul Keating is an intelligent and cultured man, an expert on classical music and a great enthusiast for French Empire clocks. When I once asked him how he could afford to collect such valuable antiques, he replied: 'Most people buy their antiques when they have been tamed,' by which he meant, found and cleaned by expert dealers who would add a large mark-up. Keating went on, 'I catch them while they are wild.' I firmly believed that Paul Keating would win his last federal election and his government be returned to power. I was totally wrong in this for, despite the fact he is highly intelligent and, furthermore, his government had the courage to carry out their ideas and had the language to sell them to the electorate, he was unceremoniously thrown from power.

Among other Labor politicians I find attractive as human beings is Bob Carr, the victor in the New South Wales election of March 1999. I will quote from a television commercial that promoted his cause during a previous election. He was asked if he would endorse President Clinton's policy of 'three strikes and you're out'. 'No,' Carr replied, 'under my plan, it is one strike and you're out. Why should we give those who commit serious crimes three chances?' Surprisingly, Carr is the most humane of men and leads the Labor Party in New South Wales with great skill and consummate ease. The politics of Australia may well be complicated, but Carr has hit on a truth that would get him elected in any country of Europe. The time has come for people to be treated humanely, not the criminals who prey on them. Bob Carr is a man for whom I have the highest regard. He is one of a small group of politicians in govern-ments the world over who actually takes the time to read a book. Literate and intelligent, Bob Carr is about as inter-esting a person to spend time with as I have met anywhere. His wife Helena is beautiful, clever and charming.

❧

Sir Charles Court, who led the Liberal Coalition and was premier of Western Australia from 1974 to 1982, believed in capitalism and he believed in his State, and under his admin-istration both flourished. He is a man with a huge personality; dealing with him was a real pleasure, nothing was ever impos-sible. It was never a question of taking ideas to Charles Court, he was full of ideas himself for developing Western Australia—he only needed entrepreneurs to carry them out. Sir Charles Court, perhaps more than any other man, set the pattern for growth that subsequently ended in tears, tears largely because the government of Brian Burke understood and liked the results of Sir Charles Court's ideas, but failed to understand how they were put into practice. In time, Carmen

Lawrence became premier of Western Australia. Billed as the clean hands that the population was told would sort out the mess, in the early 1990s she, with masterful inactivity and frenetic public relations, turned prosperity into an evil word and helped the State of Western Australia and its people not a bit. How strange is the coincidence that it has fallen to Sir Charles Court's son, Richard, to restore the State's reputation.

On my second visit to Western Australia in 1964, I was invited to lunch with Charles Court at Parliament House. He was Minister for Industrial Development and extremely powerful. I was a callow youth who had never eaten oysters before and regarded them as preferable to poison, but only just. Sir Charles was kind to me; he treated me as if I was an experienced businessman, which I most certainly was not. We sat down to lunch in the dining room at Parliament House, and the first course was served. I admired the view, and toyed with a large glass filled with tomato sauce, oysters without their shells and one lettuce leaf. Sir Charles ate his oysters with relish, carrying on a conversation at the same time. For my part, I tried to hide a dozen oysters under a small lettuce leaf. Sir Charles drew no attention to my predicament. I have since learnt that I love oysters and eat dozens of them every time I am in Australia—without doubt, the Australian rock oyster is by far the sweetest and most delicate oyster in the world.

After a long period in office, Sir Charles Court was eventually succeeded by Ray O'Connor, who took the same views about industry and the development of Western Australia but achieved little. Life dealt unfairly with Ray O'Connor when he became premier, for he inherited the tail end of Charles Court's government. A large bluff individual filled with apparent goodwill, I felt that Ray was more interested in having a good time than governing Western Australia. I first met him at lunch with John Roberts. John had invited the premier to lunch in order to introduce me to him. As a side attraction and to impress me, he had also invited Dennis Lillee, who was currently playing in a test match in Perth. The lunch was the greatest of fun—John Roberts, a brilliant raconteur, was far more impressive than O'Connor and Lillee put together.

⁂

After the days of building Western Australia during Charles Court's premiership, and the fun of Ray O'Connor's administration, came the new energy and enthusiasm of Brian Burke. The new premier, the leader of the Labor Party, believed in enlightened socialism, a mixture of free and State enterprise, a partnership between the State and its entrepreneurs. For a time, this seemed to work. Then the inevitable happened—the functionaries of the State began to behave like entrepreneurs, using the apparently bottomless resources of the State as a bankroll. The days of scandals and the crash in Western Australia will never be forgotten by those of us who ran businesses at that time. Western Australian entrepreneurs, sighting gold to be mined through the incompetence of the bureaucrats' political masters, set off to have the lion's share of that valuable substance. 'It was,' said one senior civil servant who had disapproved of the whole venture, 'as if they were taking grain from blind chooks [chickens].'

Despite all that has been said and written about Brian Burke, the premier at that time, I have never believed him to be a dishonest man. While I know full well that honesty is like pregnancy in that you cannot be a little bit pregnant nor a little bit dishonest—in both conditions, you either are or you are not—I still contend that while Brian Burke may have committed questionable actions, he was and still is, at heart, an honest man. He believed that certain aspects of how business was conducted in Western Australia needed changing, and he was right—they did need changing. Brian Burke believed that Western Australia could be set alight in a frenzy of commercial activity and that, from this activity, profits could be made for individuals and the State at the same time. The State could then use its share of the profits to finance the social policies that he deeply believed in.

Brian Burke sincerely believed that all this would be good for his State and, up to a point, he was right. Like a number of other politicians, he also believed that Western Australia's success would do his career no harm. By the time the excitement of the America's Cup was at its peak in 1987, he was suffering the hangover that comes after the high of success. Sitting next to my wife Romilly at lunch in our pavilion on the dock at Fremantle, he explained that each morning he just wanted to pull the bedclothes over his head and stay in bed; that he would rather watch 'Play School' on television than go to the office. Given this honest assessment of his own mental state, it is not entirely surprising that Brian Burke got himself deeper into the muddle that finally disgraced and sent him to jail. His crimes were not the crimes of a criminal; rather they were the actions of a man whose life had run away from him. He had been surrounded by people who genuinely believed that they could fix things and, while doing this fixing, could take a cut for themselves. Brian Burke's fate was not the well-deserved end of an habitual criminal, rather it was the final scene in a play where he unwittingly played the fall guy, while believing all the time that he was cast as the hero.

※

Peter Dowding, who succeeded Brian Burke as premier of Western Australia in 1988, was a highly intelligent politician who did the best he could, but the cycle of disaster was too far advanced for him to be able to take the action that was needed to reverse it. Try as he might to unravel the relationship between business and government in Western Australia, the task was beyond him as, indeed, it was beyond anyone else. However, Peter Dowding understood the North-West in a way that Brian Burke never could; Brian Burke could never understand that complicated place which seems at first sight so terribly simple. Peter Dowding was enthusiastic about my plans for a new Broome airport and, had he survived as premier, I have no doubt that it would by now be built and operating. Like his predecessor, he never seemed to hold against me the fact that I was a senior official of the British Conservative Party working for Margaret Thatcher. Brian Burke had appointed me to chair the newly formed Aboriginal Enterprise Board, an organisation whose object was to finance Aboriginals who would rather start small businesses than stay on the dole. We bought boats for fishermen, tractors for tractor drivers, lorries for hauliers and put up money for several arts projects. It was fascinating work and I enjoyed it immensely. We never really got all the financial backing from the Government that we were promised but I was quite used to that happening in Western Australia, so no matter.

It was, I believe, a conference in Davos in 1989 that did for Peter Dowding's premiership. He had asked me to join the Western Australian delegation and help in the effort to promote the State. His team at that conference, despite carping criticism from home, did a splendid job of selling Western Australia, an effort that was rendered worthless by the change of power in their Government. Peter Dowding was right to go to Davos, for the only painless way out of Western Australia's financial problems was colossal inward investment, and the conference at Davos was one place that might have generated such investment.

However, back home in Perth, the newspapers and the gossips were busy. They claimed that Peter Dowding and his new wife, a delightful Scandinavian, were living the life of Riley in Davos—fine wines, food galore, important people, in fact everything that the rest of the cabinet back in Australia were not getting. It was all untrue, of course, but jealousy feeds on jealousy. In Australian politics, the end for a marked premier is a quick one. His enemies laid their plans while he and his close allies were out of the country, and those enemies struck soon after his return. The truth, of course, was rather different. We were quartered in an adequate but modest hotel; Peter and his delegation ate modest meals, listened to tedious speeches and sold the idea of investing in Western Australia to whomever they could get to listen. I paid my own expenses and I took my lunch in the best restaurant in town. It has always been a principle of mine that if you want to collect honey, go where the bees are. Likewise, if you want to sell something, go where you will meet the people likely to be able to afford the goods that you are selling. On the last night, I took all the staff who were helping the delegation out to dinner at a restaurant where I knew the family of the owners. It was a riotous evening, ending with the hard core of the revellers and myself listening to a bagpiper in the restaurant's kitchens at one o'clock in the morning. The staff who served that delegation were kind and decent people, fine representatives of their State and their nation. Their attitude to life was so terribly different from the air of false sophistication affected by so many of the delegates from other nations at that conference. I had the most wonderful time that night.

Peter Dowding is a man whom I have always liked and still do. He once said to me that I had all the assets that were needed to succeed in Western Australia—energy, enthusiasm, capital to invest and the entrepreneurial spirit to invest it. Only one aspect of my situation was missing—I was not a Roman Catholic. He is a man with a sharp but dark sense of humour. When I first met him he was married to Jill, a fine-looking Aboriginal, a woman whom I always found to be extremely pleasant and who, along with Peter, introduced me to a community in Broome that I would otherwise never have met.

༒

Carmen Lawrence succeeded Peter Dowding in 1990 and almost immediately appointed a Royal Commission, which, at great length, investigated the whole affair of the State's dealings with individuals. She was almost immediately dubbed 'Dr Feelgood' by the Western Australian press. Her approach to politics was one of: 'I'm honest; you are safe in my hands'.

I worked fifteen years for Margaret Thatcher; four years as a columnist for Eve Pollard, the editor of the *Daily Express*; and for the last ten years I have worked for Min Hogg, at *World of Interiors*, as editor-at-large and a columnist. Working for all of these three women has been a most enjoyable experience as far as I am concerned; in fact, at the risk of appearing prejudiced, I would rather work for a woman than a man any day of the week.

Carmen Lawrence was, however, something else. On one occasion when she was a minister, I had a most unsatisfactory meeting with her. I entered her office. 'What do you want,' she asked. 'Nothing,' I replied, and then explained that I had come to offer the State my collection of 700 pieces of Australian furniture, much of it from the first settlement. I wished to form a trust and what I needed from her was a building in which to house this collection, a building where the public and tourists could conveniently view it. The local officials had suggested the disused customs building in Fremantle. I needed the Government to put the building into the trust, and I would put in my furniture and the money to restore the customs house. Carmen Lawrence's reaction was totally negative; she obviously had a deep suspicion of anyone who had any sort of project which could be considered altruistic. As a result of her premiership, nothing much happened in Western Australia. Soon the people did not feel good any more, throwing her out on her ear at the next State election.

After Carmen Lawrence went, her legacies to Western Australia of both the recession and the Royal Commission stayed. Her attitude to business in Western Australia could not have been more different than that of Pam Beggs, a minister in the Western Australian Government who applied common-sense to every proposition that was put to her. A distinctly feminine and highly intelligent woman, Pam Beggs was a great asset to Western Australia during its troubles. I only wish that there had been more ministers like her.

⤖

In Australia, I am, I believe, a Labor Republican, while in Britain, I am a Conservative Monarchist. I find no problem with this apparent split in my personality. The monarch is thoroughly good for Britain and should continue, if only for the reason that if the monarchy goes, the British will have Ted Heath, Roy Jenkins or even Norman St John Stevas, now Lord Fawlsey, as President, and that would be intolerable. The monarchy, on the other hand, does nothing for the Australians. Take the simple proposition of a state visit to another country. The Queen goes there to sell Britain, and often her visit will be timed to coincide with British trade missions. The Queen is the Queen not only of Britain and Australia but also of many of the Commonwealth countries. She does not, however, promote Australian trade interests in that country or anywhere else or, for that matter, the interests of any other country that she is Queen of, except Britain. The monarchy is a thing of the past in Australia; Australia will never truly be a nation while the monarchy lasts there. Britain, on the other hand, could easily cease to be a nation should the monarchy finish.

215

A large part of the population of Australia is either indigenous, comes from places that have no connection with Britain, or descends from people who have no connection with Britain. Australia's multicultural society should be the country's greatest pride. As Britain has drawn closer to Europe over the last 25 years, its ties with Australia have become looser. How strange it is that the citizens of two countries ruled by the same queen should need to have visas in order to cross each other's borders. How strange it is that Australians are restricted from living and working in Britain, when French, Germans, Italians and other Europeans can do so freely, and that there are restrictions on Britons who wish to live and work in Australia, ruled by the same queen. The situation as it exists is clearly nonsense. The overwhelming need in Australia is to find a unity of purpose. Slowly the differences with Australia's indigenous peoples are beginning to be resolved. The second and equally important stage in reaching that unity of purpose is that Australia should become its own country, owing loyalty only to the citizens of its own continent. The way to achieve this is for the Australian people to move without delay towards becoming a republic.

Never a day goes by in Britain that we do not read about the monarchy's attempts to prepare itself for the twenty-first century. A new, streamlined monarchy seems to be the order of the day; a monarchy that will fit in with a Europe of a single currency and, indeed, most likely, a European federal state. Regardless of whether or not Britain joins a single currency or a federal Europe, she will be affected by both events. The trappings of pomp and title from the past must be cast off in a new egalitarian world. Already the new Labour Government is actively reforming the House of Lords, a matter that I regard as a tragedy, but such is the fashion of the age that this will be done. With the millennium fast approaching, change is in the air. What better time for Australia to make that change? It is, after all, not such a dramatic change as might be feared, for already an Australian represents the Queen; let that person in future represent Australians. As for the Commonwealth, an organisation that often does good while giving respectability to dictators and sometimes murderers, the Queen will stay as its head, as she has said, for as long as it wishes her to fulfil that role. A nation does not need to have the Queen as its monarch to be a member of the Commonwealth, so Australia as a republic can retain its position in that important forum.

One evening, a year or so ago, I dined with Di Jagelman, a well-known beauty and a famous Sydney hostess, at her home. The dinner, as you might expect from such an accomplished hostess, was as near-perfect as it is possible to get. There were only three other guests, one of them, Malcolm Turnbull. Like everyone else in Australia, I had heard of Malcolm Turnbull and the Australian Republican Movement. Knowing little else about him, apart from his involvement in an incident that took place in my London club, the Garrick, I was not well-disposed to him personally, despite the fact that I have been advocating for many years that Australia should become a republic.

The unfortunate incident at the Garrick Club was during the Spycatcher trial in which Malcolm Turnbull represented the author and former MI6 agent, Peter Wright. It seems that Malcolm Turnbull was sitting on a lavatory behind a fine mahogany door while the British Lord Chancellor was using a urinal and, at the same time, regaling other members of his club who were also in the cloakroom with the intimate details of the trial. Something that he said was subsequently used to advantage by Malcolm Turnbull. Members of the Garrick Club, who at that time included some of the most influential politicians and journalists in Britain, were extremely put out by the use of what they considered confidential information. Malcolm Turnbull no doubt was not aware of the Garrick's rule that all conversations on the club's premises are regarded as private; not under any circumstances are they to be repeated outside the club. The Garrick Club has this rule so that members and their guests can speak with complete freedom, knowing that what they say will remain confidential. As a result, the Garrick is the place with the most interesting conversation in London. Malcolm Turnbull does not strike me as a man who would let what he might regard as the arcane rules of a London club stand between him and success in a court case. The late Michael Havers, a charming man, held the post of Lord Chancellor towards the end of his life. An amusing man, he was totally indiscreet in his conversation and I suppose paid the penalty for forgetting that, although he held the highest law office in the land, he was also a politician.

The dinner at Di Jagelman's was, from my point of view, a great success. Whether this was because of her skill as a hostess or Malcolm Turnbull's charm, I do not care to make a judgement. My misgivings about his behaviour at the Garrick were quickly forgotten and I left confirmed in my belief that Australia should be a republic and happy that Malcolm Turnbull was a leader in advocating this state of affairs.

⌘

At the time that I was first in the Kimberley, the attitude of many Australians towards Aboriginals varied from the condescending to the downright aggressive. There was considerable anger that the Government seemed to set the Aboriginal people apart. It was generally believed that an Aboriginal could arrange finance to buy a car with the utmost of ease, whereas a white man would be turned down. These new cars, it was said, were driven through the bush by drunken Aboriginals, who in the course of time wrecked them. The evidence to support this idea was the number of wrecked cars that seemed to litter the landscape. Any Aboriginals that I came across, however, took considerable care of their motor vehicles. It was much the same with drinking. Aboriginals as a generality were believed to be drunks who lived on social security and were not in the habit of holding down even the meanest of jobs, that is, if they could summon up the energy to get such a job in the first place.

This was not at all my experience. Over the years that I lived in Broome, I employed many Aboriginals in posts as simple as gardeners and as responsible as bird and animal keepers. My general conclusion is that the Aboriginal of the Kimberley is much the same as the white man of the Kimberley; like the curate's egg, they are good in parts. As, indeed, if we search our consciences, we all are—we all have our own talents and our own failings. The job of employers, however, is to get the best out of the people they employ, not to casually bar from the chance of employment whole sections of the community with opinions based on race or creed. As for drink, there are drunks in every community, but, unfortunately, they tend to hang around hotels and public places. As a proportion of their numbers, Aboriginals, considering their situation, have no greater number of alcoholics among them than do the Americans or the British.

The Catholic Church in the North-West, led by Bishops Saunders and Jobst and assisted by Fathers McKelson and McMahon and many others, has played a vital role in the reconciliation between the black and white populations. There can be no doubt that, viewed from a distance, the lot of the Aboriginal since the white occupation of Australia has not been a happy one. Equally, many of the traditional pastoralists genuinely believe that they dealt charitably with the Aboriginals in the past. Time, however, has moved on and charity has become a despised word. Rights are the nature of

219

today's ethics. To give to someone what is theirs by right should not be considered an act of charity. In the growth of a nation, history tends to be amended. If true unity is to be found in a nation, it is important that historians continue to search for the truth of that nation's history. When that truth is found, it is important that the political and religious leaders of that nation accept it, using this valuable truth as a guide for future actions. Only when Australia searches for, finds, and accepts the truth of her history, is there any chance of national unity. Australians should be searching for, finding, and accepting that truth, in the full knowledge that, without unity, it is a travesty to call their continent a nation.

The days of Stephen Hawke and Tom Stephens fighting for Aboriginal rights are over. The battle, however, can barely be considered to have been won. The fight goes on, for today the attack on minorities still exists; it is just perpetuated in a far subtler form. It is well that politicians like Tom Stephens, the member of the Upper House for a large part of the North-West, and Ernie Bridge, who really care about the population of the Kimberley, still carry on the fight against a bureaucracy working 2500 kilometres away. They have helped change the opinions of some of even the most recalcitrant of those who live in the North-West.

In my first memoirs, *Once a Jolly Bagman*, I wrote that I was sure that a great deal of what John Howard would do as Prime Minister, Paul Keating would like to have done. The reform of Aboriginal rights carried out by Keating during his term as prime minister was, in my opinion, one of the most enlightened pieces of legislation in Australia's history. I wrote that John Howard would be the man to finally resolve the Aboriginal problem in Australia. In this, I was wrong. This new volume has given me the advantage of hindsight and I am able, thank goodness, to reassess those words. In short, John Howard has destroyed the integrity of Paul Keating's

Aboriginal land rights legislation. As a matter of political convenience, legislation has been passed in Canberra that Aboriginal leaders believe robs them of 90 per cent of the benefits of Keating's bill. In this, I am inclined to agree with them. John Howard has found a formula that pleases the National Party and many of the Liberal Party's supporters, but takes away most of the rights that the Aboriginals struggled for. It is all fine and dandy to say that the Aboriginals will still have the right to use the disputed land but not the right to own it. How ironic this all is when you consider that ownership with legal title is a European concept, while the right to use land by tradition, in this case, is an Aboriginal concept. Yet the white migrants to Australia have put so much emphasis on legal title that now the Aboriginals will not settle for anything less. Paul Keating might have refined his legislation on Aboriginal land rights but I am sure that he would not have neutered the legislation in the way that John Howard has. Law, however, is only one aspect of this matter. More important by far, is the attitude of the people.

⤜

I have known John Howard for many years, first meeting him in the early 1980s when he was in Malcolm Fraser's government. He was at the time the federal treasurer. Intercontinental Hotels and my family company were trying, desperately, to build a new hotel in Sydney. At the time, the State Government in New South Wales under the premier, Neville Wran, was bending backwards to get this project under way. It had offered us a site, the old Treasury building, a fine example of Australia's heritage that was currently being used by the Transport Department. It was, I am afraid, in a shocking state of repair. State office workers on the whole are not the most congenial tenants for a heritage building. We had the finance, the hotel operator, and were all set to go; only the permission of the Foreign Investment

221

Review Board (FIRB) was needed to allow us to get our planning permission and to start work. For some reason, the FIRB appeared reluctant to give this permission. I had met with the chairman of the FIRB privately. By a fortunate coincidence, he was the uncle of Alison Brown, the wife of Bruce Brown, the Cygnet Bay pearl farmer. On my visit to the Browns, I had mentioned my frustration in Sydney, and Alison had telephoned her uncle and a meeting was arranged at the FIRB's office in Sydney.

The meeting itself was a strange affair. I arrived at four o'clock in the afternoon at the city building that housed the FIRB. The twelfth floor was where I had been told to attend, so I took the lift to the landing outside the FIRB's office. I then found that the door was locked and the office seemed unoccupied. Disappointed, I was about to leave when an elderly and immensely courteous gentleman got out of the lift and, greeting me, unlocked the office door. If these offices had seemed empty, it was because they were empty. The old gentleman turned on the lights and airconditioning in what turned out to be an extensive suite of offices. We sat opposite each other in heavy leather upholstered easy chairs, entirely alone and each with a plastic cup of water, then we discussed my problem.

I was told that there was only one man who could help me and that was John Howard, and that he needed to vary the guidelines that directed how foreign investment was dealt with. It was on this occasion that I learnt the difference between guidelines and the law. The law is a rigid thing—you are either acting legally or illegally. A clever lawyer will often find a way around a law, allowing you to act legally but still act against the intention of that law. Guidelines are, however, different; there is no convenient way around a set of guidelines.

In Canberra, John Howard received me well; after all, I was a senior official in the party that formed the British

Government. After a pleasant-enough conversation about Margaret Thatcher and her policies, we got down to business. In short, there was no way that the guidelines could be varied. Despite the fact that unemployment was high in Australia and this new hotel would create over a thousand jobs, still there was no way that the guidelines could be changed. They were the rules, did I not understand this? Of course, I understood that they were the rules, but governments make rules and only very foolish governments do not change them when circumstances have changed. At that time, I was lobbying anyone who I could lay my hands on and among those I lobbied was Philip Lynch, a cabinet minister in Malcolm Fraser's government. Philip Lynch lived just outside Melbourne on the coast. His home was most elegant, and his wife both beautiful and charming. He had in his garden a hedge that made a profound impression on me. So large was this hedge that on the occasion of my visit, three men were clipping it. During lunch in his home, we talked of my problem and he agreed that it was a problem made by bureaucracy rather than a problem caused by principle. Philip Lynch was very kind to me: he took up my cause and the problem was overcome. In the event, the Sydney Inter-Continental has been nothing but an advantage to Australia, playing a large part in achieving Sydney's aim to become the venue for the next Olympic Games. The fact that this hotel was for a time owned by foreigners seems not to have mattered at all.

❧

As for Australia realising the geographical reality of her position and accepting that she is part of a group of Asian continents and islands, John Howard has allowed the insidious lobbying of a certain Pauline Hanson to make all the running on that front. In the following pages, I will come to Pauline Hanson in some detail. At the last federal election,

Hanson's party was almost wiped out. That, however, is not enough. Had John Howard destroyed her intellectually when she first emerged, none of us would have ever heard of her again. It was not that John Howard could not have destroyed the arguments that this woman made, rather that he chose not to destroy them, hoping, I imagine, that they would destroy themselves. In this, history will judge him and I suspect the terms of that judgement will be harsh.

If John Howard has one overbearing disadvantage, it is that he is too nice. A cultured and kind individual, he has all the talents for politics. It is just that, while he relishes the chase, he holds back from the kill. One aspect of John Howard, is, however, totally beyond question, and that is his honesty. At a time when Howard was in government, his brother Stanley and his wife came to lunch at my country house, West Green. We were a party of about twenty that day, including my partner in the pearl farm, Snowy County, and his mate, Richard Ballieu. Introducing Stanley Howard to Richard Ballieu, I remarked that Stanley was John Howard's brother. 'I know your brother very well,' said Richard. 'We own a lot of housing sites together in Broome.' Stanley went white at the idea that his brother was involved in property with this rough-looking character. In fact, Richard Ballieu comes from a highly respectable family in Melbourne; he just happens to look a little on the rough side, but no matter, Stanley Howard was speechless. I let the silence hang for a moment or two and then explained that the John Howard I referred to was Australia's prime minister, while the one that Richard Ballieu referred to was the magistrate in Broome. I have never seen a man look as relieved as Stanley Howard did at that explanation.

It would be churlish to leave the subject of Australian politics without just a mention of Malcolm Fraser. It always seemed to me that Malcolm Fraser is just the stretched version of the British prime minister, Edward Heath. Neither of them are true conservatives; both of them led their parties into opposition. Purely as an insight into Malcolm Fraser's political judgement, I will recall a night during the 1983 British general election. It was in Annabel's, the fashionable London nightclub, that I met Malcolm Fraser. Most nights during elections, I went there after a day's campaigning to collect money for the Conservative Party. Sitting in the bar near the door to the restaurant where I could buttonhole likely donors, I smoked a cigar and drank mint tea. At about one in the morning, in comes Malcolm Fraser. We greet each other briefly and then, without a moment's hesitation, he launches into a dissertation on how he had studied the polls and the political situation, coming to the conclusion that the Conservatives would lose by a mile. Protesting that he was wrong, I offered him a drink, only to be stuck with this Jeremiah for some half-an-hour. Luckily, he was distracted from politics by someone he knew from Australia. When they got up to dance, I went home to bed. A few days later, despite Malcolm Fraser's gloomy predictions, the Conservatives won the election, gaining the largest majority they have ever achieved. It is, however, fair to write that, in 1978, when our political prospects did not look so good, Malcolm Fraser sent Tony Eggleton, the general secretary of the Liberal Party, over to Britain, to give us some advice. Tony Eggleton arrived, bringing with him a videotape of the Liberals' famous election broadcast, 'Memories'. It was this tape that set the pattern of the Conservative party's advertising that summer. Like the Australian Liberals, we went straight for the jugular and the following year won a victory that put the Conservative Party into power for eighteen years.

As a rule, I am generally well disposed to politicians, even when I disagree with their politics. Among the politicians that I have never met is Pauline Hanson. Of this I am heartily glad for I detest her policies, which are not really policies at all, rather a hodgepodge of statements and ideas of a despicable nature. She has no place in these memoirs, however, because her words are likely to affect the future of Australia, a country of which I am inordinately fond. I have taken space in this book to explain why I believe her words and her policies to be so destructive to the future of Australians, regardless of their race or colour. On the Statue of Liberty that stands on Ellis Island at the mouth of New York's harbour are engraved the words: 'Give me your tired, your poor, your huddled masses on your teeming shore'. For many years, the world did this, and America grew great. Australia, by comparison, adopted a rather different attitude to immigration. White was the colour of the game and when white people from Britain were in short supply, disgracefully, young orphans were transported without telling them where they were going or why they were going there.

In America, the penniless immigrant's sons and daughters became doctors and scientists. In Australia, if you were a scientist or a doctor, you could come to live here. The rich rather than the poor were welcomed, poor and white perhaps, but poor and black—never. Those days are long gone but this attitude to foreigners lingers on, and among those foreigners are numbered the indigenous Aboriginal population. This is an attitude that is deeply ingrained into the psyche of a small part of Australia's population. Sadly, this attitude is from time to time adopted by a politician, then taken up by the press and displayed in all its racist horror.

Pauline Hanson's words were first heard by a world unfamiliar with the niceties or, rather, nastinesses of Australian politics. Unaware of how Hanson has been ridiculed by both the public at the polls and the cartoonists in the media, the world still remembers those words, and suspect that the feelings they express lie dormant in Australia's subconscious.

Australia, however, is a free land, a democracy, and Hanson is entitled to her views. John Howard could not have been expected to silence Hanson; he could, however, have been expected to show the Australian electorate the shallow quality of her views. Her proposals for the Australian economy were ludicrous, such as a special bank giving loans of 2 per cent. This idea, in a country where the interest rate is a considerable multiple of that figure, was destined for spectacular failure, a formula for jealousy and corruption. She also supported tariff barriers, in a country that lives by its exports. Such measures would only bring retaliation from Australia's trading partners.

All of this is obvious to anyone with eyes, ears and a brain in between them. Just as is the canard that if a finite number of Australians can live well, due to the minerals that are dug up, the trees that are cut down and the other natural products of Australia that are exploited, then to increase the number of its inhabitants will lead to all living less well or, for that matter, the canard that there would not be enough water if the population is dramatically increased. Water is only a matter of engineering, as has been shown in Israel. Australia has never really grasped the possibilities of becoming fully populated in the same way that America is fully populated. This is Howard's mistake; it is the task of a nation's leader to lead that nation to a prosperity, not just to preside over the division of a prosperity, most of which exists largely due to the benevolence of nature and God. To 'deal with' Hanson is merely to operate in the currency of her own language and to hasten progress towards the kind of state that Hanson advocates. Happily, the Australian electorate had the good sense to 'deal with' Hanson and her followers at the polls, humiliating them and, for a time, rendering them and their successors politically irrelevant. Pauline Hanson's words, however, have been said and the poison remains in the Australian national bloodstream. To demonstrate, on the other hand, the great benefits that will come to Australia from massive immigration on the scale of nineteenth and early twentieth-century American immigration makes Hanson irrelevant. It offers to the Australian people a prosperity, a power and a culture far beyond their wildest dreams, thus removing Hanson's poisoned words from the conscious memory of the nation. Only when this happens will Australia fulfil its true destiny to replace America as the most stable, prosperous and powerful nation on earth.

In time this will happen, whether Pauline Hanson and her colleagues like it or not. It will happen, regardless of the apathy of Australia's politicians, for this under-populated continent will be filled by immigrants regardless of what care she takes in defending her boundaries. How much better that Pauline Hanson and John Howard should turn their minds to ensuring that this influx of immigration is carried out in an orderly manner. How much grander they would be, remembered as the founding fathers and mothers of a truly great nation, than as just a pair of politicians who merely stood and bickered as the inevitable course of history approached.

V

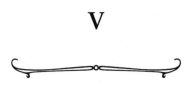

Collectors, Dealers and Artists

16

All my life I have been a frustrated shopkeeper. I love the idea of owning and running a shop. After many years, I have, however, come to the conclusion that I am rather better at buying stock than selling it. To be a successful shopkeeper, you need a reverse talent to mine. It's not that I do not enjoy selling or, indeed, that I am not personally good at selling. When my wife Romilly had a grocer's shop in London's Covent Garden and subsequently in South Audley Street, I would occasionally go and encourage her customers to buy. Without an undue lack of modesty, I believe that I was rather good at selling groceries. The customers used to go away with a myriad goods that they had no need of, let alone any intention of acquiring when they entered the premises. Romilly's shop, started before we married, bore her maiden name, Hobbs. It was a leader in its field, way in advance of tastes current in the late 1970s. Romilly only sold her shop when I became ill with the heart condition that culminated in a sextuple bypass operation. It was to her a considerable sacrifice to give up the business that she had started in order to look after me, and I am deeply grateful.

Shops that I ran myself over the years include a bookshop, an antique furniture shop and a premises that sold curiosities and antiquities. For some reason I love not only shopping, but, more so, the shops themselves. I am tempted to open a shop almost every time I see a promising premises with a sign indicating that it is to let. It is a great joy for me to sit in shops—to watch goods being bought and sold is to me a great excitement. Over the years, I have sat in dozens of galleries and antique shops around the world, gossiping with their proprietors and this, I suppose, is how I came to learn about antiques and paintings. It was certainly where I learned the trade of dealing and the principles that apply, whether you are buying and selling land or Greek sculpture. Traders are, by nature, enthusiasts; they like to trade because that is what they do best, and the activity of trading gives them pleasure. True traders may be able to walk away from particular offers, but they cannot walk away from the activity of trading. Therefore, experienced traders are life's easiest victims. Never try selling jewellery to a jeweller, for the jeweller will know its value down to the last cent; offer it instead to a picture dealer who knows it to be valuable but not its exact worth. When the goods on offer reach a price where they appear to be a bargain, the picture dealer will have no alternative but to buy. It's is in the blood, nothing can be done about it. Expert and as hard as nails at their own trade, a dealer will become putty in your hands when enticed into a transaction involving goods of whose value the dealer has only a notional idea. Dealing has provided me with immense pleasure over the last 50 years.

⁂

Given my predisposition towards owning shops and knowing that I am a better buyer than a seller, it is not entirely surprising that when I came across Joan Bowers in Sydney I became her business partner. Joan imported Indian art and artefacts. She is an enterprising woman who, when in India in the 1970s, saw the possibilities of selling the goods that they made there in Australia. Her shop was a delight; it did not matter whether it was in bronze, marble or wood, Joan's eye was impeccable in the choices that she made. In time, she was importing large chunks of India's demolished buildings to Sydney. Joan had developed a passion for India, she was fascinated with it, and adopted initially two small Indian children, a boy and a girl, and then later a second girl.

Only married recently to Stephen Bowers, she and her family acquired a larger house in a rather unfashionable suburb of Sydney, a suburb where the gracious old buildings had become ruins, their gardens repositories for rubbish. Stephen Bowers, who was an architect by profession, cleaned up the house and the family moved in. Joan was young, enthusiastic and happy with her Indian family.

For the best part of 20 years, the name Joan Bowers was synonymous with India. For me, her emporium was one great confectionery shop, with rows and rows of goods as delectable as sweets and cakes. When I called at Joan's shop, which was at least twice a year, I found nothing that I did not want to own. When I visited Sydney, I camped in her premises. I loved the atmosphere, I loved the social whirl that surrounded the place. For Joan's impeccable eye could not only spot just the right architectural details, textile, deity, doorway or pot, but the right people as well. Joan Bowers' taste is in humorous people. It does not seem to matter to her where they come from or who they are, she collects characters with as much unbridled enthusiasm as she scoured India for that perfect piece. It was the lunches and the parties, the table gossip and the casual generosity of her hospitality that made her shop a point of pilgrimage, the genius of her ability to put disparate objects together, to show them in a different light, that made her shop an outstanding success.

In the early days when Joan first opened her shop, fascinating and wonderful objects were plentiful in India. Joan never bought masterpieces in the pompous sense of the word; her interest was in the beauty of the work that came from the villages. She did not strip India of its heritage, rather she promoted the brilliance of its indigenous arts. Joan knew an India that tourists and dealers tied to a hectic itinerary could never find. For her, choosing her stock was never a matter of filling a container or knowing that she could sell a particular piece. She bought what she liked and only what she liked.

৵

Joan regularly made buying trips to India and usually stayed at the Rambagh Palace Hotel in Jaipur, where the manager was in the habit of calling her Mrs John Borris. He was, however, not the only member of his staff to be involved in a misunderstanding where Joan was concerned. A waiter at the hotel had become her friend and regularly took her home for meals with his wife and family in their village. On one occasion, Joan knew that his wife was absent and was somewhat surprised to be invited to dine there. She refused the invitation on the grounds of etiquette, leaving the waiter bitterly disappointed. That night, she dined instead with an English couple who were also staying at the hotel. During dinner the waiter approached Joan, telling her how much he loved her. She in her turn told him not to be foolish. Later that night, the same waiter returned and apologised for an apparent misunderstanding. Needless to say Joan was greatly relieved. The waiter then set about explaining the misunderstanding, telling Joan that he did, indeed, really love her. It was, he explained, she who misunderstood his words. Joan replied sharply to him, telling him to go away, but there was no stopping the man. The fateful words burbled out of him. 'I desperately need to see you without your clothes on. I mean you no harm. I love you so much, I would not lay a finger on you. I only want to see you without your clothes on and to prove my good intentions, I will have another waiter watching while I look at you.'

৵

When I met Joan, she was living in Paddington and running a very successful shop at 1 Paddington Street. Unfortunately, her partner in the shop, now dead, was not the easiest of people. Joan was in some distress about this during a visit she made to Broome. She was travelling with the Frosts and it was after some discussion under the mango trees in my garden that I and our mutual friend, Bob Frost, decided to go into partnership with her and take over her partner's interest. They all enjoyed their time in Broome: the weather was, as always during the winter season, perfect. Bob Frost is the most amicable of men, quite apart from being an extremely able accountant, financier and property developer. His role in the partnership was to make certain that a strategy for Joan's shop was in place. All went well at first but the troubles came and, as troubles will, they came all at once and from the most unexpected quarters. The landlords terminated the lease on the Paddington Street premises. Trade was brisk and the shop was now without a home. Joan, naturally enough, was in a considerable state at this turn of events. It had been decided for us that we should move, but where would we move to? Rents were at that time in Sydney at their highest, and good premises hard to find. Joan set out to explore and identified a warehouse that we could convert. For my part, I was in hospital undergoing heart surgery. We borrowed money and bought the premises freehold for $2 million; then we borrowed more, $500 000, to pay the builder.

All seemed fine at first, then came the recession of the late 1980s. Business dropped like a stone and the bank began to talk of calling in our personal guarantees. In time, with the recovery of the Australian economy, Joan refinanced the business and bought me out.

My business venture with Joan gave me endless pleasure but absolutely no profit. Joan's shop flourished and so it should have done, for she is an immensely talented woman of whom I have always been extremely fond. In time, of course, that recovery in the Australian economy began to flag and the financial situation among the Asian countries made trade uncertain. Joan sadly, but wisely in such circumstances, decided to close the shop, to close the doors of her emporium and 'retire' to India. As usual with Joan, she closed her shop as she had opened it, with great style and some of the best stock that she had ever owned.

The closure of Joan's shop, I must confess, left me with a tinge of sadness. However, our lives are so ordered that all things come to an end—good or bad. Joan Bowers' emporium of Indian Art and Antiques was high among the best of things in Sydney. These paragraphs are not an obituary to the demise of the most stylish of shops, rather a celebration that this shop and its predecessors under Joan's management existed at all, existed when Indian art was virtually unknown in Sydney, let alone Australia, and existed at a time when 'taste' of any sort was as rare as hens' teeth. Joan Bowers and her shop had both taste and style in profusion. Twenty years on, the world has changed. Joan's imitators are commonplace and the perfect object is harder to find.

The whole event had, from my point of view, been highly expensive. It was, however, a salutary lesson on the subject of buying in at the top of the market and waiting for values to recover once that market has dropped. The moral of my story is that one should cut one's losses when business dealings begin to go wrong and you are unable to put them right. Waiting for events to change your fortune is a fruit-less and folly-ridden exercise, more an exercise in conceit than business management. A number of years ago, Earl Macmillan, the former British prime minister, well-known for his cunning and mastery of political tactics, was asked by a young politician what he should be aware of in his political career. The old master replied, 'Events, dear boy, events. It's always events that bring you down.'

ॐ

Bob Frost is a polymath, a thinker and a doer. A man with a fine eye for art, an acute nose for business and a most entertaining companion, he is married to Glen-Marie North, an able and flamboyant publicist. After the considerable setback he received from his London colleagues, he set about rebuilding his career, while Glen-Marie's went from strength to strength. Their wedding was the talk of Australia. Unfortunately, I was unfamiliar with Australian weddings and did not realise that the appropriate dress for four o'clock in the afternoon was a dinner jacket. Arriving only just before the bride (I was delayed over lunch with Sidney Nolan), I was surprised to find all the other male guests in dinner jackets and black bow ties. I was in a pale beige linen suit with the garish pink and green Garrick Club tie. Trying to slip into a back pew was no solution to my problem. An usher insisted that I sit in the front row with the bridegroom. The walk down the church between rows of expectant guests was a terrifying experience. The bride entered with an assortment of bridesmaids: Sonia McMahon, widow of a former prime minister, who had arrived in an ambulance and walked with a stick; Di Kirby, an ex-model; and Jane Walker, Glen-Marie's general factotum. Happily, Glen had given each of them the material for their dresses and left the design to the individual concerned.

No sooner had the parson passed the ring to the bridegroom and he had slipped it on the bride's finger and given her a considerable kiss, than she turned to the congregation and proclaimed: 'He gets the glamour, I get the money,' at which the congregation broke into rumbustious applause. The reception was a lavish affair at Barford, one of Sydney's finest historic mansions owned by Barry and Wendy

Loiterton, the former owners of Hayman Island. The caterers came from Hong Kong and a maypole stood in the centre of the marquee, its pink ribbons trembling in the evening breeze. On each table there was an ice sculpture that slowly melted during the course of a very warm evening. Even these melting sculptures, however, could not dampen the high spirits of the guests. Primrose Dunlop, who was sitting next to me, drew up her skirts high on her thighs and threw her shapely legs across my knees, as from nowhere a photographer appeared and recorded this extraordinary sight for the Sydney newspapers. As the night drew on, the wedding reception seemed to gather momentum rather than to slow down, memorable is a poor word to describe this occasion. Outside, the streets were lined with hired limousines; there can have hardly been a limousine left to hire in all the metropolitan district of Sydney. Later that week, I watched a video of the whole event; one moment of that wedding sticks in my memory. As the camera panned to the right, an anonymous voice was heard to say, 'Move over to the right, Susan. That's where the press are.'

୬৹

It was Joan Bowers who introduced me to Margaret Olley, a considerable painter who has been portrayed at one time or another by most of Australia's great painters. Margaret Olley has a brilliant eye, and the Oriental Collection at the Art Gallery of New South Wales has often been the beneficiary of its selections. A generous woman, both with her purchases and her hospitality, dining in Margaret's house is an occasion to wonder at. It is, in fact, not one house but two or three houses with a carefully planned but overgrown garden. Room after room of objects that she has collected from different continents and cultures, a dead bird and a few dying flowers preserved for use as models in a painting among them. Room after room of her paintings, all in

238

various stages of completion. On the first visit to her house, it is almost impossible to understand the geography of the place. While guests sit in comfortable but tired easy chairs, balancing drinks on their knees—for there is absolutely no place to put down a glass, let alone another object— Margaret cooks in a tiny, untidy kitchen. Called to the table, guests are confronted with tablemats of an erotic nature and a meal that would delight the most discerning of gourmets. The conversation sparkles in much the same way that Margaret herself sparkles. Time flies, and when the polite time for the guests to leave has long passed, they begin to drag themselves away, then linger at the door, delaying to examine some marvellous object, not noticed before amongst the carefully arranged jumble. At last they leave this enchanted place, a house where time has stood still, where culture and pleasure, kindness and joy still mingle.

All my life I have been fascinated by dealers and their dealings. At heart, however, I am a collector, a collector of people like Joan Bowers and a collector of places and things and, above all, moments that remain in my memory. Not many years ago, Sotheby's gave a dinner party for many of the leading wine writers. The meal was extraordinary, and so it should have been, for it was cooked by Michel Roux of Le Gavroche. The wine defied belief. Let me record the list: Champagne Krug 1982, followed by Haut Brion 1961 en magnum; Margaux 1953 en magnum; Latour 1952 en jeroboam; Mouton Rothschild 1949 en magnum; Lafite Rothschild 1945 en jeroboam. All this was finished off with Chateau d'Yquem 1970. I asked the excellent gentleman from Chateau Latour why he chose the 1952 vintage, and he replied that Chateau Latour was famous not just for making great wines in great years, but for making good wines in bad years.

This just shows there is no such thing as an absolute value, a point wine illustrates as well as anything else. Christie's at about the same time also asked me to drink some of their fine vintages and, since I was in a wine mood, I waxed lyrical about the merits of wine. I remarked that I had seen a bottle of Cheval Blanc 1949, a superb wine, sold for £600. The lady on my left attacked my enthusiasm for this bargain: 'What extravagance!' 'But,' said I, 'we have just looked at a beautiful Cezanne due to fetch £10 million. If you were to buy that painting, it would cost you about £5000 a day in interest. You could buy a lot of wine for that.' 'Rubbish,' she replied. 'You drink your wine and it's gone. I still have my Cezanne.' Rather weakly, I suggested she must have worked out a way to take it with her when she had gone.

But the truth of the matter is that there are many types of collecting, and two are the collecting of the tangible and the intangible. Each is, I suppose, legitimate, each for quite a different sort of person. Of course, there are plenty of collectors who understand neither one nor the other.

✧

It is impossible to move in the extraordinary world of collectors and traders without coming across a good many art dealers. While I personally have never held this view, art dealers are often thought of as shady characters at best, likely to be downright charlatans, ranking in public esteem a little above criminals and politicians. This negative view, however, has a profound effect on the way the customers view their trade. It is amazing the way they feel that a dealer is obliged to give them a bargain when they buy a picture. Yet they do not feel a similar obligation to pay, delaying settlement for months on the assumption that the dealer probably made too big a profit anyway. They ignore the fact that dealers in art are no different from motor manufacturers when it comes to covering the costs of their business. Worse still, if the artist's work has failed to prosper, the customer often returns the painting to the gallery, usually in a large car driven by a chauffeur, along with a complicated message about changing the colour of the dining room walls and a request for the refund of the £200 paid two years earlier. The message ends with the news that the chauffeur will wait for the cheque. In this hostile environment, art dealers often discover that, no matter how competitive the business, they need each other.

Despite many tales of dealers' cunning and, sometimes, downright dishonesty, I have always trusted art dealers. One or two have stretched the truth but, by and large, it is a world in which honesty prospers and dishonesty gets its just reward in the end. When I was collecting American abstract expressionist paintings in the early 1960s, I made many of my purchases from Leslie Waddington, the owner of Waddington Galleries. Friends described me as quite mad, but Leslie helped me build an important collection of paintings and sculpture, and when events dictated that they be sold, his help was invaluable. Dealers and collectors are actually good for each other, for the combination of professionalism and enthusiasm is formidable.

But there are occasions on which even the shrewdest dealers can be of no help to the most inspired collector. It is, I am afraid, impossible to be both a buyer and a seller at the same time. The dealer must quote a price and the customer must decide whether or not to buy. During the mid-1980s, one particular dealer, after staying with me in Broome, set off after the big hitters among the collectors of Western Australia. The Perth collectors were at that time among the most active in Australia and were well-known for paying the world's highest prices, in fact, they actually liked to pay the highest prices. My friend, however, pitched her prices just a trifle on the high side, even for the wild enthusiasm to buy paintings that then prevailed in Perth.

She was keen, young, with a nicely turned ankle and immaculate grammar. When she came across a fine painting, it was not by chance, for it was her trade. One day, she sought out a nineteenth-century picture of horseracing in South Australia. It was not a picture that would become the subject of a scholarly article by Denys Sutton in a literary art history magazine, for example, *Apollo*, nor would it find itself on the pages of *The Burlington* magazine. It was for the collector whose taste runs more to horses than painting, and who lives in Australia. The painting was, after its fashion, a masterpiece, and was one with a ready market among the wealthy racehorse owners of Western Australia. But that made it a one-hit picture: fail with it in Australia and it is yours for life. Our dealer hesitated. Maybe it was natural caution, but she struck no deal. She did not buy the picture, but she did acquire a photograph of it and reached an understanding with the owner. Our dealer would journey to Australia and offer the painting to a client, not, I must add, a client known personally to her, but a client who collected on such a grand scale that he retained his own agent who cared about such details as authenticity and provenance.

By chance or intent—we shall never know for sure—this agent was bypassed and an appointment made with the grand client. Australia is a long way from Britain by anyone's standards, and as the kilometres passed in the dark, unsleeping hours of a night flight, the beauty of the painting grew in the mind of our dealer. So did the price: the photograph was shown to the client and a price of £225 000 asked for the painting. 'You mean dollars, my dear?' said the client. 'Pounds,' she replied. 'Not a penny less,' echoing the words of Jeffrey Archer, the writer of popular thrillers. 'Such a price,' said the client. 'Impossible.' 'But such a picture,' she replied, 'so early for Australia. It is so rare . . . such a chance . . . there are, of course, many other distinguished collectors . . . came to you first . . . admired your taste, acumen, judgement.'

She deployed all the blandishments of her trade; all the flattery that turns a bicycle's handlebars into a Picasso. Having finished her recital, she returned the photograph to its envelope but, as she made to go, the client asked to see the photograph again. He returned it to her once more. 'My dear,' he said, 'I'm afraid I have bad news for you.' 'But the painting is of great quality,' she said, thinking that he did not admire it. 'Indeed,' the client said, 'any ten collectors would have this painting in the rustling of a cheque. The painting is all that you say it is, perhaps even more. No, my dear, the bad news is that I acquired the work last week.' 'Impossible,' she gasped. 'No, my dear, quite possible. And for only £125 000.'

The moral: you must not sell what you do not own. Every collector who has sprung a dealer's careful trap may squeal with delight at this story. Everyone who has bought a silver dish or piece of porcelain that was not quite what it purported to be on the day of purchase may celebrate in the knowledge of a dealer caught. Or pause and weep, for the great dealer—and this dealer may one day be great—is the friend of the collector. Through this friendship, the dealer becomes the collector's other half, his twin in collecting, as keen to form a collection as the collector is to use such a dealer. The young lady's mistake was not the price she asked, which showed courage; it was the caution she revealed in not buying the painting in the first place. A dealer's profit is a payment for skill. In this case, our young dealer did not display sufficient skill and lost her profit.

Among the many strange beliefs held by even the most sophisticated of people is the one embraced by London dealers in the 1980s that the newly rich of Australia were an easy mark—kookaburras there to be plucked. This belief lacks logic: if a man has just made a large amount of money through his skill and shrewdness, he will surely be among the hardest of people to take it from. Nevertheless, stories abound concerning both these tycoons and the optimistic dealers of London.

⊗

This is the story of three men: a prince, a tycoon and a London dealer known for the touching honesty with which he restores furniture. The dealer is a man who scrapes every vestige of the kindness of time from a piece of furniture and returns it faithfully to its bright new condition. Now this man had a prince among tables in his possession, a table fit for a prince, so when a large slice of the wealth of Australia walked in and inquired about the price, it was only a moment before a deal was struck. A night or two later, the dealer dined with a real prince, Prince Charles, who mentioned, as I suppose princes do, that he required various fine pieces of furniture, among them a table. The solution to the supply of the table was obvious: here was a Prince, the dealer had a princely table, and the deal was struck again. The table was delivered to the Prince, and the Australian's cheque was returned. After all, a peasant must give way to a prince. This, however, is not how Australian 'peasants' view these matters. Lawyers were called. There was acrimony: to sue or not to sue. The dealer was confident: an Australian would not have the temerity to sue a prince, surely? The Australian viewed this matter with refreshing clarity. Later, I dined at this table, perhaps even a king among tables, in Australia, where it is now settled.

The moral of this tale is that antiques can be sold only once, or rather, to only one customer at a time, regardless of the temptations of the second offer. If an object you once owned is sold and sold again for ever-increasing sums, don't think about it. The important price is the one that was paid to you. As for the profit that accrues to others, smile and take pleasure in the evidence of your own good taste.

⊗

Collectors with great wealth are different from other collectors. The habits of most collectors vary from nation to nation, but for those who inhabit the stratosphere, there is an international taste that varies only from time to time. It makes no difference whether the seriously rich live in Tokyo, Paris, London, New York or Sydney, they collect the same objects: the French impressionists and French furniture, although these have now been joined by works from modern European artists and, in some cases, the abstract expressionists. All are symbols of wealth, and the wealthy fight for them. Witness, for example, the battles over the last three paintings by Vincent van Gogh to appear in the salesroom. They were purchased by mystery buyers. Much later, one at least of these mysteries was solved. The purchaser of Van Gogh's *Irises* was Alan Bond; the price he paid is still the world record, although the painting is now in the Getty Museum. The prices that these Van Goghs fetched appear even now truly remarkable, considering the provenance of many of them.

It is only six decades ago that the elder Gimpel, whose son founded the Gallery Gimpel Fils in London, left Holland with a bundle of Van Gogh's paintings. At the French customs, he was stopped and asked what they were. 'My own work,' he replied. 'I am taking them to Paris to see if I can sell them.' 'I think you will need good luck,' replied the customs inspector, whose attitude at the time perfectly reflected the buying public's view of the works of Van Gogh. Since then, France has adopted Van Gogh along with Picasso, Dali, Giacometti and a host of painters and sculptors from other nations. The French promoted them and, in the fullness of time, this chauvinistic approach to art paid handsome dividends when the volume of interested money increased at a rather greater rate than the availability of masterpieces by desirable dead artists.

Collectors, however, will go on buying what they like, and that is usually a reflection of where they come from. Each nation tends to buy its own art—the French buy French art and the Germans buy German art. The Canadians and Americans seldom buy anything other than work by native artists; the Americans have a very strong market in American art. The French, who invented the word *chauvinisme*, practise its meaning in the extreme. Let us take the case of a shrewd French collector on whose walls hung works by Monet, Manet and Renoir. In his private gallery, he had a large and magnificent Turner on an easel. His guests would declare it was a great work and ask who painted it. The collector would reply that it was attributed to an English painter named Turner, but added that it must be a fake, because no English artist painted that well.

⁂

The market for Australian art is in Australia, among Australians, with the exception of those foreigners who visit Australia and fall in love with its landscape and its people. These visitors may not even be collectors when they arrive. Usually, however, after their first visit, they leave as I did, clutching an Australian painting, only to return and to buy yet another and another. Even before I lived in Broome, I had become interested in Aboriginal culture. On my second visit to Australia in 1965, I acquired a number of bark paintings. These, however, were of no real quality. The enthusiasm for trading in this kind of painting had not yet really caught fire. It may sound perverse, but in the early 1960s, when the work of Aboriginals was not much sought by collectors and tourists, their work was harder to acquire. It is only after the idea gets around that a particular genre of painting or sculpture is likely to become valuable that much of it comes onto the market. Worth remembering also is the fact that the number of Aboriginal painters and sculptors working in those days was minuscule by comparison with the number active today. There can be no doubt, however, that the imaginative quality of their work is now far greater than it was 30 or 40 years ago.

When I moved my home to Broome, it was all different for me. I was no longer tied to acquiring my collection from the Perth, Melbourne and Sydney dealers, or at the London salesrooms where Aboriginal artefacts occasionally appeared and were knocked down for a pittance. Among the first people to help me with my collection was Father McKelson, a remarkable man, conversant with several Aboriginal languages. He introduced me to many of the artists who carved stone heads. The Kimberley and Broome were the source of a great deal of creative activity by Australian Aboriginals and I was spending much of my time at the heart of it. The carved mother-of-pearl shells worn as pubic shields fascinated me. They, along with the painted shields and boomerangs used in dancing, were objects that I had never seen before.

Mary Macha, who still deals in Aboriginal art and artefacts in Perth, has been to me for many years a guiding light in all matters Aboriginal. Mary Macha, now well on in life, is a fine-looking woman, with eyes that look straight at you, never blinking. In a conversation with her, there is no subterfuge—Mary tells it to you just as it is. She is a woman blessed with the patience of Job and this, combined with her obvious honesty, made her the perfect person to deal with Aboriginals. When the market in Aboriginal art and artefacts began to open up in the early 1970s, Mary was a driving force in its development. In 1971, she had begun working as a project officer for the Native Trading Fund, established to market Aboriginal craft in Western Australia. In 1973, Mary continued with this role for the Aboriginal Arts Board of the Australia Council. It was about this time that I first met

Mary. Her enthusiasm was infectious, her knowledge considerable and, quite apart from these qualities, she saw the need for Aboriginal artists to record their cultures. In the goods that she dealt in, Mary always maintained a strictly observed level of quality. She fought fiercely against the 'Let's make a few bucks' school of thought, with its production-line mentality. Mary was consistent in her attitude that only those with talent should become artists. She did not subscribe to the view that because Aboriginal art exists, all Aboriginals are artists—any more than all Chinese are brilliant at business, or all Italians expert lovers. This selective approach to arts and artefacts was dramatically different to that practised in other parts of Australia.

By May 1979, Mary was conducting intensive art and craft courses, assisted by her husband. Part of an adult Aboriginal education program, these courses helped Aboriginal artists identify the best materials to use in their work and the best techniques for using those materials. One artist, Mingelmangau, seeing the large canvases of Robert Juniper, wanted to work on the same scale. Without a great deal of difficulty, Mary persuaded me to commission six large canvases by this artist. In the event, I believe that only two or three of them were delivered. The first of them hung in the foyer of the Australian Bank building on St George's Terrace, a property development that I had undertaken. Often when I was in Perth, I would visit Mary at the gallery that she ran on St George's Terrace. It was through her that I obtained the most interesting pieces in my collection. One of the most unusual aspects of Mary's character was the way that she was determined to maintain equity between the artist and the collector; she had a determination to see that each deal she orchestrated was fair to both sides.

It was Mary who first introduced me to the work of Rover Thomas and Paddy Tjamati. They created a corroboree, Paddy Tjamati doing the dreaming and Rover Thomas doing the painting. The pictures, painted on large panels of plywood, the panels having been taken from crates, were carried on the shoulders of the dancers. A television crew from the BBC came to Turkey Creek to film this corroboree. They set up their cameras and lights opposite the dancers and their painted boards and started to film, at which point the choreography of the dance dictated that the dancers turn around. In time, the camera crew moved and set up their equipment on the other side of the dancers, just in time for exactly the same thing to happen all over again.

It is hard for those used to European culture to come to terms with the partnerships that often create Aboriginal art, in which the dreamer owns the right to the image and the painter owns the right to the way that image is portrayed. The boards first used by Rover Thomas and Paddy Tjamati were the tops and sides of tea chests; later, small boards were used, either square or rectangular. Irrespective of their size and shape, these boards are directly in the tradition of the painted dance boards of north-western Australia, long, plank-like objects painted with ochres and chalks.

In search of Aboriginal art, I travelled many thousands of kilometres in the North-West. Mary Macha sent me to Bathurst and Melville Islands, located about 80 kilometres north of Darwin in the Northern Territory. The home of the Tiwi Aboriginal people, the islands are often simply known as the Tiwi Islands. They are very different from the Kimberley; they are tropical islands with tall hardwood trees, their timber heavy as lead and hard as iron. I flew there in a light plane, landing on the short runway of Bathurst Island. Arakike-Apuatimi Declan, whom I had come to see, carved the hardwood timber with an old bayonet from the last war. A small man, slightly built, he was in his early sixties when we met. He was relaxed as he showed me his work, but as he talked about it, his enthusiasm became electric. We sat, we talked and finally we came to a deal. From Declan, I acquired the rights to all his work for the next three years; from me, Declan acquired a brand-new Toyota Land Cruiser. It was a good deal and we were both delighted. An art adviser of that region tried to change the terms of the deal later on. People such as that man could neither understand nor approve of people like myself who valued Aboriginal work at a proper price. According to Ronald M. Berndt, Emeritus Professor at the Department of Anthropology at the University of Western Australia, the artist Declan, like many a Tiwi, was adventurous. He travelled into what he would have regarded as foreign parts, and also worked on the luggers.

Darwin, for instance, was virtually a Tiwi outstation, even though many other Aboriginals from a variety of different cultural backgrounds were also there. Near the Bagot Road Aboriginal settlement, some Tiwi people were buried and their graves were complete with their mortuary posts. Many Tiwi were also employed on Aboriginal Army settlements or attached to other military, naval and air force units in varying capacities. Declan was amongst them.

The village on Bathurst Island is an attractive place, its buildings well-spaced and its gardens lush with tropical plants. There is a thriving pottery as well as a workshop where fabrics are printed; these ventures are now highly successful. As outside interest in Aboriginal art increased, Declan commenced producing for non-Aboriginals. He was among a number of Tiwi working through the medium of carving and painting; others are making decorated pottery of a high order and screen-printed fabrics. The collection that I acquired from Declan not only included the traditional Tiwi carved burial posts but also carvings of humans and animals. There were also a number of bark paintings in this collection, a number of throwing sticks, spear points and some saw-shark noses, all of them highly decorated with coloured stripes and dots. Many carvings and poles made by the Tiwi people were shipped from Darwin to my home in Broome. Sadly, shortly before Declan completed his contract with me, he died. Declan was not only an admired carver and painter, he was also an exceptionally gifted singer and dancer. A dignified gentleman, he died of cancer in 1984. Sir Sidney Nolan wrote the following words as a foreword to a catalogue of Arakike-Apuatimi Declan's work: 'Painting is an extension of communication. As such, it's pure, difficult and wonderful. Declan's work is all of these. In doing this, he utilised his own heritage, its unique shapes, designs and imagery, in an innovative manner.'

The collection that Declan made for me was sent on a tour of regional art galleries in Australia after his death. My appetite for Aboriginal art at that time was immense; even today it matters not a lot to me whether the work is old or new, traditional or innovative, or in wood, stone or fibre. Baskets and feathered ornaments, small carvings or large carvings—I love it all. I felt an energy in the work of Aboriginal artists that excited me as I had not been excited since I first came across the abstract expressionist painters of New York in the early 1960s. I do not truly know to this day whether that excitement came from the works themselves or the spirit of the countryside and the people who made them. In the event, where that excitement came from is immaterial, for an object that passes on the ethos of the person who made it and the place where it is made is surely a true work of art. The communicating of a distinct and unique feeling is what art is all about.

৵৹

I find that I am drawn to collect above all else the art and artefacts of the country where I am living at the time I make that collection. So it was with Australia. For some years, I had noticed that the antique shops in the cities were filled with stripped pine furniture. Every vestige of paint and patina destroyed, its wood laid bare, clean, fresh and lifeless. By chance, I came upon a dealer before he committed this calumny on a fine softwood dresser. The colours of this dresser were truly wonderful. It was, I suppose, at this moment that I was taken with the idea of collecting bush furniture, but only examples in their original state. All the while begging and cajoling dealers to resist dunking their stock in the acid tank, my collection began to grow. Graham Cornall, a Melbourne dealer, was the chief supplier of this furniture and in the end he played the part of curator to my collection as well. Once bitten by the bug, my collection grew apace. Soon I was collecting the jarrah tables, chairs and wardrobes of Western Australia, and then the fine furniture of Victoria and New South Wales. The collection grew and grew. Wooden toys were added and then a deal of colonial pottery joined the furniture. The beautiful sat side-by-side with the bizarre among the 700 pieces that formed my collection of Australian furniture, a collection that was chronicled by Graham in his excellent book, *Memories*, which I published.

In the 1980s, I was in Australia and enjoying its orgy of self-indulgence. Hardly a week went by without a sale of Australian paintings, furniture and pottery. There was also bric-à-brac, which is described as 'Australiana' and includes anything with an Australian trademark stamped on it. The enthusiasm for anything Australian seems almost boundless. Of course, this was exaggerated by the Bicentenary celebrations in 1988, a great Australian party with parades of tall ships and Aboriginals who came to protest but who, like the rest of us, enjoyed a good party as well. The Bicentenary celebrations were accompanied by a significant number of cultural events devoted to Australia's history: her way of life, her marine biology, her ships, her trains, and, indeed, a warehouse devoted entirely to her bric-à-brac. The Bicentenary not only made the multinational inhabitants of this country supremely aware that they are Australians, but also aware of their land and its art. To a random collector, all this may appear to indicate a glut on the market. But the real collector knows this is not the high point of a market, rather the beginning of a better one. Opportunities like these only occur once every two hundred years or so.

The line between rarity and obscurity is very narrow. In time, the great works by Australian painters such as Sir Sidney Nolan, John Olsen and Russell Drysdale will rise in price because they have quality above and beyond their Australianness. The best prices of nineteenth-century cedar furniture and First Settlement furniture of colossal originality will rise in price along with the best pottery. The price of bric-à-brac will remain constant and, in some cases, drop right away, only to revive and drop again in the years ahead. There is a lesson here for the discerning collector: spot a nation whose prospects are good—there will be plenty in the next two centuries—and buy the product of its people. As the country becomes rich, so will its people. And as they become rich, they will collect the work of their forebears. The shrewd collector, however, will already have discovered the value of these trappings.

సౌ

The art world abounds with stories, many of them cautionary tales and rightly so, for there is a great need to be cautious when moving in that world. Here are three stories about the dreadful effect on talented people of three great human failings: pride, greed and jealousy. They are sad stories because each of these failings destroys, slowly but with absolute certainty, its victim.

First, pride. There were two Bond Street antique dealers of great repute. Their shops were opposite each other. They were adversaries; their rivalry took the form of uttering mildly deprecating remarks about the other's stock. 'Too brightly painted', or 'Too highly gilded', one would say of a piece in the other's window display, and each was so proud of his own stock that he could not bring himself even to enter the other's shop. One of these dealers acquired a bow-fronted commode of such beauty and quality that it might have been made by Chippendale himself. This commode stood in the back of his shop and eventually attracted the attention of a discriminating Knightsbridge dealer, who bought it. By a remarkable coincidence, just as it was being delivered to his shop in Knightsbridge, he received a visit from the other grand Bond Street dealer. 'What a piece,' exclaimed the latter when he saw the commode. 'What's the price?' The Knightsbridge dealer contented himself with adding a modest profit to his purchase price—he doubled it; after all, he had owned the piece for only a few hours and here was the possibility of a quick sale.

'Where did you get it?' asked the Bond Street man. 'I'm afraid I cannot disclose where I acquired it,' replied the Knightsbridge man, a trifle pompously, 'but I can tell you that I'm frightfully pleased with it and if it is of no use to you, just let me get it into the shop and with one telephone call, I'll be able to sell it.' At this, the Bond Street man threw himself between the commode and the shop's front door. The removal man stood by, uncertain whether it was coming or going. 'It's mine,' cried the Bond Street man. 'Load it up again and deliver it to my shop. At once.' It is questionable whether he would have displayed the same enthusiasm had he known that this great commode had sat for months in the back of the shop across the road at half the price. He did not know, however, because his pride had not allowed him to cross the road and look. So he paid instead.

Next, greed. There was a shop in Mayfair that dealt in

arms and armour. It was a paradise for small boys, although I am bound to say that when I grew up, I lost none of my enthusiasm for that emporium. One day, the owner was away at a country sale and left an assistant in charge of the shop. Shortly after 3 p.m., a well-dressed man, obviously possessed of a few quid, entered the shop. The assistant did not know much about arms and armour, but he did know a rich drunk when he saw one. The customer began to enthuse about a pair of pistols, cocking them, pretending to fire them, pointing them at passers-by in the street, and indeed, making a proper nuisance of himself. As he did this, the assistant noticed that their price tag had become detached. It read £750. When the well-dressed man asked the price, the assistant told him £1500. 'Done,' was the reply and, having written a cheque on the spot, the gentleman left, taking the pistols with him.

On hearing this story when he returned to the shop, the owner, an honourable man, was not impressed by his assistant's enterprise. He telephoned the customer that same evening at his home and said that a terrible mistake had been made. The pistols were not really for sale but, since the fault was entirely his, he would be grateful if the customer would return the pistols and take a cheque for £3000 for the inconvenience and embarrassment. But greed, fed by the deep suspicion of the truly ignorant, had taken root. 'It's no good trying that one on me,' the customer said. 'If you have undersold them, that's your bad luck, a deal is a deal. Sorry.' Puzzled, the dealer kept the money, but more importantly, he retained his honour. Both his honour and his profit had been kept intact by the customer's greed.

Finally, the worst of these failings, jealousy. This story took place in Melbourne, where a dealer had the good luck, some might call it skill, to turn up a cedar bureau bookcase of Australian manufacture and to recognise it as possibly the earliest known piece of Australian furniture. It was quite fine; not a masterpiece, but its extreme rarity made it much sought-after by Australians. The find was a triumph. It was a triumph, however, spoiled by the behaviour of a rival dealer in Sydney specialising in Australiana. This competitor spent a good deal of time debunking the man from Melbourne and his bureau bookcase. He did not offer any evidence that the bureau bookcase was not what the Melbourne dealer claimed, indeed, his argument came down to this: if the bureau bookcase were any good, it would be in his shop in Sydney. He was jealous, and it was destroying him. This story contains a moral for dealers everywhere: it is better to spend time improving your own understanding than to waste time knocking the competition.

If you are a dealer and a customer reveals that he has bought an object elsewhere, and you know that it is half the quality and twice the price of one you have yourself, the best thing is to smile and say, 'Very nice; indeed, wonderful. Very good of its kind.' You must never—please, never—discourage a collector. Especially, never discourage a child who collects, even if that collection is as mundane as pebbles from the beach. One in three adults in the Western world collects something, while in America the overwhelming majority of children have up to eleven different collections each. For a dealer, every child that collects may one day become a customer.

༄

My first shell collection came from the beach at Bournemouth in England. Like other little boys, I found these pretty, useless objects irresistible and took them, covered in sand in a plastic bucket, back to the hotel and washed them in a basin—to the distress, I suppose, of the hotel's maids. In those days, it was my firm belief that small fish were born from seashells. I did not realise that the seashell is a mollusc, an entity in its own right. My second collection, enriched by the shells I got from Kerry Sharp, grew in leaps and bounds, not least from shells washing ashore that I found while walking each morning along Cable Beach at Broome. Cable Beach is uncluttered by surfboards or beach umbrellas. The air is fresh with the smell of bush plants growing in the dunes. Sea eagles coast above the beach and migratory wading birds that, like me, have flown in from northern Europe, rise in clouds from the gentle surf. The sea is a highway for migrating whales and a resort for turtles and dolphins; on the beach, phalanxes of seashells glisten colourfully in the sun. I cannot resist them, though life for the adult collector is not as easy as it is for little boys. Shells gathered in the early morning quickly dry out on the breakfast table. As if cursed by an appalling mystical force, they become dull and lifeless; like the ones I collected in Bournemouth, despised when they lost their lustre.

The glistening gems accumulated by true shell collectors have to be plucked from a reef deep in the ocean or dredged from its bottom. Then, when the inhabitant of this strangely shaped skin is killed and removed, time stops for the shell and its lustre is preserved forever in its pristine state in readiness to join a collection. Collectors, however, must beware the little-known phenomenon of the killer seashell. Some of the cone shells—*Conus textile* and *Conus stratus*, for instance—are among the nine or so varieties that sometimes fight back. These are violent creatures, fish-eating shells that shoot a small dart of poison into their victims. Paralysis and death follow, suggesting that it can be deeply unwise to look down the wrong end of a loaded cone shell. In Australia, paralysis and death are not the only fates that can befall unwary shell collectors. Large areas of the coastline are national parks, and collectors caught plundering the shells are subject to heavy fines.

No laws prevented the early explorers of the southern hemisphere, such as William Dampier and Captain Cook, from bringing excellent examples of Australian shells to Europe, where they were mounted on silver or gold. Indeed, shells from around the world have a place in history: primitive people used them for dress, and Pocahontas, the American Indian princess who befriended the early settlers, wore them as wampum. The nautilus shell is the image of the renaissance and the model for Sydney's Opera House. Hawaiians used the golden cowry as a symbol of royalty; cowry shells have surfaces so smooth and a texture so perfect that they are called *porcelain* by the French, and they are the pride of any shell collector's cabinet. As stamps are kept in albums, so shells are kept in cabinets. As in all forms of collecting, shell specialists have their eccentricities. Some collect freaks— misshapen or discoloured shells—cones, spiked shells or white shells. Some collect giant clams; others, cowries so small that they can be observed only under a magnifying glass and picked up with tweezers. Collectors of Victoriana prize particularly the pretty shells arranged in patterns in boxes made by seamen on long and lonely voyages. The sums of money that pass between a dealer and a collector trading in shells are considerable. Of course, primitive people also used shells for money—the *Cowry moneta* was one of the earliest forms of currency, so perhaps shells are money after all. Perhaps that is why people collect them.

My boyhood interest in collecting seashells was renewed upon my arrival in Australia, inspired by the shell collection of Paul Jones, the Australian botanical painter. I first came across Paul when I found one of his botanical paintings reproduced in a magazine and, as a result, I determined to meet him. A painter of flowers and sometimes shells, he was a man who could catch a moment of nature and commit it to paper with pencil, brush and colour. Not the easiest of people, Paul was given to grumbling at imagined slights and omissions of attention. For three years, he came in the spring to paint portraits of the flowers in my garden at West Green in Hampshire. There are well in excess of 40 portraits that he painted during those three years. I gave them to my wife Romilly and they used to hang in our home at West Green. When we sold the contents of that house, they were almost the only things that we kept. Now they decorate our new home in southern Italy. There is something both timeless and restful about Paul Jones's paintings of flowers. While difficult with people, he was at one with nature. On each of my frequent flying visits to Sydney, I visited Paul. I sat listening to his grumbling conversation and all the time I looked at the beauty that he had caught on paper with his brushes and paints.

Possibly the only advantage of jet lag is that you are fully awake at times of the night when you would otherwise be unaware that there was anything worth waking to see. The last hours of full moon, for instance, as it hovers over Sydney Harbour; the first hours of light before the sun comes over the horizon; the sunrise that paints each ripple on the surface of the Harbour's water and gleams on the shiny arcs of the Opera House. Then there is the freshness as you walk in the Botanical Gardens, a freshness that comes with dawn, a few moments caught between the stifling heat of antipodean night and the blazing sun of day, moments when the birds sing just for the joy of singing. None of this has changed since I first set foot in Australia 40 years ago. None, that is, except the Opera House: in those days, it was just a building site jutting into Sydney Harbour.

In my hunt for rare seashells, at the beginning of that strange enthusiasm, I came across Lance Moore and his shop, which was hidden in The Rocks not far from the Opera House, behind the Sydney Harbour Bridge. Lance Moore sold shells, seashells in a thousand shapes and colours. I say a thousand, but he may well have had ten thousand varieties in his narrow shop. All I know is that there were shells everywhere: great baskets of common shells, rare varieties carefully wrapped in cotton wool and pulled from a drawer filled with unpaid bills and unanswered letters, scraps of paper each with a telephone number or an address on them. A filing system from hell, a bundle of addresses with no names, and names with telephone numbers that no longer answered, would be pulled from a drawer with a shell he was showing a serious collector.

I know little of Lance Moore's background. He seemed once to have been a sailor or at least spent time on ships; clearly, he was a diver and a collector of live shells. I write 'clearly' when, in fact, I do not know, for Lance was to me quite as mysterious as the sponges and corals that decorated his walls. Giant crayfish and crabs of vast proportions hung there too, among the rows of sharks' jaws and turtle shells. His back office was a salon, not of writers or painters, other than Jonesy, as he used to call Paul Jones. No, his was a salon of fishermen, divers and collectors of shells, a salon in which your intellect was judged not by the sparkle of your wit or the depth of your education, but by whether you could put a name to an obscure mollusc. Shells were taken from cases, laid in raffia baskets, lifted and examined, occasionally compared to examples in reference books, but more often name-tagged and put away. Paul Jones sat with a discriminating eye, looking for the perfect example, for he only collected the most perfect of shells which he kept in a single cabinet, each tray a work of gleaming beauty. Cowries were the shells that attracted him the most, but not exclusively, for his collection was wide-ranging, but a rare and perfect cowry visibly excited him. Shells have that effect on those who love them, like the effect that gold, diamonds and pearls can also have. As far as

I know, men do not kill for shells, but they come close to it.

Lance Moore had only one leg, and hopped among those gathered in his back room, distributing tea and often cake. He held court at these gatherings, generous with his knowledge, careful with his friendships. Along with the stuffed fish, baskets of shells and various pieces of equipment which cluttered up the space, Lance also had two very large dogs, both of which gave one the impression that they would have been very angry if you trod on them. Lance was in the habit of taking a nap with his dogs under the table in his back room. It was a surprising sight for customers who wandered in, to find a single leg sticking out from under a table. Today, Lance Moore is dead and he holds court no longer; Australia has lost an epicentre of real culture.

⊷

I have never forgotten an experience that I, always an enthusiastic collector, suffered as a child. Invited for a day's salmon fishing on the lower reaches of the River Test in England's county of Hampshire, I stayed with my hosts the night before the expedition in order to make an early start for the river. That evening, my hosts had a dinner party, in which I joined, although I was only about twelve years old. The conversation moved about the table until a woman sitting on the other side of the table quite suddenly addressed a question to me. 'What do you do, Alistair, what are your hobbies?' She may not have used my name, perhaps she just called me 'little boy'; I do not remember. The question was innocent enough, but my answer clearly did not measure up to the standard of reply that she expected. 'I collect things.' 'What sort of things?' she asked. I suppose she had expected me to say that my hobbies were cricket or football, or even train-spotting. 'I collect arms and armour,' I responded. At which point, this woman addressed the entire table—there were eleven others apart from me sitting there—'Arms and armour! When I think of

261

armour, it is synonymous with boredom. Armour is the most boring subject that I can imagine.' The hostess, I believe, then changed the topic of conversation, which was not hard because the entire dinner party had been struck silent, expecting, I suppose, that I would burst into tears.

❧

I often think back on my varied career as a collector and my collections. From Australia, I collected paintings and bush furniture, Aboriginal art and artefacts, modern and contemporary paintings, furniture, bush furniture and Australiana, books on Australia and by Australians, seashells, parrots and other wildlife, and not forgetting the historic buildings of Perth, Fremantle and Broome. These were the physical collections that I owned; the experiences that I had while living and travelling in Australia, they are yet another collection. Then there were my collections of ties, marbles, Venetian beads, books, manuscripts, English furniture, garden implements, rare breeds of pigs, chickens, ducks and geese, sheep and shepherds' crooks, nineteenth-century policemen's truncheons, stuffed animals, farm implements from tractors to pitchforks, and, of course, arms and armour. Today, I still collect; currently, only ties, marbles, beads, glass and political badges. I try to keep my collecting under control. Slowly but remorselessly, however, the collection of odd-shaped stones in our house grows and grows.

As I have written, my interest in arms began when I was still a boy. Over the years, my collection grew to include Highland edged weapons, English pistols, long guns and, most particularly, nineteenth-century revolvers. One pair of pistols that I found in England went to Australia. Many years later, I came across them again in the collection of Warren Anderson, the Australian property developer and Colt pistol collector, who sold them in America for £250 000. When I had bought these pistols, I had paid £2000 and sold them for £5000; the first dealer to own them had paid the equivalent of £2.50. These pistols took only thirty years to reach the amazing figure that they fetched at auction in America. Warren Anderson kept his gun collection in his historic house, Fernhill, on the slopes of the Blue Mountains. It was certainly the best collection in Australia, and in respect of his Colt revolver collection, was beyond doubt among the best in the world. Tall and built like a brick wall, with a craggy face and a head of blond hair that would do credit to a thatched cottage, Warren Anderson is descended from a Norwegian sailor who jumped ship in Australia.

One winter, I visited Warren at Tipperary, his station in the Northern Territory, bordering on Darwin. With me were John Roberts and Bob Frost, my partner in the venture with Joan Bowers. We flew from Broome in a small jet, landing on Warren's airstrip. The three of us had to share a room. It was a large room but not one of us could be described as small. In the north, I always travelled with a bathplug tied to my car keys with a piece of string. This bathplug was the subject of much comment, not to say considerable hilarity, among the people who knew of its existence. 'Why would you need a bathplug?' I was often asked, usually in the bush a few hundred kilometres from the nearest bath. Well, the answer was simple: the Australians take showers while the British take baths. In my whole time travelling in the north, whenever I came across a bath, while the shower worked, the bathplug was missing. This was also the case at Anderson's station.

We arrived early in the morning and spent the day with other guests, flying across Tipperary in a trio of helicopters. John Roberts sat between Bob Frost and myself. It was the sort of helicopter that has no doors and only two seat belts in the back, so we tied John in with a piece of rope and off we flew, happy as Larry. Then the pilot spotted a cow and, like a Stuka pilot, he dropped our helicopter from the heavens in a sideways dive. Frankly, I was terrified as we skimmed the trees. Tipperary is the most beautiful of places, and we flew from its mountain ranges, across rivers, over rainforests, on to the swampland near the mudflats that edged the sea. It was on the swampland that Warren decided to land. As we stepped out of the helicopter, all around us were the nests of crocodiles. Warren, it seems, is immune to fear; for myself, already frightened by the flight, I was downright terrified by the ground where we had landed and desired nothing more than to be airborne again.

As we flew back to the station homestead, we skimmed the tops of forests, the black and white Torres Strait pigeons rising in clouds as we passed over them. Below us were the nests of jabiru storks with the immature birds staring up at us, their beaks opening wider and wider expecting a delivery of food. The natural wildlife of Tipperary is quite remarkable, both in its quantity and variety. On the outward trip, several members of the party had shot with rifles, out of the open side of the helicopters, a large number of the feral pigs that infest the north. These pigs ruin the countryside, ripping up native growth with their rutting as they search for food hidden in the earth. Because of the massive damage they do to the land they have to be regularly culled. As we returned, I expected to see the line of carcasses that we had left behind us. There was not a dead pig in sight; the crocodiles had in the course of an hour or two disposed of over a hundred of them. As we landed, a group of station hands nearby were handling a bull buffalo, trying to get it from a truck into a cattle race. One of these men had blood running from a bandage on his leg—a bandage is rather a grand word for the covering of what was clearly a serious wound. In fact, he had simply tied a dirty handkerchief around his leg, and that handkerchief was now soaked in blood. 'What happened to you?' Warren asked, pointing at the man's leg. 'That old fellow got me as we were putting him on the truck.' 'You'd better get that seen to,' said Warren, looking at the ghastly wound and then at the sharpness of the buffalo's horns. The man looked at his watch and then replied, 'I'll be finished in a couple of hours, I'll get someone to look at it then.'

The men of northern Australia are hardy men. That night, Warren gave a party. All the workers on the station turned out to eat and drink, and a few of them to dance. Bone meat was the dish that I had for dinner, its bone touching both ears as I tore at its middle with my teeth. 'It's really good for your virility,' one swarthy individual informed me. Without doubt, he did not need much bone meat to pep him up as he lurched from station female to station female. John Roberts and I were frankly exhausted after our day's outing, so we decided to retire to our beds, beds that were the best part of two kilometres away. It was pitch dark and we were fearful of the crocodiles we had seen around the homestead that afternoon. They had lain like giant maggots sunning themselves on the nearby river bank. 'We stick to the road,' John instructed. For myself, I could not see how a road was going to protect us from a hungry croc whose tastebuds had been alerted by the scent of the barbecue. Not long after we had set out, a truck's headlights could be seen behind us. 'Good old Warren,' says John, 'he's sent one of the men to give us a lift to our quarters.' As the truck drew level with us, a female voice enquired, 'Wouldn't you two fellows rather be coming with us?' As our eyes became used to the bright lights, they focused on two of the most toothless old hags one might ever meet. If there had been a third, they would have been straight out of Shakespeare's *Macbeth*. John and I looked at each other and then at the hags. 'Oh, thanks a lot,' says John, 'but I think I'll walk, it's a lovely night.' With a serious belch, the driver of the vehicle commented, 'Youse fellows don't know what you're missing.' Then they drove off.

17

Travelling in Australia, or rather urban Australia, which is where ninety per cent of the people live, I am struck by the interest in art—not art in general, but Australian art, particularly nineteenth and twentieth-century Australian paintings in the European idiom. There is hardly a restaurant in Melbourne or Sydney that doesn't hang works by Australian painters. Certainly no bank is without a twentieth-century Australian painting or sculpture in its foyer, or a nineteenth-century Australian painting in the boardroom. The art of France, America, Britain, not to mention Spain, Italy and the rest of Europe, has no place here. The names of the great icons that we Europeans admire are to be found in art galleries but not in houses, office build-ings or banking halls. Australians collect Australian art or, at least, the most prudent of them do.

The first Australian artists were visitors from other coun-tries, recording the plants and animals of Australia to show an astonished world what a kangaroo looked like. Convict painters first recorded life in the colonies or, in the case of William Buelow Gould, death in the colonies: heaps of dead game and fish, carefully recorded, complete with blowflies. The first serious school of Australian painting was located in the bush not far from Melbourne at a place called Box Hill, where three painters named Roberts, McCubbin and Abrahams lived in the 1880s. They painted in the style of the

French impressionists. They painted on empty cigar boxes because they gave a good texture and surface to paint on—and were free. Abrahams's father was an importer of cigars. He was, incidentally, also grandfather to Sir Denys Lasdun, the British architect and designer of London's National Theatre. In 1889, this group of painters held an exhibition that was called '9 × 5 Impressions'—nine inches by five being the size of a cigar-box lid. Australians, in those days, were clearly not smoking Laranaga Magnums which come in a somewhat larger box. These antipodean impressionists, whose most recent exhibition was called 'Golden Summers', drew a mist of happiness over their harsh and dangerous landscape. Their work is in vogue and fetches great sums.

Australian painting trundled along without arousing much interest among European collectors until the Second World War, when a group called the Angry Penguins emerged. These were painters and writers whose trumpet was a magazine by that name, and who were fighting one of the obscure battles that seem to obsess the art world but which have no relevance for the collector. By this time several artists were painting the Australian outback, but none caught the reality of the bush in the way Sir Sidney Nolan first did in the late 1940s. Nolan's bush strikes fear into the urban population of Australia. He painted the bush where one man never asks another man where he is from, or where he goes to, where laughter is crude and unforgiving and violence equates with humour, where a joke can be made of death. This landscape predates man by millions of years. The bush has resisted almost every attempt by Europeans to destroy it: it has resisted cattle, sheep, mining, litter, and even the demand for Aboriginal bark paintings. This is the hard bush, and Nolan painted it as it is. Many other painters paint it as they imagine it to be: a bush that does not disturb the peace and comfort of a Sydney drawing room.

Arthur Boyd put strength, not into the landscapes, but into his figures—savage brides and beasts and bulls. Russell Drysdale painted soft landscapes with strong people. John Olsen's bush is knowing, lonely and distorted, empty but full of humour. John Percival painted *Demented Swans*, no kidding. As is the fashion, there is also a mass of painters working in the modern idiom, from Tim Storrier down—or on. Slowly, the styles of the painters in European idiom and those of the indigenous people merge, this is art that is conscious of Australia's proximity to the Far East.

Art in Australia takes two paths: there are paintings about the country as a place and as a nation. There is freshness in the sunshine, in the people, in the cities and in the paintings, whether they are good or bad. If you are excited about Australia, you will be excited about its art. I suspect this strange continent creates collectors of paintings. In Sydney, the doyen of the dealers was Barry Stern. While Barry has given up dealing, the Gallery Stern still exists, now run by Dominic, and Dominic's exquisite and catholic tastes make this gallery a good place to start.

The first Australian painting that I ever bought came from Barry Stern. It was of emus dashing across a red landscape— Barry had an eye for a good painting and without doubt was an extremely able dealer. I enjoyed drinking a cup of coffee and catching up on the gossip with Barry when he was in business and I enjoy doing the same with his successor. When Barry moved to Morocco, he left in style with a splendid sale at Sotheby's. One lot in particular amused me. It was of twelve saucers and two cups—clearly designed for the family which keeps a lot of cats!

৵

A painter who has a real sense of humour is Elizabeth Durack. She managed to pull the best joke on the art establishment of Australia and its attendant flock of dealers since

Ern Malley, when two young Australian writers, fed up with what they regarded as the drivel published by trendy magazines, fancied a practical joke. With the help of the works of Shakespeare and a dictionary, they wrote a number of modern poems under the name of Ern Malley and sent them to an avant-garde magazine called *Angry Penguins*, which enthusiastically published them. When the truth came out, all Australia laughed at how the art establishment of Europe and America was fooled. Elizabeth Durack, however, is no mere practical joker, rather a serious and talented painter. It was, I suppose, out of a sense of mischief that she started to paint under the name of Eddie Burrup. Three of these paintings were submitted for an exhibition, 'Native Title Now'. With the paintings went a fake biography of Burrup, a name that many assumed to be Aboriginal, when in fact it was that of an Englishman who gave it to a peninsula on the Western Australian coast. Along with the biography was an interview in which Burrup refers to 'the olden day track place where dreaming time . . . bin . . . put'm first time'. Not content with this, Elizabeth Durack also entered one of Burrup's paintings in the competition for the Sulman Prize.

When the hoax was pointed out to him, Edmund Capon, the Director of the Art Gallery of New South Wales and the least pompous of men, merely remarked that artists, like writers, often used pseudonyms. Most of the painters who painted in Renaissance Italy are known by the names of the towns where they originated, rather than by their real names. Go back 600 years and you find painters with curious names such as the Master of the Lily. Edmund Capon was quite right, of course, in his assessment of the situation. In the world of conceptual art, what is taken as a hoax would, in fact, be a complete work of art. Painting, biography, interview and invented name—all part of it. What a shame that Elizabeth Durack did not enter her 'hoax' for the annual

Turner Prize offered by Britain's Tate Gallery; she would most likely have won it.

Humour is the key essence of communication. With her humour, Elizabeth Durack, whether she intended to or not, was making a considerable statement. Aboriginal art, primitive art, conceptual art, abstract art, figurative art—is all art and should be judged by the same set of standards. The setting aside of any particular strand or type of art is just misleading, for it is a work's quality that matters, not the style in which that work is painted. Unfortunately, the statement by the director of the Kimberley Aboriginal Law and Cultural Centre—'We are upset that someone who claims to have an understanding of and respect for our Aboriginal culture should act in a way that can only be interpreted otherwise'—adds fuel to the ever-smouldering fire of prejudice in Australia.

Artists are artists the world over, nothing more, nothing less. Where they come from and the style in which they paint are simply matters of incidental interest; it is the quality of their work that matters above all else. As for the idea that Elizabeth Durack was abusing Aboriginal culture by painting in a style reminiscent of that culture, the notion is ill-founded. Aboriginal culture is one of the strongest cultures in the world, and one from which in the past many people have drawn, Picasso's X-ray paintings, for instance. What is more, many people will draw inspiration from Aboriginal art in the future. Once a culture is discovered by the art world it, of necessity, becomes the property of all artists. There are in the twentieth century a legion of examples to demonstrate this fact. Matisse's use of African tribal art, Henry Moore's use of the sculptural images from the Mayan culture and, not least, the use of European images drawn from European twentieth-century culture in innovative Aboriginal sculpture, painting and music. The people who harm a culture are those who distort its history and invent for it new traditions, in the way that the English destroyed the clan culture of the Scottish Highlands during the eighteenth and nineteenth centuries. The Australian Aboriginals, however, have had their share of this, with foreign best-sellers identifying curious Aboriginal customs as spurious as those allegedly practised on an American writer, in which she was buried up to her neck in the ground. Such ideas owe more to spaghetti westerns and the book *The Songlines* by Bruce Chatwin (now disclosed in his widow's autobiography as more the product of his fertile imagination than carefully researched text) than anything Aboriginal. In the event, however misleading these curious notions may be, they draw attention internationally to the existence of the Aboriginal people as well as to their grand and powerful culture. In the end, this attention can only help those people in a struggle for the recognition of their rights.

No sooner had Elizabeth Durack's hoax hit the news than a publishing company in Broome set up to publish only Aboriginal writing was taken in by a Sydney man masquerading as an Aboriginal woman. So long as there are publishing houses that practise a racial policy and art exhibitions that exhibit work based only on race, there will always be fraud. The argument used by Magabala Books Aboriginal Corporation that it was set up to help Aboriginals who found it hard to get their work published is spurious. There are people all over the world who would like to have their books published and cannot achieve their ambition.

For many years, I have known Edward Capon and I regard him as among the most civilised of humans and a good friend. It was for this reason that in the late 1990s I decided to give not only a large number of works by Sir Sidney Nolan to the Art Gallery of New South Wales, but also my collection of twentieth-century fashion photographs by European photographers and a much smaller collection of photographs by Australian photographers. Among the former collection there is a group of about 70 photographs by my friend, the late Terence Donovan, along with those of his friend David Bailey and others of their generation. In the early months of 1997, Terence Donovan committed suicide; a less likely candidate for that end I could not imagine. Overcome, however, by deep depression from a severe outbreak of eczema and the cortisone that he was given to cure it, he took his own life.

ॐ

Whether there for business or to find pieces to add to my collections, I thoroughly enjoyed my visits to Melbourne, finding that city both attractive and highly civilised. When I first went there in the mid-1960s, there were two apparently first-class hotels to stay in—the incredibly stuffy Windsor Hotel, where Sir Halford Reddish always stayed, and the brighter but less comfortable Southern Cross. The food and the beds at the Southern Cross were dreadful. As a hotel, it crossed the spectrum from the garish to the downright uncomfortable, yet it boasted four stars. For my money, I would not have given it any stars at all. However, the Southern Cross did have one asset: it was run by one of the most remarkable hotel managers that I have ever come across. John Carrados had two main interests, racehorses and women, and these interests worked greatly to the advantage of the Southern Cross. The racing crowd met there and there were always glamorous women about, one of the few things to recommend the place. John's personality gave the hotel life—there were people there most of the time, which is more than you could say for the Windsor Hotel which was, as far as I could tell, empty whenever I went there.

My association with the Southern Cross did not start well. The first time that I visited the place, my first wife, Sarah, and a girlfriend were left alone for lunch. I was out engaged on business. When I returned, I discovered two very angry young women. It seemed that they had walked into the hotel's grill room, a pleasant restaurant decorated much like a London club. Seeing no head waiter, they found themselves a table; Australia being the land of self-sufficiency, this seemed to them the right thing to do. Settled at the table, they set about getting the attention of the waiter, who studiously ignored them. Sarah, not being the most patient of souls, summoned the head waiter, who had by this time appeared. Before she was able to complain about the lack of service, he announced, 'You can't sit here.' 'Well, where can we sit?' Sarah asked, and began to move towards another empty table. 'You can't sit anywhere in this restaurant. It's for men only.' This was a concept that was new to Sarah: a hotel restaurant that only served men. She and her girl-friend protested vehemently, only to be summarily thrown out of the Southern Cross's grill room. Sarah seldom returned to Australia, a country that she believed to be hostile to women and, I have no doubt, or so she believed, to her in particular. Happily, Australia began its great change after this and the Southern Cross began to serve all comers, male or female.

John Carrados was among the most amusing of men. He explained to me that when flight crews checked into the hotel, he watched for the best-looking women among them. Then, having noted their room numbers, he called on them with a bottle of whisky. 'Don't you get a lot of rejections?' I asked, for he would suggest to these attractive young women that they share the bottle with him. Then he would stay on a little longer. 'Of course,' he replied, 'but I also get a number of girls who are delighted with my idea and invite me into their rooms.' When John's time at the Southern Cross expired, Intercontinental Hotels sent him to manage the Mark Hopkins Hotel in San Francisco.

It was while I was staying at the Southern Cross that I met and made friends with the art dealer Julian Sterling, who owned an art gallery in the arcade below the hotel. Over the first five years of the 1970s, I bought from him a number of Sidney Nolan's early works, among them *The Dog and Duck Hotel*, painted in 1948, which I had fallen in love with when I first saw it reproduced on a Qantas menu: Burke dying under a tree, the deserted mine, and a policeman with his head down a wombat hole. Along with these paintings, I also bought *The First-class Marksman*; it is one of the few of Nolan's famous Ned Kelly series exhibited in London and still in private hands.

John Adams, my lawyer in Western Australia, often stayed at my home when he visited England; usually, he slept in the same guestroom. On one occasion in, I believe, 1966, he asked me about the painting that was hanging in that room. 'Is it a copy of Russell Drysdale's painting *The Cricketers*?' 'No,' I replied, 'it's the real thing.' John looked a trifle shocked. 'That's Australia's most famous painting.' He was right, of course; it was then and it still is. I had bought the picture from Julian Sterling for £6000. Its sale was reported in the *Financial Times* as the highest price ever paid for an Australian painting. A few years later, I sold it for £12 000 and was very pleased with the deal. Today, that painting must be worth well over $500 000. I love Russell Drysdale's work and bought several more of his paintings. At his exhibition in London's Leicester Galleries, I missed the chance to buy what I regard as one of his most haunting works, *The Barmaid in Broome*, as I had arrived at the exhibition only minutes after it was sold. I had never heard of Broome in those days, so my judgement was not coloured by my affection for that town. The painting was pure magic, far better than *The Cricketers*. The new owner was a man I knew quite well, but he would not part with it, despite being offered a considerable profit. The picture remained in his collection until his death; afterwards it was sold at auction by Sotheby's in London, along with the rest of his impressive collection of Australian paintings. By this time, Russell Drysdale had died and the prices for his pictures were running into hundreds of thousands of dollars.

Lauraine Diggins was another dealer from whom I bought some wonderful paintings. Imaginative and energetic, she always seemed to be able to lay her hands on just the right sort of paintings, a talent displayed by few in her trade. On one occasion while I was in Melbourne, John Olsen asked me to open an exhibition of his work at the National Gallery of Victoria. To do this was for me a pure pleasure, because I have always admired John's work. At one time I owned a number of drawings and watercolours that he had done of Broome and its inhabitants. John Olsen and his elegant wife Catherine had fallen in love with Broome, and some years later, after visiting the town each winter, bought a house not far from the town. As for John's paintings, they have a quality and a content that surpasses the natural attractions of Australian painting. His pictures would be as at home in New York or in London's winter light. Somehow, John seems to have caught the light of Australia in his pictures, rather than just relying on the Australian light to be reflected on them. Among the friends that I have made in Australia, John Olsen stands out. I regard him as Australia's greatest living painter. Of the people I most enjoy spending time with, he and his wife Catherine are high on the list.

၎

I first met Sidney Nolan in 1978, when he was brought to see me by my friend, the painter and typographer, Gordon House. They visited me at my bookshop in London's Cork Street to ask if I would be interested in publishing Sidney's own poems. The bookshop was laid out like a sitting room, with armchairs and sofas. The books that I sold were extremely eclectic and included twentieth-century contemporary poetry and novels, as well as second-hand and antique books. While the shop specialised in fine eighteenth- and nineteenth-century botanical and natural history colour-plate books, there was, however, another aspect to the stock that I kept at 31 Cork Street. On the shelves was a large selection of *beaux livres*, among them a copy of Matisse's great work, *Jazz*, in a fine contemporary French binding. Works illustrated by most of the great painters from *l'école de Paris* were there. One book in particular, I remember, was a thin book of poems illustrated with four cubist etchings by Picasso. Sidney bought this book for a small price and I have often wondered what happened to it.

Sidney Nolan was very taken with my bookshop and set about taking books from the shelves with a wild enthusiasm, while Gordon House was diffident about the purpose of their visit. 'Sidney thinks that perhaps you don't like his work.' It was not surprising that Sidney should have come to that conclusion because, at the time, I collected abstract colour sculptures, mostly by artists from the St Martin's School of Art. I also collected American abstract expressionists and the colourist painters of the New York school. I have always liked Sidney's work, at least, since I began collecting paintings in the early 1960s. I had in my collection at the time at least three of his paintings. Reassured, Sidney began to talk about his poems and how he would like the book containing those poems to look. The book was to be called *A Paradise Garden*.

A month or so later, I was invited to Sidney's house in Deodar Road in Putney. When I saw the paintings that would illustrate *A Paradise Garden*, I had the shock of my life, for there were well over 2000 of them, small paintings each about 30 centimetres square, that when joined together made up the large painting called *Paradise Garden*. Later, Sidney painted two more sets of these oils on paper, which made up a painting called *Shark,* and after that an even larger painting, *Snake.* These three pictures were huge.

I was deeply impressed both at the quality and the scale of his work for the project, so it was only a matter of moments after seeing these paintings, stacked against the wall of the studio, that I agreed to publish Sidney's poems. Gordon House designed *A Paradise Garden* and in less than a year I had delivery of the copies from the printer. Despite the fact that *A Paradise Garden* was a beautiful book in every respect—no expense had been spared in its production—I was only able to sell a small number of copies. As for the painting of the same name, a work nearly 30 metres long, it was only years later that I saw it all in one piece. Sidney and I, along with Lord Clark and Sir Norman Read, then director of the Tate Gallery, had made a trip to Dublin to see a retrospective of Sidney's work exhibited in Dublin's Agricultural Hall. *A Paradise Garden* was hanging there in all its size and glory. There was no doubt in my mind after seeing that exhibition that Sidney Nolan was a great painter. When he was the director of Britain's National Gallery, the art historian Lord Clark was the one person who realised the importance of Sidney's work. He had been to Australia in the 1950s and could see the paintings in their natural context. While Lord Clark had always held that view, Norman Read went along with it as well after seeing the exhibition in Dublin.

A Paradise Garden was, I believe, the most original and impressive book that I have ever published and I very much enjoyed working on it with Gordon House. The fact that it sold rather badly did not stop me embarking on a second book illustrated by Sidney Nolan. Like *A Paradise Garden, The Darkening Ecliptic* was a fine publication. With poems written by Ern Malley, illustrated by Sidney, it was perhaps not quite as lavish as *A Paradise Garden* but of that order. However, in common with the first book, it did not sell in any great number. A glutton for punishment, I continued to publish books, all of them illustrated by a variety of artists and on a variety of subjects, of equal quality to the books illustrated by Nolan, with an equal lack of commercial success.

When Sidney first showed in London, his pictures caused a sensation. Many people believed that he was an abstract painter, that it was impossible for landscapes to have the shapes and colours that he painted. While Sidney Nolan certainly understood the abstract quality of the Australian landscape, his colours, however, were true to life. During the mid-1960s, the Art Gallery of Western Australia bought a large painting by Sidney Nolan from Rose Skinner, the West Australian art dealer. Made up of eight panels and called *The Desert Storm*, it depicts the bright red landscape of the Pilbara with a purple storm and is among Sidney's greatest works. Because its colours seemed so unnatural, this was exactly the sort of work that made collectors in England and America believe him to be an abstract painter. The art gallery trustees of the day viewed the painting and Rose told them in all honesty that it was a masterpiece. When the deal was all set to go, there was a snag—the art gallery's wall was too short and the painting far too long. Rose had the answer: the painting came in eight panels, so why not take only seven of them? The gallery trustees agreed and for years only seven panels hung in the Art Gallery of Western Australia. Later, Rose Skinner sold me the eighth panel for £220, never mentioning that it was the tail-end of a much larger painting. Many years later, Cherry Lewis, now the doyenne of the Perth art dealers, tried to have this panel reunited with its fellows. The trustees of the art gallery at this time seemed content with the panels that they owned, despite the gallery having been rebuilt with larger walls. In time, I gave the eighth panel to the Art Gallery of New South Wales, along

with many other paintings and a large collection of photographs. It is my hope that they will lend the eighth panel to
the Art Gallery of Western Australia and then Sidney Nolan's
work can once again be seen complete.

Cherry Lewis and her late husband sold me many pictures
during the 1980s. Their gallery was an intimate space; their
stock small but of a very high quality. The pair of them had
a brilliant eye when it came to selecting the best of
Australian paintings. Quite apart from their ability as art
dealers, I enjoyed their company. Often, I would leave my
offices at about eleven o'clock in the morning to take a walk
and stop by their gallery; at other times, I would visit them
at home for a cup of coffee and gossip to relieve the pressure
of a hectic day's work in the office. To take time talking to
the Lewises was to enter a different world from that of
planning permissions, tenants, architects and banks, which
made up my day from seven-thirty in the morning to late at
night. The Lewises, along with Mary Macha, the dealer in
Aboriginal art, were the people who really put the joy into
my life in Perth.

I was somewhat perverse in my dealings with Sidney
Nolan, for I used to buy his early works in Australia, the ones
that everyone wanted, and swap them with him for his later
pictures, the ones that nobody seemed very interested in
owning at the time. Sidney needed his early work, first as a
reference from which to move forward and then to give to the
art gallery at Lanyon near Canberra. Over the years, Sidney
and I saw a lot of each other. On several occasions, he visited
my home at West Green, but mostly we met in my shop or at
the National Gallery, where he could usually be found sitting
in front of Piero della Francisca's three great masterpieces. On
at least one occasion at West Green, I showed him my collection of chickens. It was this collection that caused him to paint
a whole series of works entitled *Oedipus*. The strange-looking

creatures in these paintings were my rare breeds of chicken; I had at the time over 75 different breeds.

On a number of occasions, Sidney and his second wife Mary came to Broome. Often we would have lunch at the Mangrove Hotel at a table and chairs placed on the lawn overlooking Roebuck Bay. We sat and watched the blue waters of the Indian Ocean, eating quantities of its produce and then we talked. Always we talked, each of us inventing stories more implausible than the last tale told by the other. Other times, we would sit under my mango tree with a bottle of wine and gossip. He told me of his experiences with Xavier Herbert, who was undoubtedly Australia's greatest novelist, easily comparable to Dickens in his robust treatment of social issues. Sidney told how Herbert had taken his hand and squeezed it until he was forced to his knees. 'My legs are filled with steel,' Herbert told Nolan, and then released him so that he could get to his feet again. Sidney felt that Herbert badly treated the local telephone operator in the Queensland town where he lived. She was, in Sidney's opinion, really Herbert's slave, a situation that he found in contradiction to Herbert's socialism. Endlessly, Sidney would recite a story by Herbert about Herbert. He entitled it 'My Grief'. It told of the death and burial of Herbert's wife. Mary tried to stop Sidney telling this awful story but he was incorrigible. As for Patrick White, Sidney intended to be revenged for the slight that White had given him in his autobiography, *Flaws in the Glass*. (Patrick White had said that Mary moved in too quickly after Sidney's first wife, Cynthia, died. This throw-away comment sparked a feud that ended only in death.) In the event, Sidney's revenge was terrible. He painted a portrait of White as a dog with his hindquarters being sniffed by his homosexual partner. The painting is one of the best works to come from Sidney's brush, and I still own a study for it. Sidney loved feuding and the feuding with White seemed never-ending: not a day passed without Sidney devising some new jibe to launch at White; no press or television interview was complete for Sidney without the ritual trashing of Patrick White. Each day under my mango tree, Sidney would plot and plan the next move in his vendetta.

Back in England, Sidney Nolan painted Broome. The Sun Pictures, my cinema, became the subject of a masterpiece; my portrait appears on a poster to the left of the picture house's door. The Bungle Bungles again became the subject of another masterpiece, which is now in the collection of John Roberts; there was a series of paintings of the Mitchell Plateau and the Kimberley bush, wonderful pictures on a scale that Sidney had never attempted before. For a man who normally painted cabinet pictures, these pictures were huge. Large pictures were now the order of the day: two metres by two metres, and larger. Larger and larger grew his work and, as the size of the canvases grew, so too did the quality of his work. Like Titian in his old age, Sidney painted relaxed, easy paintings. The agony, the anger, and the despair were gone from his palette. In their place were the colours of a lyrical beauty, each easily finding its place on these vast canvases.

One year in Broome, Mary and Sidney were joined by her son, Percival, whom I commissioned to paint the people and the places of the Kimberley. Strangely for a young painter, he did not catch the way that the Kimberley was changing. His paintings were fine works that caught the violence of the landscapes and the nostalgia of its people but not the spirit of change that was abroad. Sidney Nolan, who had painted all over the Kimberley in the late 1940s and early 1950s—the stations belonging to the Vesteys were often his favourite subjects as they had sponsored his travels there—seemed to me to have no trouble with the way that the place was changing. The mobile telephone, the fax machine, airconditioning, helicopters, four-wheel drives, and all the late twentieth-century equipment that vehicles carry today. Sidney was a modern man: he understood change, delighted in it, and used that change to push his work in advance of many of his contemporaries. Sidney took to the spray can beloved of young German painters in the 1980s like a duck to water. They had made their way to fame through using this technique, but for Sidney it had the reverse effect. Dealers or collectors unfamiliar with the German school, whose work was fetching hundreds of thousands of dollars, saw the use of this style as a sign of laziness, a desire to speed up the time taken to paint a picture. In time, however, some of these works will be considered to be among Sidney's best paintings. The comment 'I really much prefer his earlier work' was always much used about Sidney and, indeed, if Sidney Nolan was to have an epitaph written for him by the art dealers of Australia, it would be those very words.

Towards the end of Sidney Nolan's life, I commissioned him to paint a series of pictures for an office block on St George's Terrace in Perth. Sidney finished the paintings and attended the opening of St George's Square. These paintings, like many of Sidney's later works, were difficult to accept; I am, however, without doubt that these paintings will one day be regarded as among his greatest works. At the same time that I commissioned these paintings, I arranged for Sidney to carve a dozen marble sculptures for the gardens of the office block. Sidney was just not able to complete them—he made one, the rest remain only as drawings and, somewhere I suppose, there are maquettes for others. Certainly, Sidney was a fine sculptor as well as a great painter; the series of small sculptures that he made in gold bear testament to that and they certainly are among his finest work. Faced with problems from the British Inland Revenue—Sidney had only the vaguest notion that sometimes you had to pay tax—he went into a decline. I did not see him in the months before his death. As the years pass, my admiration for his paintings grows rather than wanes. Sidney was a most unusual man and a great painter. As I wrote in my earlier memoirs, *Once a Jolly Bagman*, when Sidney Nolan died, a joy went out of my life, for I miss him and his company.

∽

As a collector of contemporary art for all my adult life, it is not entirely surprising that a number of artists should have offered to paint my portrait. It was, however, something of a surprise to me when Elizabeth Frink, the British sculptress, now sadly dead, asked me in 1965 if I would let her make a portrait of me in bronze. I turned down Elizabeth Frink's offer.

In truth, I did not believe in people arranging to have themselves immortalised in stone, bronze or paint. In retrospect, I regret the arrogance of this opinion and the fact that Elizabeth, an artist for whom I have a great respect and of whose work I once owned over a hundred examples, did not make a portrait of me. Or did she? For, within a few months of asking if I wanted such a portrait and her offer being refused, Elizabeth Frink produced a life-sized bronze of a naked man. This bronze bore a striking resemblance to me. It was not, as I had imagined, because Elizabeth Frink thought that I might become famous or was a particularly interesting person, nor, indeed, was it because I had become a considerable patron of her work. Rather, she wanted to make a portrait of me simply because I had the right-shaped body. For some years, *The First Man* stood in my garden in England before it was removed to the Parmelia Hotel in Perth. While it was in England, I posed beside it, and it was hard to tell us apart in a photograph that was taken. Elizabeth Frink liked, in those days, to make sculptures of men with well-turned legs, narrow hips and vast, heavy bodies topped with block heads. This description exactly fits her work

The First Man—and it also fits the way I looked then.

From time to time, Sidney Nolan included me in his paintings. Kinder to me than the Frink portrait perhaps, his depictions of me are slight images that are usually not central to the painting. I also featured on sketches drawn on menus in restaurants while lunching with Sidney. John Olsen drew a brilliant cartoon of me buying an antique Chinese pot. Apart from these occasions and one other, portraits of myself are something that I have never encouraged.

Clifton Pugh's portraits I had always admired and, in a weak moment, I had agreed with myself that if ever I had my portrait painted, I would like him to be the artist. In 1983, I received a letter from Clifton Pugh. He said he would be in London before Christmas that year; could he paint my portrait? A day or so before Clifton's letter arrived, I received notification that I was to be made a life peer. In future, I would have the privilege of sitting in the House of Lords. The announcement of this appointment would be made on 1 January 1984. Clifton Pugh and his wife duly arrived in London a few weeks before Christmas. We arranged that our first meeting would be at my political office in the Conservative Party's headquarters at 32 Smith Square. The Pughs arrived, were shown into my office and I offered them champagne. In those days, the walls of my office were decorated with smaller versions of the giant 48 Street posters that the Conservative Party had used during the recent successful election campaign. One of these posters caught Clifton's eye. It read: 'The Conservatives talk sense even when they talk rubbish'. This legend referred to the ability of Conservative councils to improve rubbish collections. I doubt if I would run that advertisement today, in an age when many of the Conservative shadow ministers are clearly not talking much sense about anything. Indeed, they seldom say anything constructive, confining themselves to carping criticism and snide jibes at a Labour Government which seems to me, for all the world, to behave like the Conservatives; while the last Conservative government, led by John Major, appeared to behave just like the Socialists. No more of that, however, for 1983 was a vintage year for Conservatives and Conservative policies.

Clifton Pugh asked me if I could get him copies of these small posters that decorated my office walls. A week later, I visited him at his house in London, just off Kensington Church Street. He stood before a large canvas on which he had made a collage of the posters that I had sent him. Then he began to paint my portrait on top of this collage. I sat on a bed, facing him, my jacket unbuttoned, the Garrick Club tie covering a small part of a large chest and abdomen. After five sittings, the portrait was finished. When it was delivered by the Pughs to my home at West Green so that I could see it for the first time, it was wonderful. Even my wife Romilly, a stern critic, loved this work. Afterwards, we ate lunch, talked and drank. Then we walked in the garden at West Green; despite the season being winter, the sun shone. It was a perfect day.

For ten years or so, this portrait hung in my home in Broome. When I sold that house, I gave the portrait, along with many other paintings, to the Art Gallery of New South Wales. I found Clifton Pugh, an important painter, to be an amusing companion. It had been a pleasure to sit and talk to him as he worked. When Clifton visited London on that occasion, to paint my portrait, it was the first time that we had met. After the portrait was finished and delivered, we never saw each other again. It is like that with myself and artists. Sometimes enduring friendships are formed, sometimes they just pass in the night. With me, this has nothing whatsoever to do with whether they are great painters or merely painters with a specific talent. My friends are few but they are my friends, chosen carefully for reasons that go far deeper than a mere facility or even a serious talent.

⁒

It would be something of a travesty to end this chapter on the art world of Australia without mention of two other people, neither of whom are dealers or artists. The first is Leo Schofield, a man who comes and goes from my life, a considerable wit, brilliant conversationalist and a true Renaissance man. The other is Lucio, the proprietor of the restaurant named after him. Lucio is host to the art world in Sydney and serves the best Italian food outside of Italy. People who genuinely enrich one's life are hard to find. Both of these men have made my years in Australia the richer for their acquaintance and I am grateful to them.

It is almost forty years to the day that I first set foot on Australian soil. By far the largest part of my life has been closely involved with that continent. When I travelled on the *Oriana*, it was the stretches at sea that interested me, rather than Australia's cities. Those days between ports gave opportunities for the pursuit of young Australian women; tall, fit, blonde, I had never seen anything like them in the London of the 1950s. Brown and healthy, clad in the briefest of bikinis, they were so unlike the ladies in large hats and long white gloves of Sydney and Melbourne. Susan and Virginia Campbell were stars in this firmament. We became friends but when we spoke, it was not of Australia; they were interested in London and I was interested in telling them of that place. In all honesty, even four years later, when Sir Halford Reddish made the telephone call that sent me speeding across the world, it was not the prospect of visiting Australia that excited me, rather the prospect of going somewhere and doing something on my own.

It was by chance that I went to Perth and fell in love with that city. Chance chose for me a path to hoe and, as I look back, chance chose a hard path. It would be a trivial life indeed, that after forty years had not taught a lesson or two. In that respect, I believe I learnt much in my days in Australia. When I set out in the early 1960s to start a business, I found the Australian attitude to life refreshing, the Western Australians direct in their dealings. It seemed that Australia was a simple place that had worked for years according to well-regulated and sensible rules. Now I realise how terribly wrong I was in that judgement. Australia and the Australians are more Machiavellian in their approach to life than the courtiers of any Florentine court.

In my early days, just married, I knew nothing of life, yet I believed that I knew all of it. Life and death were strangers to me; birth, divorce, death, all experiences of which I had no knowledge. Young as I was, confidence filled me; humility was a virtue unknown to me. I took life at a run, not thinking about where I should put each foot until it hit the ground. Taking friendship at face value, making enemies lightly. I am, as I look back, surprised that with my simplistic approach I survived so long in a country as byzantine as Australia. In my passion, I was, however, remorseless—and my passion was Australia, Australia and all things Australian. It was this pervasive passion for Australia that influenced my every action and coloured my every reaction, both inside that continent and out of it. The people, the places, the things of Australia—I desired to know them all and for many of those years, my view of life and its individuals was through Australia-tinted spectacles.

I learned during the high days of the 1980s that the end does not justify the means, that there is no short cut to success that leads to joy. I learned in the 1990s that in any life there must be moments of pleasure, joy and excitement, and that these moments are balanced by failure and dismay. If a life does not have its dark gorges, how on earth can it expect to have its high peaks? In Australia, there were for me the lean years as well as the years where I lived off the fat of the land. When I left Australia, my affairs were in an orderly fashion; materially, I left much as I had come. Mentally, however, it was a different matter: I left Australia a truly rich man.

The memories that I have of Australia are but a taste of that wealth. No day goes by that I do not recall some aspect of the Australian countryside and my heart beats a little faster. No day passes that I do not remember a dear friend with sadness or a treacherous friend with anger, but the anger seldom lasts. I learnt in Australia that scale is important; these treacherous friends are no more than pimples on the chin caused by lavish eating, gone in a week of abstinence. More often, I sit in a Venetian campo or take tea among the crowds in front of Monte Carlo's casino, and chuckle as I remember Charlie Diesel and Snowy County, telling tales around the camp fire in some distant desert. I laugh out loud as I recall the gossip of the Pearlers Rest Bar in Broome. Bitterness is a poison that rots the soul and, in time, the body that contains that soul. Laughter is the medicine that cures all ills. However it may seem, Australia is still the lucky country, lucky in the people who live there, lucky in the beauty of the place. Australia is a serious place, a competitor in the world's economies, yet it is also a place where humour abounds, even though the source of that humour is as likely to be a tragedy as a triumph. There is, however, whatever its cause, always a joke to be told in Australia.

Index